The
Gentlemen's
Club

The Gentlemen's Club

International Control of Drugs and Alcohol

Kettil Bruun
Lynn Pan
Ingemar Rexed

THE UNIVERSITY OF CHICAGO PRESS
Chicago and London

KETTIL BRUUN is research director of the Finnish Foundation for Alcohol Studies.

LYNN PAN is coordinator for the International Research Group on Drug Legislation and Programs in Geneva, Switzerland.

INGEMAR REXED is secretary to the Nordic Research Council on Criminology and magistrate of the Court of Appeals in Stockholm.

Library of Congress Cataloging in Publication Data

Bruun, Kettil.
    The gentlemen's club.

    (Studies in crime and justice)
    Bibliography: p.
    Includes index.
    1. Narcotics, Control of—International cooperation. 2. Liquor problem—International cooperation. I. Pan, Lynn, joint author. II. Rexed, Ingemar, joint author. III. Title. IV. Series.
HV5801.B73   363.4'5   74-21343
ISBN 0-226-07777-2

The University of Chicago Press, Chicago 60637
The University of Chicago Press, Ltd., London

Contents

Tables and Figures

FIGURES

Foreword

Transnational crimes, crimes crossing state borders—smuggling, hijackings, blackmail and bombings by terrorist groups, economic and currency frauds percolating national boundaries—all present increasingly threatening problems of crime control. If they are to be at all contained, and the need to contain them is obvious, effective international collaboration will be required far in excess of what has been achieved by past efforts at drug and alcohol control.

Bruun, Pan and Rexed have been prominently involved in these efforts. They write from a rich experience. Bruun is the research director of the Finnish Foundation for Alcohol Studies in Helsinki, Pan is the coordinator of the International Research Group on Drug Legislation and Programs in Geneva, Rexed is the secretary of the Swedish Narcotics Commission and also an appellate judge in Stockholm. Their manuscript was prepared under the auspices of the International Research Group on Drug Legislation and Programs, a group formed in Geneva following a special meeting in 1970 of the United Nations Narcotics Commission. The aim of this group, commonly called the Consortium, is to provide information useful for the planning of international collaboration in drug programs and controls. The Consortium has undertaken a number of research projects, several of which have resulted in published works; *The Gentlemen's Club* is the most recent of these.

The authors submitted their manuscript for critical commentaries by leading authorities in this country as well as in England, Finland, Norway, Sweden and Switzerland. It is comprehensive, authoritative and original. All this sounds forbiddingly and aridly academic but the the impression is false. To a field rich in demagoguery and fertile in opinionated ignorance, the authors bring facts and wit.

It is a sad tale they tell. Of prejudiced pressure groups and national representatives with elephantiasis of the ego combining most courteously to preclude effective international control of the growth, manufacture, export and distribution of opium, heroin, cannabis, the psychotropic drugs and alcohol. We have all paid heavy costs for these repeated failures of international collaboration—and we will continue to pay.

Why should this book be part of a series on crime and justice? The many links between drugs, alcohol and crime are clear enough, as is the link with the crime of smuggling; but there are more fundamental reasons why this book is important both to the scholars of problems of crime control and to the administrators of all criminal justice agencies. It speaks with compelling power to the challenging tasks of international control of transnational crime, which present a larger threat to all societies than crime has ever done before. Further, it is an important study in another issue of central concern to scholar and practitioner alike: the dominant role of half-baked ideologies, catch phrases, law and order promises, and powerful but inaccurate affirmations as substitutes for knowledge in devising crime control policies.

Bruun, Pan and Rexed do not stop short at a precise if depressing history of failures. They offer recommendations, immediate and long-range, to turn a gentlemen's club of seasoned veterans of ineptitude into an effective international instrument of social control.

NORVAL MORRIS

Acknowledgments

The debts we have incurred in the making of this book are twofold. First of all, we are indebted to those who helped in 1970 to bring the International Research Group on Drug Legislation and Programs (the Consortium) into existence, and those who subsequently supported its work. Among the first group are the delegates to the UN Narcotics Commission of Australia, Canada, Denmark, Finland, Hungary, Iran, Sweden, the United Kingdom, and the United States; to their support was added the assistance of other officials and individuals in Canada, Egypt, Finland, Italy, Japan, Mexico, Norway, Sweden, Switzerland, the United Kingdom, the United States, West Germany, and Yugoslavia. Among international organizations the participation of the United Nations Social Defence Research Institute is particularly appreciated. Among government-affiliated agencies giving financial support, we wish to acknowledge with thanks the Finnish Foundation for Alcohol Studies, the Swedish National Board of Health and Welfare, and the United States Bureau of Narcotics and Dangerous Drugs. Among private institutions the Consortium is indebted to Stanford University, California, and the Institute for the Study of Drug Dependence, London. A grant from a group of European pharmaceutical firms is also gratefully acknowledged. The research reported here was supported in part by a grant from the Drug Abuse Council, Inc., Washington. All this support notwithstanding, little of the Consortium's work would have been accomplished without the unflagging energy and able efforts of its chairman, Richard Blum.

Secondly, we wish to thank all those who assisted us at various stages of the work reported in this particular publication. We are grateful to those named in the list of interviewees appearing in the Note on Sources for giving so generously of their time and knowledge. As it has been the rule of the Consortium to distribute drafts of its project materials for comment and criticism, this book has benefited enormously from the considerable consulting which has occurred in its preparation among both the members of the Consortium and other experts. We are particularly grateful for the editorial assistance of Richard Blum, Dick Joyce, and Jasper Woodcock. We have been fortunate in having Lawrence Hoover, Jr., as our consultant. Comments on the book in draft form were also received from Peter Beedle of the British Home Office, London; Pekka Kuusi of the Finnish State Alcohol Monopoly, Helsinki, and Kjell Skjelsbaek of the Peace Research Institute, Oslo. Their help is gratefully acknowledged. We also wish to record our thanks to Göta Friman, Pamela Hulls, Barbara Redman and Anita Tombez, who carefully typed successive drafts of the manuscript. In particular, we would like to thank Agneta Bruun and Catherine Stenzl for valuable assistance in the compilation of data.

Because each person participates in the work of the Consortium as an individual, even though he may simultaneously be an official elsewhere, it is important to stress that no participant, consultant, editor, or agency, nor any institution or nation, can take responsibility for what any individual author has written in any of the Consortium's publications.

                                                  Geneva, July 1973

Abbreviations

AID   Agency for International Development
AMA   American Medical Association
AMS   Administrative Management Service
BNDD/DEA   Bureau of Narcotics and Dangerous Drugs/
    Drug Enforcement Administration
CND   Commission on Narcotic Drugs
DSB   Drug Supervisory Body
ECAFE   Economic Commission for Asia and the Far East
ECOSOC   Ecomomic and Social Council
FAO   Food and Agriculture Organization
GIIP   Groupement International de L'Industrie
    Pharmaceutique des Pays de la Communauté
    Economique Européenne
ICAA   International Council on Alcohol and Addictions
ILO   International Labor Organization
IMS   Intercontinental Medical Statistics
INCB   International Narcotics Control Board
INTERPOL   International Criminal Police Organization
IPC   International Police Commission
JIU   Joint Inspection Unit
KMT   Kuomintang

NGO	Non-Governmental Organization
OAC	Opium Advisory Committee
PCB	Permanent Central (Opium/Narcotics) Board
PIA	Pharmaceutical Industries Association in the European Free Trade Area
UN	United Nations
UNCTAD	United Nations Conference on Trade and Development
UNDP	United Nations Development Program
UNESCO	United Nations Educational, Scientific and Cultural Organization
UNFDAC	United Nations Fund for Drug Abuse Control
UNIDO	United Nations Industrial Development Organization
UNTA	United Nations Technical Assistance
WHO	World Health Organization

Introduction

China looks ... to the fullest co-operation of all the
civilized Powers in her attempt to throttle the opium evil.

T'ang Kuo-An, Chinese delegate to the International Opium Commission, 1909

The principal object of all inter-State action against the
illicit liquor traffic is to arrive at an agreement ... under
which each state will undertake to control the exportation of alcohol to the effect that all exportation for illicit
purposes be suppressed.

Väinö Voionmaa (Finland), International Conference against Alcoholism, Geneva, September 1925

In his Government's opinion, amphetamines and the
other stimulants of the central nervous system possessed
all the characteristics of narcotic drugs, and he therefore
urged the Commission to take the necessary steps without
delay....

Dr. Rosen, observer for Sweden, CND, twenty-
second session, 1968

It is in the world interest that the narcotics traffic be
curbed. Drugs pollute the minds and bodies of our young,
bring misery, violence and human economic waste. This
scourge of drugs can be eliminated through international
co-operation.

Richard Nixon, message to the UN on its twenty-
fifth anniversary, October 1970.

Behind these quotations can be seen the
stages of development of international cooperation in the drug
field. They mark the various points in time when different
countries have looked to international support to deal with what
each has considered to be a serious drug predicament within its
territory. The drugs involved have been different: opium in one
case, alochol in another, and manufactured substances in yet
another.

The responses to these and similar appeals have varied widely. In
some cases a long process of international negotiations has been
initiated and a series of international control agreements reached;

1

in others, even the principle of international control has not been accepted.

How does one account for these differing responses? We examined the large literature of historical and contemporary works, legal commentaries, and official documents relating to the subject of international drug control, and found that, while some questions had been satisfactorily analyzed, others had been overlooked. Insights into the complex control machinery itself gained through our personal encounters with it made us skeptical, moreover, of the claims which have frequently been made for the success of international drug control.

Our study begins with a recapitulation of the history of the control system and proceeds to an analysis of its goals and operations. A central concern has been to identify the chief sources of influence—individual persons, agencies, and countries—and the interests which bear upon the decisions and processes in the machinery. As a technique for analysis and presentation, we selected a series of key issues in the development of international control and used them as case studies of the way in which problems have typically been perceived, the manner in which they have been handled, and the different positions which have been taken on them. From all these we have drawn conclusions regarding the successes and failures of the control system and have arrived at a set of recommendations for the future direction of its efforts. That we have offered recommendations at all is a reflection of our view that the international organs concerned should be an object of critical scrutiny and that their future objectives and activities should be a matter of constant public debate.

Our study also addresses a number of neglected perspectives in its attempt to:

—look behind the formal legal structure at the less overt workings of the control machinery;

—consider the League and the UN periods within a continuous historical compass;

—include alcohol control attempts in its discussions;

—quantify observations where feasible.

Setting ourselves these objectives perforce implies a narrowing of the scope of our study to only the drug-centered agencies of the total international system. Quite clearly, to many countries drugs pose less of a problem than, say, poverty, the unequal distribution of wealth, and the pollution of the environment. Yet, even though exaggerations of perceived drug problems often occur, the consequences of the widespread use of some drugs do provide sufficient grounds for countries to work together to devise and implement controls. Some causes of death, some illnesses, and some breakdowns in social relations are closely associated with at least some types of drug-taking. To take two examples of familiar phenomena, alcohol is involved in half the highway fatalities and homicides in the United States and is a causal factor in at least four out of five cases of death from cirrhosis of the liver in France, where such deaths number seventeen thousand annually (Martini and Bode, 1970:316–17). In Britain, over two thousand deaths by barbiturate poisoning were recorded in 1967 (Zacune and Hensman, 1971:117). However, the precise nature of the relationship between drugs and outcomes of use is still a matter of debate and ongoing research. Well-founded opinions vary and sometimes clash over the question of where the core of the problems related to drugs is to be located. The issue is complicated by the fact that drugs which entail risk and which warrant control are often widely used for their beneficial effects in medicine. Discussions concerning harmful and beneficial effects of drugs are, moreover, hampered by difficulties of measurement and the unavoidable intrusion of value judgments. Furthermore, drugs are big business and contribute significantly in some countries to the national economy. The emergence of the pharmaceutical industry as one of the most dynamic sectors of modern economy after the Second World War has greatly added to the vested interests already held in the drug field by, for example, the alcohol industry. The protection of such interests has naturally led to resistance against attempts at control.

There are additional complicating factors. Drugs occupy different places in different cultures; across cultures, attitudes towards drugs with similar properties can vary quite considerably. Thus alcohol use is condoned in France but forbidden, as being against the religious code, in Libya; coca leaves are chewed daily in parts of Peru but not in the United States; use of cannabis leaves is permitted in parts of India but is a crime in Norway, and so forth. Likewise, within the range of pharmaceutical products significant differences exist in the extent to which society deems these products problematic. Thus drugs are not only substances affecting behavior; they have symbolic value and culturally based meanings which influence expectations of effects and, in turn, actual experience.

Some clarification of terminology is necessary. We shall use the term "drugs" to refer to what are variously known in the international vocabulary as drugs of abuse, or as dependence-producing drugs. Thus we include alcohol, the classical narcotics, and other psychoactive drugs. As regards the concept of control, we have not included within the scope of this study such types of control as the monitoring of adverse reactions to drugs, the testing of drugs for efficacy and safety, the application of procedures for the quality control of drugs with which the World Health Organization (WHO), for one, is becoming increasingly concerned. We include under the terms "control" all those factors which bear on the legal, economic, and physical (the "real") availability of drugs to the individual (WHO/FFAS, 1974); it embraces all efforts, whether penal, preventive, educational, or therapeutic.* The concept of "international control" is limited to those forms of intervention which are embodied in international treaties or are dealt with by international organizations, or both. The term "international" refers to relations among and between governments, and between governments and international organizations; it is also used to refer to the behavior of the United Nations system. The UN system is the complex of organizations made up of the UN itself and the specialized agencies such as WHO and the Food and Agriculture Organization (FAO). The UN, on the other hand, is either the body of member states acting through the principal organs, or the Secretariat (the secretary-general and his staff).

* This usage is in keeping with the stance adopted at the 1973 Helsinki meeting of the International Research Group on Drug Legislation and Programs.

I   Perspectives from the Past

1 A Historical Overview

> Suppose there were people from another country who carried opium for sale to England and seduced your people into buying and smoking it: certainly your honorable ruler would deeply hate it. ... Naturally you would not wish to give unto others what you yourself do not want.
>
> Commissioner LinTse-hsu in a letter to Queen Victoria, 1839 (translated from the Chinese).

Before embarking on a historical review of drug control, we should perhaps stress that the drugs discussed represent only a selection from the range of psychoactive substances in existence and that the period covered by our review does not span the entire history of drug control endeavors. Since ancient times most societies have sought to regulate the substances men have used as drugs, whether tea or coffee or opium. But for this study we have abstracted from the range of drugs a limited number and from the historical sequence a circumscribed period of time. This was a period marked by increasing international cooperation, beginning in an opium conference attended by thirteen states and culminating in twelve multilateral treaties.*

The historical development of international arrangements for drug control parallels other forms of international cooperation and is in a sense neither novel nor unique. Its pattern of evolution closely resembles that of other subjects of international concern: the abolition of the African slave trade was one such, and the

---

* For detailed historical accounts the reader is referred to Eisenlohr (1934); Lowes (1966); Musto (1973); Owen (1934); Renborg (1947); Taylor (1969); Terry and Pellens (1928); and Willoughby (1925).

traffic in women and children towards the close of the nineteenth century was another. The sequence of international response seems to run from the convening of a conference of interested states and the passing of resolutions, to the drawing up of treaties, the setting up of international machinery, and the working out of intergovernmental arrrangements within the framework of the League of Nations and, later, the United Nations.

The sources of international action in the different fields of concern share a common context characterized by a rising public conscience at a particular time. This crystallizes into movements and pressure groups in individual countries. Few movements wielded as great an influence or had quite as many repercussions as the antiopium protest at the turn of the century. Among its overall consequences was the creation of a number of enduring international control instruments. In contrast, the results of the temperance movement against alcohol—at least insofar as international action is concerned—are of a far more modest order.

The lesser impact of the temperance movement occurred in spite of the fact that initially the antialcohol movement had a wider support than the antiopium movement. As early as 1808 the first American temperance society was founded in Saratoga, and twenty-five years later a total of six thousand local societies, with a membership of one million, had sprung up in the United States. In 1851 the state of Maine passed the first alcohol prohibition law. Then, from a home-based campaign, the movement went international. Its influence spread to Ireland, England, and the Scandinavian countries, and it gathered much political momentum. In 1878 the first international alcoholism congress was held in Paris. In 1906 an international association was set up, and in the following year its headquarters was established in Lausanne, Switzerland, where it still functions. In 1910 some twenty-seven countries joined this organization. Meanwhile, a more radical counterpart, the International Prohibition Federation, had come into being. In spite of the pressure which these associations could exert upon public and international opinion, little headway was made by them in countries where wine was in daily use and was important economically. Although the temperance movement was essentially a feature of Western societies, its goals would have found much sympathy in the Muhammadan world.

In contrast to the antialcohol movement the antiopium movement was less widespread. It was primarily a British campaign leveled against the British-Indian-Chinese opium trade. The sentiment of opposition it represented was preceded by the Opium War of 1840–42 between Britain and China, which ended in China's defeat and laid it open to foreign trade and missionaries. In 1874 the Society for the Suppression of the Opium Trade was founded in London and steady pressure was applied on the British Parliament from that time onwards to relinquish the opium trade. Towards the end of the nineteenth century the proportion of members voting in the House of Commons for the suppression of the trade showed a progressive increase (Lowes, 1966), signifying the growing support that the antiopium movement was gathering. A corresponding movement was underway in China and later in the United States. Years later, an antiopium bureau was set up in Geneva by A. E. Blanco, an ex-employee of the League of Nations and a former expert in the League's Opium Section. The bureau took upon itself the task of criticizing, for its ineffectiveness, the committee formed under the League to deal with the opium question.

These moral movements cannot be seen independently of other social forces. The British antiopium movement, encroaching as it did upon strong vested interests, would have had less success if it had not been for American backing. The U.S. adopted an antiopium position partly because there were economic reasons for doing so: it was a way of eroding the European domination of the trade with China. Thus the objectives of the moral crusaders coincided with, and were reinforced by, economic objectives (Musto, 1973:24; Taylor, 1969:30).

The Shanghai Commission, to which these developments eventually led, was to have far-reaching consequences. No comparable event marked the history of alcohol control; there the closest approximation to collective effort was in the African-based regional control arrangement arrived at between the parties to the General Brussels Act of 1889–90 and included in the essentially antislavery provisions of the act. The antialcohol campaigners' efforts were largely home-directed, whereas antiopium sentiments were leveled against an essentially foreign habit. The prevailing social climate within which the two groups worked was thus dissimilar. However, it will be remembered that, paradoxically, opium was first used in the West; it was taken to China by Arab traders as a medicine, and the smoking of opium derived from tobacco smoking, another Western import, believed to have been introduced by the Portuguese to Formosa and from there to the mainland of China.

In 1906 a new edict banning opium was issued by the Chinese government in yet another effort to suppress opium, but the ban proved impossible to enforce as long as the system ushered in by the treaties ending the two opium wars held sway (this system placed what were in practice severe limitations on China's sovereignty). In that same year, two significant events occurred which provided some of the impetus for an international opium conference. First, the British Parliament passed a resolution in the House of Commons accepting the proposition of the anti-opium movement that the opium trade should cease. Second, Bishop Brent, a member of an opium investigation committee that had been set up to look into the use of opium in the Philippines (which had been ceded to the United States as a result of the Spanish-American War), wrote a letter to President Theodore Roosevelt proposing that steps be taken to secure international action over China's predicament. The committee had found that opium smoking was a serious problem in the Philippines and that domestic legislation prohibiting the import of nonmedical opium had proved ineffective in reducing the illicit trade; it realized that domestic legislation had to be complemented by international action.

U.S. diplomacy then worked towards this end, and in January 1909 an international opium conference opened in Shanghai with the participation of thirteen powers. Prior to the conference an agreement had been reached between China and Britain for a one-tenth reduction of the Indian opium trade annually.

Among the nations gathered at the conference, the U.S.A., Great Britain, and China naturally dominated. The documentation prepared for the conference largely followed the U.S. format and provided some idea as to the size of the opium problem in the world. Neither the presentation of the various reports nor the discussions to which they gave rise obscured the underlying conflict of interests between the participating countries. The debate revolved around, among other issues, the type of control to be advocated—whether prohibition or regulation, the latter being pressed for by the British, anxious to protect their Indian-

Chinese trade. One of the matters of dispute was the scope of the commission's terms of reference: initial resistance to a discussion of the domestic drug situations of the participating countries gave way under the pressure of international opinion. Another issue was the question of whether the conference was competent to discuss matters of a medical nature: the proposal to consider medical matters was narrowly defeated (by a majority of one), the objection being that expertise for such a task was not sufficiently represented at the conference.

The conference ended in the adoption of nine resolutions, some of which were based on Chinese propositions, others on American and British proposals, and yet others on compromises struck between these two groups of propositions. A number of resolutions dealt exclusively with the Chinese opium question, but there was a resolution addressed to all governments calling for the general suppression of opium smoking (opium eating was not mentioned). Resolution 3, which stated that the use of opium for other than medical purposes was held by "almost every participating country" to be "a matter for prohibition or for careful regulation," represented a compromise between the American and British positions. What was surprising, and perhaps more important, was a resolution on the problem of morphine and an injunction to take "drastic measures" to control its use, which was thought to be spreading. Control of trade was covered by Resolution 4, which pointed to the responsibility of all countries to prevent the export of opium to countries which had prohibited its import.

The Shanghai resolutions required a follow-up, and in fact another meeting was convened three years later, in 1912, this time at The Hague. Again, it was the United States which, through its diplomatic channels, made all the preparations. Conflicting interests were already apparent at this preparatory stage. The meeting was postponed at the request of Great Britain, which insisted on a formulation of the scope of the agenda so that it might include consideration of cocaine and morphine, the latter already touched upon in Shanghai. The British conditions were only partially met in that the detailed statistics on cocaine and morphine, which Britain insisted upon having for the conference, were not as thorough as they had been for opium; nevertheless, compiling them provided the British with some stalling time. In

May 1911 an agreement consolidating the ten-year reduction of the Indian-Chinese trade was concluded, and this made the prospect of the planned conference more palatable to the British. An Italian suggestion to include cannabis in the agenda was not taken up, nor was a similar but independent proposal by Henry Finger to the American delegation, which he was to join. In addition to suggesting that something be done about "Hindoos" in California who demanded cannabis, he also proposed that a friend of his be allowed to supply, free, the finest California wine for the conference banquets—a proposal which Hamilton Wright, a senior member of the U.S. delegation, brusquely rejected.

Although there was no increase, over Shanghai, in the number of countries participating in the Hague meeting, the occasion nevertheless marked the beginning of a shift from a preoccupation with China to a true internationalism. The old disagreement between the U.S. and Great Britain continued, but a new conflict also appeared. Germany, the leading country in drug manufacture at the time, was opposed to the control of cocaine. It attempted, but did not succeed, in removing the drug from the convention which was approved at the conference. It insisted, moreover, that the convention should have universal signature before it could go into effect. This was obviously a strategy to postpone controls. The text of the Hague Convention was by no means a strong one; it left the interpretation of control to the individual governments, and the regulations it called for on production and distribution were domestic rather than international. In addition to the convention a protocol was signed which pointed to the necessity for international control over the mailing of drugs and investigation into the problem of cannabis. Because of the peculiar ratification procedure maneuvered by the German delegation, the Hague Convention did not come into force before the First World War broke out; however, a large number of countries became parties to the Hague Convention through their ratification of the Versailles Treaty. It was the British government which took the lead in securing the ratification of the convention by this method (Buell, 1925:57, 107).

While these international moves were being made to bring opiates and cocaine under control, the adoption of strong measures against alcohol was being contemplated in a number of countries. In the United States, Iceland, and Finland these took the shape of prohibition, while in Canada and Norway they amounted to a partial prohibition. At the international level a measure of control was exercised by the League of Nations through its Permanent Mandates Commission, which supervised the working of the convention on the liquor traffic in Africa, which was signed at Saint Germain-en-Laye in 1919 and superseded the alcohol stipulations of the Brussels Act. As the League of Nations was almost entirely European, and alcohol use is deeply embedded within the European culture, attempts by some countries to interest the League of Nations in alcohol control did not succeed. France, in defense of its wine industry, was the chief opponent of controls.

At the Paris Peace Conference, the involvement of the League of Nations in the drug question was secured by including in the Covenant a provision entrusting to the League "the general supervision over agreements with regard to the traffic in opium and other dangerous drugs." At the first assembly of the League, an Advisory Committee on Traffic in Opium and Other Dangerous Drugs was created. The original European members of the Committee* were countries with opium monopolies in their Far Eastern colonies. Membership increased as time passed. The United States—a nonmember of the League—was not a member of the Advisory Committee, but it managed to participate actively in the work of the committee in a "consultative capacity." But it was the colonial powers and the drug manufacturing countries which largely dominated the picture. If the provisions of the Hague Convention were vague, the terms of reference of the Advisory Committee were equally so. That the control attempts it supervised were not effective was hardly surprising since those countries that would most feel the pinch of control were the ones supervising its application. The nickname which the committee earned—"the old Opium Bloc"—well illustrates this. Admittedly there were difficulties with obtaining adequate information from governments—this was as much, if not more, of a problem then as it is now—and this no doubt hampered the committee's work; but the fact remains that the economic interests which the members served were directly opposed to controls.

* The committee was composed of China, France, Great Britain, Netherlands, India, Japan, Portugal, and Siam.

In other quarters forces were at work to bring about more stringent controls over the production of drugs. In the United States a resolution was passed in Congress in 1923 enjoining the president to exert pressure upon opium and coca-leaf producing countries to agree to direct limitation of production. In deciding in 1927 to widen the membership of the Advisory Committee to include "victim" countries, so that the dominance of those countries "most interested in manufacture or revenue" (Gibberd, 1933) might be diluted, the Assembly of the League was seeking the same end. Renewed talks at another international conference were proposed, and concrete proposals for a quantitative limitation of production were brought before the Advisory Committee by the U.S. These proposals were so controversial and so unwelcome that when they came to be discussed at the Second Geneva Conference in 1925, and acceptance of them was not forthcoming, the U.S. delegation walked out of the conference. At about the same time the Chinese delegation also withdrew because of the failure of the conference to agree on the suppression of opium smoking.

Between 1924 and 1931, several new drug treaties were drawn up. Although the goal had been to achieve a system of quantitative limitation of drug production and manufacture, the form of control agreed upon by the contracting parties was not quite so comprehensive. The most salient features of the new legislation were: the regulation of drug distribution by the Geneva Convention of 1925 and the limitation of the manufacture of opiates to the amounts necessary to meet medical and scientific needs by the Limitation Convention of 1931. (During this same period there was much public alarm at overproduction by drug manufacturers and massive diversions from legal supply channels.) Another important feature of the measures was the inclusion of cannabis in the 1925 convention on an Egyptian request, although this was not an item on the agenda.

By these conventions, new control organs were created. In 1929, the Permanent Central Opium Board, later renamed the Permanent Central Narcotics Board (PCB) began its work.* To avoid governmental control, the PCB was composed of eight experts

---

* The abbreviation PCB will be used here, although PCOB and PCNB are more commonly used in other works.

appointed in their personal capacities, not as government representatives. The 1931 Convention, which set up a system of estimates of national drug requirements, imports, and manufacture, also created the Drug Supervisory Body (DSB) to administer the system. The International Health Office in Paris (the Office International d'Hygiène Publique) and the Health Committee of the League of Nations (and, after 1946, the WHO), were among the appointing bodies. The official representation of international health authorities is a development worth noting.

The creation of new control bodies was prompted by, among other things, the ineffectiveness of the Advisory Committee on Traffic in Opium; conferring supervisory and administrative powers upon wholly new bodies was a tacit affirmation of the committee's unsuitability for the new tasks. As it was constituted, after all, the old committee had little chance of developing and pursuing rigorous control strategies. In contrast, the position which the new bodies took toward governments was firmer, but this firmness derived less from their members' relative freedom from governmental claims than from their being less overwhelmingly dominated by representatives of countries with vested interests in drugs.

Much of the work of the new bodies was concerned with obtaining reliable statistics from governments on drug production and transactions. This work was impaired by the political climate in the late 1930s and the period immediately before the outbreak of the Second World War. While the results of their work, insofar as the effectiveness of control is concerned, are difficult to assess, the extensive information they collected provided a starting point for a sound data base, a prerequisite of planning.

On the other hand, the impact of the implementation of the 1925 and 1931 treaties was discernible in the sharp decrease in the supplies coming from legal drug manufacturers into the illicit market. But illicit drug trafficking did not abate, for clandestine factories were increasingly appearing as substitute suppliers. In 1936 a treaty designed to suppress the illicit traffic was drawn up and called for harsher punitive measure against drug traffickers in the penal systems of contracting parties. The initiative for this stemmed from the International Police Commission, the name by which the International Criminal Police Organization (INTERPOL) was once known.

After the Second World War the United Nations inherited the primary responsibility for drug control. The League of Nations machinery for the control of drugs was transferred almost wholesale into the institutions of the new system. The Advisory Committee on Traffic in Opium was replaced by the Commission on Narcotic Drugs, a functional commission of the Economic and Social Council (ECOSOC); the committee's standing secretariat services, hitherto provided by the League, were taken over by a section of the UN Secretariat which was designated the Division of Narcotic Drugs.

The UN period of drug control differs from the League days in several respects, one of the most significant of which is the number and variety of international agencies which became involved in the drug question in the later era. The expansion of the UN itself is reflected in the progressive increase in the number of countries (especially non-European ones) participating in drug affairs. An effect of multiagency involvement has been an increase in the number of contacts between different approaches to the drug question. Of the related agencies that have come into the picture, the most important by far is WHO, a specialized agency. WHO has an obligation under the drug treaties to evaluate the properties of new drugs to determine whether they should be controlled. The part played by WHO in developing international drug policy is particularly noticeable in the increased emphasis upon treatment as a preventive form of control. Another potential contribution is the initiative WHO recently took to bridge the gulf between the handling of alcohol and of other psychoactive drugs. Previously in WHO, alcohol has been the province of the Mental Health Unit, while other psychoactive drugs have been the concern of the Drug Dependence Unit. Recently, a merger between the two at the administrative level has occurred, giving effect to what has been called the "combined approach," which sees the usefulness, in some instances, of considering alcohol and other drugs together.

The concentration upon opium continued after the Second World War and considerable effort was invested in the creation of an international opium monopoly. The project failed, however. Instead, an Opium Protocol, which was adopted in New York in 1953, attempted to limit production by less direct means than those envisaged by the international monopoly project. The most notable provision of the 1953 protocol was the limitation of the number of legitimate producers of opium for export to seven: Bulgaria, Greece, India, Iran, Turkey, USSR, and Yugoslavia. Other provisions were in a similarly stringent vein; not surprisingly, this treaty took ten years before receiving enough ratifications to allow it to come into force.

The next major development was the consolidation and unification of all the treaties entered into since the Hague Conference of 1912. This effort resulted in the Single Convention on Narcotic Drugs of 1961, which was aimed at replacing all but one of the earlier treaties, namely the 1936 treaty on the suppression of illicit traffic.

But the Single Convention was not a mere technical instrument for bringing together disparate pieces. In the control of cannabis, it signified a new policy—prohibition. Nominally, the convention effected a change in the structure of the control machinery: the PCB and DSB, which were in practice already unified (see chapter 6), were merged to form the International Narcotics Control Board (INCB). Furthermore, the convention contained recommendations to parties to provide facilities for the treatment, rehabilitation, and care of drug addicts.

The Single Convention nevertheless left outside its scope a number of substances which were causing disquiet in several countries and were considered suitable for control under this convention. As will presently be shown, the variety of psychoactive drugs which became available after the Second World War increased considerably. In 1949 the WHO Expert Committee on Habit-forming Drugs had commented upon the abuse of amphetamines, but this was not discussed by the Commission on Narcotic Drugs until 1955. In the case of barbiturates and tranquilizers, concern in WHO circles dated from 1950 and 1956, respectively, and in the Narcotics Commission from 1957. But action at the international level was not taken until much later, as all the while the international community was endorsing a policy of control at the *national* level. Initiatives taken by Sweden to have amphetamines placed under international control found growing support until, at a conference in Vienna in 1971, a Convention on Psychotropic Substances, including amphetamines, was adopted.* At the last count (February 1974), this

* In the terminology of the Vienna Convention, "psychotropic substances" are depressants and stimulants of the central nervous system (tranquilizers, barbiturates, and amphetamines) and also hallucinogens.

convention had acquired only sixteen ratifications, a number insufficient to bring it into force.

All these developments have not affected the international community's long-standing preoccupation with opiates. In March 1972 another UN conference was convened, following a U.S. initiative, to consider amendments to the Single Convention. The stated objective of the conference was to strengthen the convention's provisions to deal more effectively with the illicit traffic in opiates. It is widely accepted that the Single Convention controls over opium production represented a relaxation of those arrived at in the 1953 Opium Protocol; thus what was attempted by the amendments was to bring about a return to the stiffer controls agreed upon by the parties to the 1953 protocol and rejected by the conference which adopted the Single Convention of 1961.

In 1970 the proposal was formally made by the United States that a special United Nations Fund for Drug Abuse Control (UNFDAC) be set up, to be administered by the secretary-general and to be sustained by voluntary contributions from different sources. Accompanying the proposal was an initial pledge of $2 million by the U.S. government. In April 1971 the fund came into being.

During the last three-quarters of a century the international interest in the drug question has clearly changed in scope as well as in outlook. This change was accompanied by a change in vocabulary. In the official documents of today words like "evil" and "vice" appear less often, and "addiction" is now often referred to as "dependence." One of the more popular contemporary phrases is "drug abuse control," which has come to be synonymous with curbing illicit use, reducing illicit supplies, treating addiction and a host of other activities. Confusion is inevitable and is not helped by the continued use of the word "narcotics" (which means, pharmacologically, drugs capable of producing both sleep and analgesia) for all the internationally controlled drugs, in spite of their different modes of action. Even so, the tendency is towards greater precision in terminology. The choice of words does have practical social consequences, but the change in UN parlance may not necessarily reflect changes in underlying beliefs and approaches (Christie & Bruun, 1968). Much lip service has been paid of late to the concept of affecting consumer "demand," but the thrust of international efforts is still being directed towards controlling supply.

It may be of help to the reader to tabulate the drug treaties according to their age and status. This is done in table 1.1. As the intention of this chapter has been to provide a background to the contemporary workings of the control system, rather than to offer detailed historical recapitulation, some of the treaties appearing in the table have not been mentioned in the text, being of lesser importance.

Running parallel to the events just recounted were changes in drug production and use in the world at large, changes closely interwoven with the progressive elaboration of international treaties. A look at the changes in the quantity and variety of drugs that have been produced over the years will provide a clue to the changing world drug economies which control endeavors have sought to influence and to which they have had to adjust.

In table 1.2 changes in the level of production of a number of drugs are shown.* Figures are provided for four points in time only, with intervals of twenty-five years between each of the first three points, beginning from 1909, the year of the Shanghai Commission, commonly regarded as the starting-point of international drug control. It was for the Shanghai Commission that data on opium production were first collected on anything like a world scale. The twenty-five-year time span was selected so as to minimize the effects of the two world wars and artefacts created by short-term fluctuations of a possibly random character. A few notes of explanation may be necessary on the data presented.

First, it should be noted that there are considerable gaps in the data. For some drugs no production figures are available. This is the case, for instance, with barbiturates and amphetamines. Currently, the only source of comprehensive information relating to sales totals by country of such drug groupings as barbiturates seems to be the Intercontinental Medical Statistics (IMS), an organization which, among other activities, supplies on contract to individual pharmaceutical manufacturers such information as the share of the market which a firm has in the sale of its products in a particular country. This information is confidential and is

---

* International treaties distinguish between production and manufacture, but here the term "production" is used to mean either or both.

TABLE 1.1
Multilateral Treaties on Narcotics and Psychotropic Substances

Date and place signed	Title of Treaty	Date of entry into force	Number of ratifications[a] (1 November 1972)
23 January 1912 The Hague	International Opium Convention	11 February 1915[b]	102
11 February 1925 Geneva	Agreement concerning the manufacture of, internal trade in, and use of, prepared opium[c]	28 July 1926	55
19 February 1925 Geneva	International Opium Convention[c]	25 September 1928	78
13 July 1931 Geneva	Convention for limiting the manufacture and regulating the distribution of narcotic drugs[c]	9 July 1933	91
27 November 1931 Bangkok	Agreement for the control of opium smoking in the Far East[c]	22 April 1937	
26 June 1936 Geneva	Convention for the suppression of the illicit traffic in dangerous drugs[c]	26 October 1933	31
11 December 1946 Lake Success, New York	Protocol amending the agreements, conventions and protocols on narcotic drugs concluded at The Hague on 23 January 1912, at Geneva on 11 February 1925 and 19 February 1925 and 13 July 1931, at Bangkok on 27 November 1931, and at Geneva on 26 June 1936	11 December 1946	59
19 November 1948 Paris	Protocol bringing under international control drugs outside the scope of the convention of 13 July 1931 for limiting the manufacture and regulating the	1 December 1949	109

	distribution of narcotic drugs, as amended by the protocol signed at Lake Success, New York, on 11 December 1946	8 March 1963	52
23 June 1953 New York	Protocol for limiting and regulating the cultivation of the poppy plant, the production of, international and wholesale trade in, and use of, opium		
30 March 1961 New York	Single Convention on Narcotic Drugs	13 December 1964	119
21 February 1971 Vienna	Convention on Psychotropic Substances		7 (32)d
25 March 1972	Protocol amending the Single Convention on Narcotic drugs, 1961		0 (47)d

aIncluding states having declared themselves bound by the treaty, the application of which had previously been extended to their territory.

bOn this date China, the U.S., and the Netherlands put the convention into force among themselves. Norway and Honduras joined them later that year. But not until the convention was made part of the Versailles Treaty in 1919 were its obligations assumed worldwide.

cAs amended by the protocol signed at Lake Success, New York, on 11 December 1946.

dThe number in parentheses is the number of signatures.

TABLE 1.2
World (Licit) Production of Dependence-Producing Drugs

	1909	1934	1959	1970
Raw opium (tons)	25,800	6,800	1,000	1,200
Poppy straw (tons)	–	–	12,600a	31,300a
Morphine (kg)	?	26,800	108,200	177,000
Heroin (kg)	?	1,100	80	100
Codeine (kg)	?	17,200	98,000	169,000
Ethylmorphine (bionine) (kg)	–	1,700	8,200	9,200
Pethidine (kg)	–	–	14,200	14,800
Coca leaves (tons)	?	?	11,300	18,600
Cocaine (kg)	?	3,400	900	1,900
Cannabis	?	?	?	?
Barbiturates	?	?	?	?
Amphetamines	–	?	?	?
Tranquillizers		–	?	?
Distilled spirits (1,000 hectolitre)	44,557b	40,600b	21,224	44,457
Wine (1,000 hectolitre)	157,262	207,300	219,017	286,149
Beer (1,000 hectolitre)	295,919	179,900	382,707	630,157

SOURCES: 1909 opium figure: International Opium Commission, Shanghai, 1909.
1934 opium figure: analytical study by OAC (C.305.M 203. 1937 XI).
All other figures except those for alcohol: PCB/INCB statistics.
Alcohol: 1909 figures from Gabrielsson (1915); 1934 from Voionmaa (1939); 1959 and 1970 from UN publication
Growth of World Industry (1968, 1970).

aThese figures refer to the volume of poppy straw used in the manufacture of morphine.
bThese figures include quantities of industrial alcohol. The 1909 figures are means of figures for the period 1906–10.

strictly for the use of those firms which subscribe to the service in question. But no data on aggregate production of the so-called "psychotropic drugs" are currently available on a world scale.* Statistics on these substances are being compiled by the International Narcotics Control Board in anticipation of its duties under the Vienna Convention (see chapter 16). The figures which appear in the table are mostly derived from statistics supplied to INCB by governments under their treaty obligations. But even with drugs for which statistical reporting has long been required, production information is incomplete. This is the case, for instance, with cannabis.

For another reason, caution should be exercised in interpreting the data presented. All the information given is based on declared, or reported, data supplied to the UN by individual countries; the information is thus only as good as the data of the country from which it is obtained.

The number and variety of drugs have greatly increased over the period under review. This reflects the rise of the pharmaceutical industry from before the First World War to its prominent place in the commercial sector after the Second World War. The period after the war was unique in its alertness to the importance of psychiatric illness (Hordern, 1968), and it was in this climate that the major tranquilizers made their appearance. More recently a number of minor tranquilizers such as chlordiazepoxide (Librium) and diazepam (Valium) have come on the scene. Predating all these were the barbiturates, the clinical use of which began at about the same time (1903) as nations were foregathering to lay the foundations of international drug control. Hordern notes that prior to the latter part of the nineteenth century "natural" hypnosedatives, such as alcohol and cannabis, were widely used, "and the new drugs that were introduced into clinical practice differed from the older agents in being synthetic, and in being free at first from the degradation and social misery the others sometimes produced" (1968: 117). Also preceding the tranquilizers were the amphetamines, first used for depression in 1936. But the ones to arouse the most public interest among the new "psychotropic substances" were the hallucinogens, notably

---

* John Borland, who heads IMS in Britain, is said to be writing a book which contains these data.

LSD. To provide some idea of the importance which psychoactive drugs have come to assume, we reproduce below some figures on prescriptions for hypnotics, tranquilizers, and antidepressives, and ingredient costs of psychoactive drugs for one country, Britain.

Number of prescriptions (million)*		% of total prescriptions
1961	26.2	12.6
1968	42.2	15.8
1971	45.1	18.2

Net ingredient cost (million £) of psychoactive drugs (unspecified)†		% of total drug ingredient cost
1965	10	12
1966	12	13
1971	22.7	16

The figures imply not only the wide extent to which these drugs are used but the heavy financial investment they represent.

To return to the world production table, it should be noted in relation to the figures for opium that the bulk of the world's licitly produced opium is converted to morphine, most of which (about 90 percent in some countries) goes in turn to make codeine. Since, under the international system of control, licit production of opium is more or less limited to the amount required to satisfy medical needs, the production figures can be taken roughly to indicate legal consumption level. However, the apparent decline in the consumption of opium, morphine, heroin, and cocaine must not be taken to mean an actual decrease in use; to these figures should be added illicit or unsupervised consumption. For opium, illicit production is estimated to be around 1,200 tons a year (INCB, 1969). During the earlier period (1909–34) non-medical consumption accounted for a large part of the opium

---

* Source: Zacune and Hensman, 1971:57
† Sources: Hordern, 1968: 148; *Annual Report of the Department of Health and Social Security for the Year 1971* (London: HMSO).

produced, while morphine manufacture absorbed a considerably smaller quantity. The picture for the later years has altered, and the quantity of opium smoked or eaten out of the total amount produced licitly is negligible. Most licit opium is consumed in the form of codeine. The alcohol statistics may not be entirely reliable either, and the comparability of the figures for distilled spirits, especially between the first and second points in time, is open to question. However, subject to this qualification, it is noteworthy that production of beer and distilled spirits decreased between 1909 and 1934. The effects of control attempts, the First World War, and the scarcity of raw materials may have contributed to this decrease. The increase of production between 1959 and 1970 appears to have affected the world pattern of drinking (Sulkunen, 1973).

Table 1.3 illustrates the geographical distribution of drug producers. Opium, coca leaves, and cannabis are produced predominantly in the economically poorer, or less-developed, countries while manufactured drugs are products of industrialized societies. This pattern reflects production economies generally, regardless of drug, in which primary products form the bulk of the exports by poor countries to rich countries. The division is less apparent in the figures for alcohol production, but on the whole the industrialized countries predominate.

This pattern has implications also for the relation between production and consumption. In 1909 the leading producers of opium and alcohol were also big consumers. Industrialization and the development of international trade have weakened the link between production and consumption. Nevertheless, it is still manifest in the high level of alcohol consumption in the top two wine-producing countries, France and Italy, and in the large share of the world's consumption of pharmaceutical products by those countries which manufacture the bulk of them (Wortzel, 1971). There are exceptions: Algerian wine production, for example, is unrelated to Algerian consumption, and Turkish opium production to Turkish use of opium. Thus the distribution among countries of the total world production does not always correspond to the distribution of consumption.

Finally, we offer some general observations which will be elaborated in later chapters.

TABLE 1.3
Main Licit Drug-Producing Countries

	1909	1934	1959	1970
Raw opium	China India Persia	China Persia India	India Turkey USSR	India USSR Iran
Cannabis	India Pakistan	India Pakistan	India Pakistan	India Pakistan
Coca leaves	Peru Bolivia	Peru Bolivia Netherlands (East Indies)	Peru Bolivia	Peru Bolivia
Cocaine		Japan U.S. U.K.	U.S. France Japan	U.S. Peru
Morphine		U.S. Germany Japan	USSR U.K. U.S.	USSR U.K. U.S.
Heroin		Japan U.K. Germany	U.K. Belgium	U.K.
Codeine		Germany U.S. France	USSR U.K. U.S.	USSR U.K. U.S.
Ethylmorphine		Germany	France	France

Pethidine		U.S. Switzerland	West Germany U.S. U.K. West Germany	U.K. West Germany U.S. U.K. West Germany
Distilled spirits	Russia Germany U.S.	USSR France U.S. Germany	U.S. Japan U.K. Brazil	U.S. U.K. Japan West Germany
Wine	France Italy Spain	France Italy Spain	Italy France Algeria Argentina	Italy France USSR Spain
Beer	U.S. Germany U.K.	U.S. Germany U.K.	U.S. West Germany U.K.	U.S. West Germany U.K.

Column group headers: USSR / West Germany (third group); U.S. / Switzerland (second group).

SOURCES: For 1909: International Opium Commission, Shanghai, 1909.
For other years (barring alcohol data): PCB/INCB statistics.

NOTE: The three leading countries are given in descending order of production level except where, as in the case of coca leaves, two countries have a virtual monopoly over production, or where fewer than three countries are involved in licit production of any significance (e.g., for heroin), or where the fourth country produces close to the quantity produced by the third.

1. International drug control was initiated in response to a specific problem in a specific area of the world—opium in China. Opium and its alkaloids came to be the main focus of subsequent control efforts.

2. The pattern of international control evolved from measures to check unbridled opium trade and to suppress opium smoking to the regulation of international trade and the limitation of manufacture and production.

3. The introduction of cocaine into the international control scene was due to the delaying tactics of an opium power (Britain); its classification as a drug needing control was based on incomplete documentation and uncertain evidence. Cannabis control appeared to be extempore.

4. International supervision of alcohol control was confined to Africa between the two world wars. Efforts to expand such control were unsuccessful.

5. WHO's role became more prominent as the number of medically prescribed dependence-producing drugs increased. This allows, in theory, more emphasis to be placed on the treatment of the drug addict rather than on the use of criminal sanctions.

6. Initiatives for more forceful control have mostly come from the U.S. Behind these initiatives were moral pressures, confidence in regulatory codes, economic incentives, and an active diplomacy.

7. The main obstacles to statutory international control have been the vested interests of the opium monopoly countries in the early phases, and of the drug manufacturing countries in subsequent periods.

8. The drug control system of the League of Nations was inherited by the UN. WHO's participation in international drug control is based on a statutory responsibility for evaluating drugs for control, and on an interest in the medical aspects of drug use. It has evolved a "combined approach" towards alcohol and other dependence-producing drugs.

9. Structural social changes between 1909 and 1970 were accompanied by:

   —the appearance of a large variety of new dependence-producing industrial pharmaceutical products;

   —shifting sources of the illegal trade in drugs under inter-

national control;
—marked changes in licit production, for example, a decrease in opium and heroin production and, although no general trend was discernible, an increase in the production of distilled spirits and beer in the 1960s.

II The System

2   A Note on Evaluation

> ... the Commission has done truly constructive work.
>
> By now the problems have been clearly defined and some of them have been solved, or the instruments of their solution have been created: non-medical consumption of opium, coca leaf, cannabis, and of the drugs manufactured from them is outlawed in principle and is bound to disappear after transitional periods of adaptation....
>
> "Twenty Years of Narcotic Control Under the United Nations—Review of the Work of the Commision on Narcotic Drugs," *Bulletin on Narcotics* (1966)

      We turn now from the historical development of international drug control to a consideration of the present situation, without, however, altogether abandoning the historical dimension. In this chapter we will discuss the legal framework which has evolved, and the related international institutions, in terms of structure, resources, policies, and functions. We shall try to see the forces which shape the overall legal framework as well as the patterns of power found within the institutions and the way in which these forces shape the decisions which emerge.

There has been no systematic evaluation to date of the workings of the international drug control machinery. The above quotations, taken from a UN publication, are examples of the kind of unrealistic and self-commending appraisal that does exist. In this and other reviews of its work, the Commission on Narcotic Drugs, like many other organizations, affirms its own value as if this was an assessment of objective reality. In fact, it was agreed by the commission before the review was written by the UN Secretariat that "it should focus attention on the achievements of the Commission" (E/CN.7 / SR.559, 1966).

Yet the survival and growth of an organization may also require periodic review of its performance; the acknowledgment of difficulties or inadequacies is, after all, a ground for further investment and change. But the public debate of issues and the continuous scrutiny of systems and institutions within a society that take place at the national level have no parallel in the international sphere. Here such criticism is either absent or tacit, or else it is always "unofficial."

The absence of proper evaluation and a constructively critical attitude towards the activities of international bodies is what makes it so difficult to study them. Despite the fact that we encountered, during the course of our own study, many cooperative individuals within the international organizations, there was in general a resistance to requests for data, the lack of which has no doubt affected not only the analysis attempted of the work of the international drug control bodies but also the conclusions at which the study will later arrive.

That this resistance is not due to any particular antagonism towards the authors themselves is borne out by the fact that access to the information sought has been denied other investigators. In fact the role played by members of the secretariats of international organizations may be seen as an occupational role close to that of the diplomat and of the civil servant (Galtung, 1966), two roles that carry with them a resistance to open discussions of their work and a corresponding belief in the virtue of secrecy. No doubt there are reasons for, and utility in, a good deal of work-related secrecy, but these reasons are too readily used to protect the prevailing policy against criticism (Lowry, 1972). Yet the importance of an evaluation of the work of international organizations has frequently been pointed out, not least by the organizations themselves. Within the UN system the existence of a Joint Inspection Unit (JIU) and an Administrative Management Service (AMS) attests to this need. Indeed, according to the reports of these units, there are real inadequacies in the administration of programs by the UN and its related agencies (Bertrand, 1971). Robert Jackson's "Study of the Capacity of the UN Development System" (DP/5, 1969), a critical evaluation of the UN agencies' management of development programs, similarly found it to be a system "without a brain." In WHO steps are said to have been taken to evaluate its activities. Such work, however, is usually carried out by "insiders" (Sacks, interview), who are likely to be bound by loyalty and self-interest and to be partisan. The AMS, for instance, is staffed by a segment of the UN Secretariat, and, when a unit is under review, the AMS is assisted by the staff of that unit; although outside recruits and consultants are used, the AMS team is essentially an internal one. Furthermore, AMS reports are restricted to high-ranking UN officials, and outside investigators have no access to them.

Much of the literature on international organizations, some of it containing valuable material, consists of work by people who have either been employed by, or have been closely associated with, the organizations. A history of the League of Nations written by F. P. Walters, who worked closely with the first secretary-general, is one such work (Walters, 1952). Perhaps the best example of what can be achieved by combining critical evaluation on the one hand with intimate inside knowledge on the other is Landy's study of the International Labor Office (ILO) (Landy, 1966).

All this is not to say that international organizations are impervious to research. On the contrary, much of the research on these organizations has been done with the assistance of the officials working in them. While such research often yields insight into the nature of international organizations, much of what is done is seen as irrelevant as far as practical appplications of findings is concerned (Dittert, interview). Good and relevant studies—such as that on the decentralization of WHO (Berkov, 1957)—certainly exist, but more of these might be done if it were not for the likelihood of official cooperation being withdrawn as soon as sensitive topics are broached (Anderson and Nijkerk, 1958).

These comments are not to be construed as implying criticism of those international civil servants who have aided our information-gathering. We are articulating a typical attitude of scientific investigators. We believe that outsiders have a contribution to make. In saying this, we are of course taking a stand on the issue of the relative merits of the "outsider" and "insider" positions. Whereas the "insiders" will argue that you *must* be Caesar in order to understand him, the "outsider" will argue that you *must not* be Caesar to do that. Both arguments may be vaild to a degree: insiders having "acquaintance with" and outsiders reaching "knowledge about" a phenomenon may arrive at the same point in understanding. Be that as it may, the broader perspective still comes more easily to the outsider, as is generally acknowledged in the social-behavioral tradition. Although we consider ourselves outsiders, we have tried, through observation of the system at close quarters and by interviewing the insiders, to benefit from the advantages of both positions.

Our approach to international organizations may be said to fall within a school of thought which holds that:

Every status quo—societal, organizational, or factional—thrives on myth and mystification. Every group in power ... tells its story as it would like to have it believed, in the way it thinks will promote its interests.... Every group in power profits from ambiguity and mystification, which hide the facts of power from those over whom power is exerted and thus make it easier to maintain hegemony and legitimacy. A sociology that is true to the world inevitably clarifies what has been confused, reveals the character of organizational secrets, upsets the interests of powerful people and groups (Becker & Horowitz, 1972: 54-55).

3   Goals and Means

> Broadly speaking, the system established by the[Single]
> Convention is extremely simple. Narcotic drugs can be
> consumed only on medical prescription or at least in the
> legal performance of a therapeutic function.
>> Paul Reuter, "The Obligations of States under the
>> Single Convention on Narcotic Drugs."
>> *Bulletin on Narcotics* (1968)

The international system of drug control rests on a legal framework provided by the written international agreements of governments and brought into being by diplomatic conferences. The implementation of these agreements is supervised and monitored by decision-making and administrative bodies. The different forces which influence the system—and in a sense are part of it—are traceable not only to the international institutions but also to the participating nations and, ultimately, to the different interests within each nation. We will discuss how these forces interact. Because of the central role occupied by the international bodies, as both the agents and the arenas of these interactions, we have made them the focus of our analysis.

We will begin with an analysis of the stated objectives of the system and proceed to an overview of the types of control subsumed under that system, seeing these as an end-product of international efforts. We will then go on to examine the formal mechanisms and procedures that are used in the international setting to achieve certain ends.

Goals

The avowed aim of the control system is to combat drug abuse. In examining this goal we are compelled to raise a series of questions. Is the goal the total suppression of abuse or is it the achievement of a tolerable level of undesirable drug use? Does the system recognize other goals? Is it possible to discern more specific, operational goals?

The International Opium Commission at Shanghai, in 1909, formulated its resolutions against the background of the Chinese problem but stated in general terms that:

the use of opium in any form otherwise than for medical purpose is held by almost every participating country to be a matter for prohibition or for careful regulation and that each country in the administration of its system of regulation purports to be aiming, as opportunity offers, at progressively increasing stringency.

Contained in this statement are some of the questions which have since bedevilled efforts to evolve a workable international drug control policy. One of these questions concerns availability of drugs for medical use. Another is the choice between prohibition and "careful regulation."

The aims of the international drug treaties may be inferred from the preambles. The following excerpts illustrate the differing formulations of goals in the various conventions:

The Hague Convention, 1912. Determined to bring about the gradual suppression of the abuse of opium, morphine and cocaine, as also of the drugs prepared or derived . . . .

The Geneva Convention, 1925. Convinced that the contraband trade in and abuse of these substances cannot be effectually suppressed except by bringing about a more effective limitation of the production or manufacture of the substances, and by exercising a closer control and supervision of the international trade. . . .

The 1931 Limitation Convention. Desiring to supplement the provisions of the International Opium Convention by rendering effective by international agreement the limitation of the manufacture of narcotic drugs to the world's legitimate requirements for medical and scientific purposes and by regulating their distribution. . . .

The 1936 Convention on Illicit Traffic. Having resolved, on the one hand, to penalize offences contrary to the provisions [of earlier treaties] . . . and, on the other hand, to combat by the methods most effective in the present circumstances the illicit traffic in the drugs and substances. . . .

The 1948 Protocol. Desiring to supplement the provisions of that [1931 Limitation] Convention and to place these [synthetic] drugs, including their preparations and compounds containing these drugs, under control in order to limit by international agreement their manufacture to the world's legitimate requirements for medical and scientific purposes and to regulate their distribution....

The 1953 Protocol. Determined to continue their efforts to combat drug addiction and illicit traffic ... considering, however, that it is essential to limit to medical and scientific needs and regulate the production of the raw materials....

Single Convention 1961. The Parties, concerned with the health and welfare of mankind, recognizing that the medical use of narcotic drugs continues to be indispensable for the relief of pain and suffering and that adequate provision must be made to ensure the availability of narcotic drugs for such purposes, recognizing that addiction to narcotic drugs constitutes a serious evil for the individual and is fraught with social and economic danger to mankind ... considering that effective measures against abuse of narcotic drugs require co-ordination and universal action, understanding that such universal action calls for international co-operation guided by the same principles and aimed at common objectives ... desiring to conclude a generally acceptable international convention replacing existing treaties on narcotic drugs, limiting such drugs to medical and scientific use, and providing for continuous international co-operation and control for the achievement of such aims and objectives....

Vienna Convention 1971. The parties, being concerned with the health and welfare of mankind, noting with concern the public health and social problems resulting from the abuse of certain psychotropic substances, determined to prevent and combat abuse of such substances and the illicit traffic to which it gives rise, considering that rigorous measures are necessary to restrict the use of such substances to legitimate purposes, recognizing that the use of psychotropic substances for medical and scientific purposes is indispensable and that their availability for such purposes should not be unduly restricted....

Conceptions of the problem have evolved from the threat that was represented by Chinese opium smoking in 1909 to the danger that was envisaged to the health and welfare of mankind in 1961. This change may be partly one in the manner of expressing the problem, but not entirely so. The problem which engaged the attention of the international committee in 1909 was opium smoking, facilitated by the unrestricted import of this drug into China. By 1912 the perception of the problem had extended to the "abuse of opium, morphine and cocaine," whereas the concept of "addiction"—a narrower one than "abuse"—was introduced in 1953. The Single Convention refers to both addiction and use, but the concept of addiction is given much emphasis and is expressed in emotionally charged terms ("addiction constitutes a serious evil"). Of all the definitions of the problem, that expressed in the Vienna Convention is the broadest: "the public health and social problems resulting from the abuse of certain psychotropic substances." Most of the treaties, including the Vienna Convention, also refer specifically to the problem of illicit trade.

As some treaties were enacted to supplement earlier ones, they omitted, as may be expected, a definition of the problem. They do attest, however, to the failure of the earlier treaties to resolve the problem and to the need for additional arrangements.

The definition of concrete objectives also has undergone changes. In 1909 the "gradual suppression" of opium smoking was recommended and the nonmedical use of opium was to be subjected to "prohibition or careful regulation." Only the "gradual suppression" of abuse was mentioned in 1912. The 1925 convention sought to suppress "effectually" contraband trade and abuse. By 1931 the goal is stated as a "limitation of manufacture to legitimate [i.e., medical and scientific] requirements."

There are two sides to controlling drug availability: on the one hand medical and scientific supplies have to be ensured; on the other supplies for other kinds of use have to be withheld or restricted. In view of the need to protect the interests of medicine and science and simultaneously to "prevent and combat" drug addiction, the control system is said to have dual goals.

A clear-cut separation of goals and means is not possible. Ultimate goals—such as "the health and welfare of mankind"— are sought through processes which often come to acquire the values of ends; thus prevention of "drug abuse" as a step towards universal health and welfare has come to be an end itself. Farther down on the scale between immediate and ultimate objectives, such means for achieving drug control as regulation of international trade, law enforcement, international cooperation, and the like acquire more than instrumental value and come to assume the importance of goals in themselves. Excluded from the treaties is a statement of their levels of aspiration in what they seek to do.

A treaty should ideally be an instrument of some duration, and this militates against the setting forth of a very specific set of goals in the treaty itself. Moreover, its international character behooves it to avoid goals that have relevance for only a single nation. That the dual goals of ensuring medical/scientific availability and preventing other kinds of use are not always commensurable makes it all the more difficult to set specific objectives.

We might well note in this context that these two goals do not only coexist but also overlap. Scientific and public debate is by no means agreed on what constitutes medical need as opposed to nonmedical, or on alternative ways of minimizing the risks involved in drug use; nor is speculation ended as to how factors such as fringe medical needs or alternative drugs and treatment modes may affect the balance between availability and control. Where are the lines to be drawn, if indeed any lines can be drawn?

The formulation of the two goals has undergone a slight but significant change in the last drug treaty. While the preamble of the Single Convention notes "that the medical use of narcotic drugs continues to be indispensable for the relief of pain and suffering and that adequate provision must be made to ensure the availability of narcotic drugs for such purposes," the Vienna Convention formulates the idea in this way: "the use of psychotropic substances for medical and scientific purposes is indispensable and ... their availability for such purposes should not be unduly restricted." The latter, in not tying the definition of medical needs down to pain and suffering, would seem to broaden the category of medical use to the practice, for example, of enhancing or suppressing emotional behavior or performance.

To reach ultimate, necessarily long-term, goals, there is first a need for short-term goal-setting. This also applies, of course, when no specific goal is set but only a direction of action. What may be termed operational goals which general or specific programs are designed to attain are not formulated in the international agreements, nor are they often made explicit publicly. One reason for this may be that specific objectives and plans by which the overall goal can be reached are not readily definable; another may be that, in a situation of limited resources and options, to be precise is often to court criticism for subsequent failure to attain the objectives set. Perhaps, too, a treaty might be harder to agree on if it were to attend to more concrete affairs. Nevertheless, a clear definition of operational goals is a necessary part of planning. The natural forums for reaching such definitions should be the sessions of the Commission on Narcotic Drugs and ECOSOC.

When it comes to executing these programs, the various international agencies will derive their operational goals from those set for the tasks assigned to them. However, it is characteristic of most organizations that, regardless of these assigned goals, one of their prime concerns will be to increase their existing allocation of resources and power and to maintain the interest of individual functionaries even if these ends prove inconsistent with those formal mandates set forth as their tasks.

Both at the international and the national level drug policy is usually only part of a more comprehensive public policy, and the objectives of one must conform to, or fit within, the goals of the other. A country may wish, for example, to allocate its resources to education or to development of an industrial infrastructure, rather than to finding substitutes for drug-bearing crops or to enforcement of drug laws. In this case little headway will be gained by proponents of drug programs, at least not as long as the priorities remain that way. If, on the other hand, the drug policy agreed upon by the international community is in line with the government's own general policy, the government will pursue it and will brandish it at international gatherings with a suitable underlining of its contribution to international solidarity.

Other goals, such as a desire to safeguard national sovereignty and commercial interests, will influence the position of a country vis-à-vis the development of treaties and its subsequent willingness to adhere to them. Once a state becomes a party to a convention, fulfilling its obligations under the convention may become an end in itself. However, even within these obligations there is often room enough for the contracting state to aim for the furtherance of a variety of interests. Such interests are not a priori less legitimate, nor do they invariably reflect commercial interests. The Vatican state, has, for example, suggested that the safeguarding of human rights be considered an important goal in the area of drug control.

These diverse goals interact on different levels, sometimes in conflict and other times in concordance. Their realization depends on what possibilities exist in the means for attaining them and what forces and interests will prevail in the final decision and action. The choice of goals and actions is based upon concepts of what the problems are, how they have come about, what various measures can do to counter them, and how drug policy relates to other interests.

Attitudes towards drug control range from opposition to all controls to belief in the need for total prohibition. The former attitude may be based on a number of notions—that the problem does not exist, or that controls will not bring about any improvement in the situation, or that society should not interfere with what is perceived as the private conduct of the individual, or that possible improvements would be outweighed by the costs of producing them, or that it is more important to protect commercial interests connected with production and sale. The revenue-oriented policy of the British in the Indian-Chinese opium trade at the close of the nineteenth century might be an example of the last position. Variations of the same position were taken by the drug manufacturing countries of Western Europe towards international control in the early days of the League of Nations. Illustrations of the prohibitionist attitude might be drawn from the alcohol field. Here there are some examples of implemented prohibition policies, although the use of alcohol for industrial purposes has seldom been questioned. As has been mentioned earlier, the two prongs of international control are, first, ensuring medical supplies and, second, minimizing nonmedical use. Insofar as it is only over nonmedical and nonscientific use that control is to be exerted, the international approach may be seen as one of partial prohibition. That even this is not wholly accepted is suggested by the fact that under the Single Convention, for instance, reservations can be made to certain provisions so as to allow the continued nonmedical use of some of the substances it covers.

A number of intermediate positions between laissez-faire and total prohibition can be identified. The position taken by a group or nation is not necessarily determined by a particular philosophy but may have to do with actual possibilities, given local legal tradition, resources, and expectations of outcome.

From the texts of treaties two crucial concepts emerge—coordination and evaluation. Both the Single Convention and the Vienna Convention point to the necessity for coordinated action. However, the conflict of interests, such as that between civil rights and law enforcement, between scientific interests and regulatory purposes, pose serious challenges to drug policy formation; it is usually not possible to give every interest its due. Nevertheless, it is important for conflicts between goals to be brought out into the open. The other point is the importance of evaluation. The preamble to the 1925 Geneva Convention attributes "results of great value" to the Hague Convention, although this could hardly have been determined. A fact which is still being overlooked by the international drug control system is that the assessment of the outcome of efforts made in pursuit of goals is a necessary element in policy-making.

Means

The word "means" is understood to refer to any institution, rule, or action employed in pursuit of an end. Some means are *international*: treaties, the international agencies created to administer them, and international cooperation fall into this category. However, the application of international control is based on *national* legislation and exercised through national executing devices. National action is, of course, determined to a very large extent by treaty obligations, but nations are also, within the limits prescribed by international law, relatively free to organize their drug control strategies to fit within their own institutions.

There are two points of general significance which must be stated. First, "drug abuse" is not an isolated phenomenon but is a part of a whole set of personal and social conditions. Although our discussion will be limited to policies and actions designed specifically to control "drug abuse," their relationship to the general pursuit of social policy must be borne in mind. Second, not all measures of drug control are designed to prevent "drug abuse." There has been a growing interest in establishing consumer safety procedures and setting standards and requirements for drug purity, nomenclature, labeling, marketing, pricing, and statistics. We do not deal with these forms of drug control, but we do not deny their relevance.

Which type of control measure is to be used in a problem situation is determined by the context. At the international level the scope of action has been limited to legal-administrative measures aimed at controlling the supply of drugs and the intervening activities between supply and demand, both licit and illicit. At the national level the range of options is wider and may encompass treatment, social welfare, law enforcement, education, and so on. Furthermore, controls will vary depending on the type of drug, drug-related behavior, and the drug-taking group to which they are directed.

Finally, the scheme of control adopted will be affected by the rules governing the process whereby controls are decided, codified, and implemented. Such rules pertain to the criteria for control, the responsibilities for initiating controls, and the relations between individual states and international organizations.

The Treaties

The Single Convention, since it unified the treaties preceding it, will form the basis of the following discussion. The two treaties not yet in force—the Vienna Convention and the 1972 Protocol amending the Single Convention—will be touched upon, the former especially, since, on the basis of an ECOSOC resolution, it is to some extent being provisionally applied. First, however, we will summarize the salient features of the earlier treaties. The 1925 convention established a system for regulating international trade; a country had to have the approval of the importing country before it was allowed to export narcotics. The 1931 convention introduced the estimates system, under which drug needs had to be anticipated and manufacture tailored to these needs. Under the 1948 treaty a range of synthetic narcotics came under control. The 1953 treaty provided for controls over the production of raw materials.

The parties to the Single Convention are obliged to cooperate with the international organs and with each other in the execution of the treaty provisions. Although this obligation seems a less than meaningful abstraction, it is not in fact so. The efficacy of control relies to a large extent on the goodwill of the parties and on the mutual observances of the rules governing international trade.

The national obligations under the Single Convention include the following (see E/CN. 7/484/Rev.1, 1966):

(a) establishing or adjusting national legislation to conform to the convention;

(b) maintaining a system of licenses (for manufacturers, wholesalers, and others), permits and prescriptions (for dispensing of drugs), record-keeping, reports, controls and inspections;

(c) establishing estimates of national requirements of drugs, transmitting them to INCB, and enforcing the established estimates;

(d) maintaining a system of export and import authorizations and import certificates;

(e) maintaining statistics and other documentation, and transmitting them, respectively, to the INCB and the secretary-general;

(f) coordinating preventive and repressive actions against illicit traffic and arranging for treatment of addicts;

(g) cooperating with other nations and the international agencies in counteracting the illicit traffic and in extradition and other questions relating to the punishment of offences.

Some of these obligations are subsumed under the Vienna Convention. A notable exception is the absence of the estimate system.

International intervention involves the following procedures:

(a) placing new drugs under control or altering the regimes of control;

(b) documentation and evaluation of the operations of the control system;

(c) establishing (by INCB) of drug-need estimates for different countries and supervising the working of the control system;

(d) employing sanctions, ranging from criticism to the imposition of an embargo, against countries in breach of the treaty provisions;

(e) technical assistance;

(f) inducing changes in the system of control, ranging from recommendations to the elaboration of new treaties.

With regard to the placing of drugs under control (which determines their level of control) it is as important to ask which drugs are controlled as how it is done. What critieria apply? Who takes the initiative? What is the procedure?

The Hague Convention of 1912 included opium, heroin, morphine, cocaine, and certain of their salts and preparations. The Geneva Convention added cannabis. Under the 1931 Limitation Convention more compounds of the drugs listed in the earlier treaties were included. There is a basic technical difference between the way drugs are controlled under these treaties, and the way they are controlled under the Single Convention and the Vienna Convention. In the earlier treaties the drugs are named in the text, which means that, as a rule, to change the type of control to which a drug is subjected, the treaty must be amended. The more recent treaties arrange drugs in separate schedules, corresponding to different regimes of control. A change in the degree of control of any drug can be brought about by moving it into another schedule, without amending the treaty.

Drugs have been brought under all treaties individually, not in groups. An exception to this practice may be found in the 1931 Limitation Convention. No trade or manufacture for trade was allowed in a country for any of the phenanthrene alkaloids of opium or for the ecgonine alkaloids of the coca leaf, subject to a decision by a government and to an international review process.

As to the procedure for extending control to additional drugs, both individual governments and WHO are entitled, under the Single Convention, to take the initiative. However, almost all initiatives have so far originated from countries. Other countries are then notified. If WHO finds that the drug is liable to similar abuse and is productive of similar ill effects as the drugs already controlled, then WHO will have to notify the Commission,* which will decide for or against the inclusion of the drug in a specific schedule. If WHO does not provide an assessment, then the controlling process will not be able to run its course. The decision of the Commission may be reviewed by appeal to ECOSOC, which in fact has the power not only to accept or reject the original

* "The Commission" will be used hereafter as an abbreviation for the Commission on Narcotic Drugs.

WHO proposal but also to alter the proposal (by placing the drug in a schedule other than the one proposed).

Under the Vienna Convention, WHO is required to spell out in greater detail the criteria it applies in evaluating a drug for control. The Commission has the right to seek advice other than that of WHO (except on medical and scientific matters) and may alter the proposal. Another departure from the Single Convention is the requirement of a two-thirds majority in the Commission when voting on such a question.

Changing the System

With the exception of the Hague Convention all the drug treaties have been concluded under the auspices of the League of Nations and the United Nations. Considering the recognized authority which the UN has come to have for drug control, it is unlikely that future drug treaties with any claim to universality will be concluded outside the UN framework. However, bilateral and regional agreements may well be concluded, and do in fact exist. In another category is an agreement between a state and an international organization, such as the one between the INCB and the minister of public health of Bolivia (PCB, 1964: xiii–xiv).

We will now see what possibilities there are in the process of enacting UN drug treaties, for states and international organizations to pursue their own goals and to initiate or resist proposals for action.

The 1969 Convention on the Law of Treaties (CA/CONF.39/27) provides a framework for viewing UN treaties. The convention does not lay down rules for the treaty-making process, and decisions leading up to the convocation of a conference to consider a draft convention are dictated by UN procedure in general. A pattern has been established for the creation of drug treaties. National initiatives are first raised in the Commission. When a necessary majority has been obtained, the initiative goes before ECOSOC, which adopts a resolution asking the secretary-general to convene a plenipotentiary conference according to article 62 of the UN charter. The ensuing preparatory work for the conference is usually performed by the Division of Narcotic Drugs of the UN Secretariat. Invitations to the plenipotentiary conference are issued to member states of the UN and to certain nonmembers. However, in spite of the universal application of the drug treaties, invitations have not been issued to all states, and this has been a matter of some contention at the plenipotentiary conferences.

It follows, given the central role of the Commission in the process of taking initiatives and making preparations, that a state which has a place on the Commission will have an advantage over those which do not when it comes to raising issues or deflecting them. These "outsider" states may attend the Commission meetings as observers, as do certain nongovernmental organizations and other UN agencies not exclusively concerned with drugs, so the opportunity does exist for them to wield some influence. But they cannot vote, nor can they take part in the management of the Commission (through such activity as deciding on agendas, and the like); thus their contribution to the making of important decisions will be only marginal. As the Commission initiatives have a decisive effect on subsequent ECOSOC standpoints, participation in the latter forum will barely compensate for the lack of representation at the Commission level. The actual preparation of draft proposals and the analysis of preliminary government responses are carried out by the Division of Narcotic Drugs, and such interests as the secretariat officials may have will probably manifest themselves at this stage.

The deliberations in the Commission and the plenipotentiary conference will be affected by what alternatives to the proposals are offered for discussion, but the way those responsible for the initial drafting of proposals have phrased them will also affect the outcome (see chapters 13 and 16, on the cannabis issue and the construction of the Vienna Convention).

The secretary-general provides a UN plenipotentiary conference with such material as provisional rules of procedure, memoranda on the topics to be discussed, and a provisional timetable.* These rules, which are generally adopted by the conference, do not confer advantages or disadvantages unevenly upon the participating states. However, as the time allotted for any conference is limited—it was roughly two months for the confer-

* Work performed in the name of the secretary-general in the field of narcotics and other drugs is done by the Division of Narcotic Drugs, except for legal matters, which are usually handled by the legal adviser. Although documents prepared by the Division bear the name of the secretary-general, the term "the Division" will be used hereafter in reference to such documents.

ence which adopted the Single Convention and three weeks for
the conference which considered its amendments—there is bound
to be some bias in favor of draft proposals circulated in advance
and of better-staffed delegations. Time pressure will require
several committees to work simultaneously, and only if the
delegation is a large one will a state be able to provide personnel
for all these committees. The area of deliberation is provisionally
defined by those participants who have submitted proposals; thus
they will have a lead in steering the discussion along the lines
which particularly interest them. In the negotiations which ensue,
they will seek the general acceptance of their proposals. The
strategy in the past for those participants who were bent on
strengthening controls has been to work for mandatory regulations, administered by international organs and automatically
binding on the contracting parties. Those participants who have
wanted to minimize such controls have had recourse to other
types of action. If the intention is not to be bound, then a state
can either refrain from taking part altogether or it can take part
in the bargaining process, vote against the proposals, and then
refrain from signing the concluded document. Clearly, those
aiming at increased control are usually willing to settle for less
than all they aspire to, out of consideration for the need to have
a treaty which contains only such undertakings as a sufficiently
large number of states are prepared to accept. This has not always
been the case, however. Recall that when the American delegation
failed to secure acceptance for its plan to control opium at the
source during the Geneva Conference of 1924-25, it withdrew
from the conference. The Protocol of 1953 was a move to reinstate
this plan, while the proposed amendments to the Single Convention were yet another effort along the lines of the original
attempts in the 1920s. Another way of reconciling different
interests is to narrow definitions down to a point where there is
common agreement: the definition of cannabis in the Single
Convention, which excludes those parts of the plant other than
the flowering or fruiting tops, is a case in point.

States opposed to controls will strive to render the proposed
rules more permissive; what is originally intended to be a
mandatory provision can, in the course of negotiations, be toned
down into a recommendation. For example, at the New York
Conference of 1961, it had been intended to subject cannabis to

mandatory suppression, but after a Burmese intervention general assent could only be had for a recommendation that strict control be applied (art. 2, pars. 2 and 4).* Similarly, rules concerning cultivation leave it to a state's discretion to determine whether it will opt for prohibition: if "prevailing conditions" render the prohibition of cultivation of the opium popy, the coca bush, or the cannabis plant "the most suitable measure," in the opinion of the party, for protecting health and welfare and preventing illicit traffic, then prohibition shall be carried out. Other such qualifications are: "so far as possible," in relation to the uprooting of wild coca bushes (art. 26); "if . . . economic resources permit," where establishing treatment facilities is concerned (art. 38); holding a practice "desirable" rather than obligatory, such as the indication of the WHO nonproprietary names of drugs (art. 30).

Rights and duties are conferred sparingly. This is exemplified by article 14, by which the INCB "may" call the attention of the parties, ECOSOC, and the Commission to the failure of a government to give a satisfactory explanation for untoward occurrences. States are generally wary of investing international organs with too much authority. However, this is not to say that they are invariably more concerned about securing maximum relief from international jurisdiction than with giving sufficient leeway to the international organs and to themselves.

But escape clauses do exist, such as the one relating to the right of parties to export drugs to a country in spite of an embargo having been declared, if exceptional circumstances—such as the need of such drugs for the treatment of the sick—can be invoked. And, certainly, one of the most important devices for reconciling the interests of those pressing for controls and those hesitant about them is the possibility of making reservations. States can avail themselves of the provision which allows reservations to several highly important parts of the convention to be made at the time of signature and at the time of ratification or accession:

(a) the right of the INCB to request and establish estimates

* During a discussion on changes in the scope of control, U Ba Sein, the delegate from Burma, said that in his country cannabis was still used medically. "It was, for example, administred to elephants used for the transport of timber. The prohibition of cannabis in Burma would be a severe blow to the timber industry." Later, his fellow delegate made a similar intervention (E/CONF.34/24: 20, 61).

in respect of countries and territories not bound by the
convention;

(b) the right of the INCB to question statistics and take
action against governments;

(c) certain limitations on the export of drugs in excess of the
estimated requirements of an importing country;

(d) the prescribed manner of settling disputes, including
recourse to the International Court of Justice.

The transitional reservations embodied in article 49 allow a
party to permit, throughout a specified period of time, the "quasi-
medical use" of opium smoking, coca-leaf chewing, and the
nonmedical use of cannabis, cannabis resin, and so on. Allowing
for the continued use of cannabis is ironic considering that it is
included in article 2 among the drugs purported to have "particularly dangerous properties."

The manner of a treaty's entry into force is often another
compromise struck between the proponents and opposers of
control. As its entry into force is subject to ratification or
accession, the number of ratifications required to bring it into
force will have a profound effect on how quickly it will be
implemented. Recall the German insistence on universal
adherence to the Hague Convention as a precondition of the
convention's entry into force in 1912. The Single Convention
follows the standard model in requiring forty ratifications, a
number representing about a third of the number of UN member-
states at the time of signature. The Vienna Convention requires
the same number of ratifications, although between 1961 and
1971 the UN membership had increased.

The Single Convention can be altered through amendments
(art. 47) and can be terminated as a result of denunciations or by
a new treaty. Amendments to the treaty can be secured without
convoking a conference (proposals can be circulated to the
contracting parties), but this has not happened. Nor is it
likely to, considering that eighteen months must elapse after the
circulation of the proposals before a decision can be taken and
considering that it takes only one party to dissent for the
proposals to be rejected.

Finally, to illustrate the constellation of forces which have to be
reconciled before a treaty is brought into being, we have tabulated
the declarations and reservations which qualify the acceptance by

the states concerned of the text of the Single Convention (see Appendix A). These throw light upon the positions which individual countries maintain towards the controls embodied in the treaty. In many cases they have little or no bearing on drug control, as such, but have to do with political relations in the world at large. The refusal of the socialist states to submit to international arbitration, and the declaration made by the UAR that ratification of the treaty did not imply recognition of Israel or that any treaty relation would be forged between the UAR and Israel, serve as examples.

4   Key Organs

> Evidence is growing that international agencies are fully
> capable of developing vested interests and "empire-
> building" tendencies.... The pacts concluded between
> the central organization and the Specialized Agencies
> are, in large measure, agreements to agree.
>
> Inis L. Claude, Jr., *Swords into Plowshares*

Many organizations within the total UN
system are concerned in one way or another with matters closely
related to drugs. It is not our intention to examine the activities of
all these organizations. Instead, attention will be confined to a
few key organs which have formal and de facto responsibility for
drug control under the UN system. How the drug control
structure relates to the overall organizational structure of the UN
is shown in figure 4:1; the organs in boxes are those we will be
dealing with. A word on their selection is necessary.

The highest body of the UN, the General Assembly, can make
important decisions concerning drugs. However, these are usually
based on recommendations by the Economic and Social Council
(ECOSOC), which in turn draws from resolutions drafted by the
Commission on Narcotic Drugs. In fact, only 2 percent of the
sessional time of ECOSOC is devoted to drugs (Woodcock,
1974:306). The Commission, which succeeded the League of
Nations' Advisory Committee on Traffic in Opium and Other
Dangerous Drugs, is the chief policy-making organ in the drug
area. The International Narcotics Control Board (INCB), established by the Single Convention and taking over from the
Permanent Central Board and the Drug Supervisory Body in
1968, is charged with the supervision of drug treaties, particularly

FIGURE 4.1

Organizational Structure of the International Drug Control Machinery, 1972

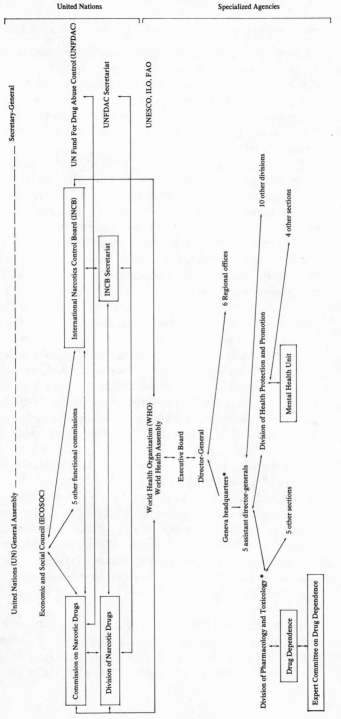

*Prior to reorganization

of those provisions pertaining to quantitative control of drug production and distribution. It is said to enjoy a special status (one of technical independence) vis à vis the UN—this is a point of contention to which we will return—but its secretariat is an integral part of the UN secretariat. Both the Commission and the INCB report to ECOSOC but, unlike ECOSOC, their entire concern is with drugs.

The other principal components of the drug control apparatus come under the World Health Organization (WHO), a UN specialized agency. The central organs of WHO are: the World Health Assembly, the executive board, and the secretariat headed by the director-general. WHO is decentralized to a very large extent but its regional offices do not administer drug matters. Work on drugs is primarily carried out by the headquarters in Geneva, specifically by the Divison of Pharmacology and Toxicology, one of twelve divisions of WHO. This division breaks down into six sections, one of which—the Drug Dependence Unit—is, as its name implies, concerned with that aspect of drug use to which international controls are directed. WHO acts in an advisory capacity under the treaties, providing information and expertise of a pharmacological, pharmaceutical, and medical nature to the other drug control bodies. In doing this, it draws upon the opinions and knowledge of an Expert Committee on Drug Dependence, periodically appointed by the director-general. The terms of reference of the Drug Dependence Unit do not provide for action in the field of alcohol, so that alcohol has, in the recent past, been a concern of the Mental Health Unit in WHO's Division of Health Protection and Promotion. This unit is in a different category from that into which the Commission, INCB, and the Drug Dependence Unit fall; its field of attention embraces subjects other than alcohol, whereas the other units are exclusively concerned with drugs. We should add here that changes in the organizational structure of WHO occurred in August 1972 at headquarters and that in consequence "alcoholism" and "drug dependence" have been united at the administrative level.

The secretariats of the key UN drug control organs have a dual source of authority: on the one hand, they serve the Commission and the INCB; on the other, they have to respond to decisions and directives from the secretary-general and other higher officials of the bureaucracy. The impression gained from interviews with various staff members suggests that in the area of drug control administration the role of these higher officials is sufficiently minor to justify their exclusion from our analysis. Also excluded from our analysis of the drug control machinery are organizations like INTERPOL, the Customs Cooperation Council, the Universal Postal Union, and the Food and Agriculture Organization (FAO). While these are all involved in varying degrees in drug control matters, they are peripheral to the central apparatus, and we will thus consider them only when their activities or attitudes bear on the policy and actions of the central organs. The following discussion is confined to the contemporary drug organs, but it will be remembered that these organs have predecessors in the League of Nations. Figure 4.2 illustrates their descent.

Objectives of Control Bodies

The Commission on Narcotic Drugs was established in 1946 "in order to provide machinery whereby full effect may be given to the international conventions relating to narcotic drugs, and to provide for continuous review of and progress in international control of such drugs" (ECOSOC: 1st, 1946). More specifically, The Commission would:

(a) assist the Economic and Social Council in exercising general supervision over the application of international conventions and agreements dealing with narcotic drugs;
(b) carry out such functions entrusted to the League of Nations Advisory Committee on Traffic in Opium and Other Dangerous Drugs by the international conventions on narcotic drugs as the Council has found necessary to assume and continue;
(c) advise the Council on all matters pertaining to the control of narcotic drugs and prepare such draft international conventions as may be necessary;
(d) consider what changes may be required in the existing machinery for the international control of narcotic drugs and submit proposals to the Council;
(e) perform such other functions relating to narcotic drugs as the Council may direct.

The Commission's terms of reference imply that it should function as a policy-maker, but they are sufficiently vague to allow the Commission considerable flexibility in adjusting to changes in the world drug situation and climate of opinion, and in

FIGURE 4.2

Key Drug Control Organs and Their Predecessors

Political bodies

> *League of Nations*
> Advisory Committee on Traffic in Opium and Other
> Dangerous Drugs (1921–40)
>
> *UN*
> Commission on Narcotic Drugs (1946–)

Expert Bodies

> *League of Nations and UN*

PCB   Permanent Central Opium (or Narcotics) Board (1929–67)
DSB   Drug Supervisory Body (1933–67)
INCB   International Narcotics Control Board (1968–)

Health bodies

> *League of Nations*
> Provisional Health Committee (1921–23)
> Health Committee (1924–45)
>
> *WHO*
> Expert Committee on Habit Forming Drugs (1949)
> Expert Committee on Drugs Liable to produce Addiction
>   (1950–55)
> Expert Committee on Addiction-Producing Drugs (1956–64)
> Expert Committee on Dependence-Producing Drugs (1965–67)
> Expert Committee on Drug Dependence (1968–)

Secretariats

> Opium Traffic Section of the League
> UN Division of Narcotic Drugs
> INCB Secretariat
> WHO Drug Dependence Unit, now Drug Dependence and
> Alcoholism

modifying its strategies accordingly. Shifts of position have occurred: in 1951, for example, a discussion took place in the Commission over the question of coca-leaf chewing and it was pointed out by a representative that before continuing the discussion "the Commission should decide whether the chewing of coca leaf was to be considered an addiction, in which case the Commission would be competent to deal with it, or as an economic and social problem outside its competence" (CND: 6th; 1951). Today, the Commission would be the first to insist on its competence to handle the social and economic aspects of drug-related problems.

The Commission has quasi-legislative and administrative functions and obligations under the Single Convention as well as policy-making authority. Article 5 of the Convention provides that:

The Commission is authorized to consider all matters pertaining to the aims of this Convention, and in particular:
(a) To amend the Schedule in accordance with article 3;
(b) To call the attention of the Board to any matters which may be relevant to the functions of the Board;
(c) To make recommendations for the implementation of the aims and provisions of this Convention, including programmes of scientific research and the exchange of information of a scientific or technical nature;
(d) To draw the attention of non-parties to decisions and recommendations which it adopts under this Convention, with a view to their considering taking action in accordance therewith.

The functions of the INCB have been defined by the Single Convention, and its goals are basically those of that convention. The 1972 protocol amending the Single Convention has added a new dimension to the INCB's responsibilities by providing that it would "endeavour to limit the cultivation, production, manufacture and use of drugs to an adequate amount required for medical and scientific purposes, to ensure their availability for such purposes and to prevent illicit cultivation, production and manufacture of, and illicit trafficking in and use of, drugs." Hitherto, the Board's task had been very largely that of keeping a watch over the working of the treaties in relation to licit trade, but this new provision allows a much more *explicit* involvement in control over illicit drug production, distribution, and use. Earlier, the Board has been regarded as an administrative and semi-judicial body in some contrast to the policy-making Commission, but new functions assigned to the Board by the protocol have a tendency of making the INCB's scope of action broader, so that this distinction is perhaps less sharp. To offer another illustration: the Board has been authorized by the protocol to recommend technical or financial assistance to countries to help them carry out their treaty obligations. There would seem to be an overlap between this mandate—which in fact makes explicit what has already occurred informally—and the sphere of action of the Commission, to which the recommendation of technical assistance programs to supplement the treaty system has hitherto been attributed. The INCB, however, does not see an overlap and considers that its action will be limited to identifying countries in need of assistance (as distinct from the amount required and the source from which it should come) and to reviewing the situation after the assistance has been given to see if further action is warranted. In any case, the authorization merely confirms a practice which the Board has followed for many years (INCB, 1972: 32).

Although the WHO constitution contains no specific reference to drug addiction prevention, the general goal of the organization ("the attainment by all people of the highest possible level of health") would imply a responsibility to consider this problem, insofar as drug dependence is judged to be a health problem, as indeed it is by WHO definition. The second article of the constitution enumerates a number of subgoals but these are not assigned by reference to particular organizational units; instead, all the units have to keep all of these goals in sight, at least as far as is applicable. Under the treaty system WHO is required to evaluate and to identify the drugs that may warrant international control (a task once performed by the Health Committee of the League of Nations). But, for WHO, international control implies not only control of availability but also the reduction of demand through treatment and rehabilitation. Where alcohol is concerned, the objectives are again not explicitly stated but are to be inferred from the general WHO purpose of fostering an improved state of health, defined as a "state of complete physical, social, and mental well-being and not merely the absence of disease.'

The common purpose guiding the work of the key drug bodies does not preclude or completely override the existence of personal or group interests within the total system. The tendency of groups in formal organizations to favor actions that will maintain or augment their own power, prestige, and share of resources has been remarked upon by a great number of scholars (for example, Downs, 1967). And international bureaucrats, like national bureaucrats, are not free from the "instinctive interest" in the expansion of the activities of their organization by embarking upon new programs (Symonds and Cader, 1973: xvi). To some officials, the stability and cohesion of the agency to which they belong may be the prime consideration. In the early days of WHO, when the question of birth control programs was becoming a subject of debate in the international forum, the attitude of WHO's first director-general, Brock Chisholm, was that the first priority was to ensure that the future of the organization was not jeopardized by raising what was likely to be a highly controversial issue (Symonds and Carder, 1973: 59-60)

But these separate intersts relate more to means than to ends, and no doubt there are many officials who do not assert the primacy of the interests of their own organizations. In this they are supported by the consensus which is to be found among the international organizations that the "rules of the game" are to be preserved. While the organizations are not all agreed on all matters, they tend nevertheless to agree that the unspoken rules of the game upon which the entire international system rests should not be broken. This is often done by an avoidance of what may be considered radical measures or proposals. Another way of maintaining overall harmony despite factional interests is for members of one body to nominate or appoint the members of another (Skolnick, 1967), and for the same individual to be alternately a representative on the Commission and a member of the INCB, to take one of several examples (see chapter 9).

Resources

Table 4.1 gives a picture of the development of manpower in the four secretariat units of the key drug organs. For purposes of comparison we have provided similar data for the UN, WHO, and ILO. We have also compiled budgetary data on all these organizations for the period under review, and the comments which follow can as easily have been derived from these. But because identical conclusions can be drawn from both sets of data we have limited ourselves to the less cumbersome set. Both may, however, be used as indicators of the development of the resources of the bodies concerned.

The Division of Narcotic Drugs and its predecessor have always been the strongest unit as far as resources are concerned. Until 1929 the Opium Traffic Section was effectively the only secre-

TABLE 4.1
Manpower of Drug Control Secretariats, 1925-72

Year	League Opium Traffic Section/UN Division of Narcotic Drugs	Secretariat of PCB/DSB and INCB	WHO Drug Dependence Unit	WHO Mental Health Unit[a]	UN	WHO	ILO
1925	5	–	–	–	–	–	353
1930	6	5	–	–	–	–	399
1935	7	6	–	–	–	–	411
1950	25	8	2	3	3,908	?	613
1955	29	9	2	4	3,996	948	671
1960	28	9	4	5	5,546	1,410	914
1965	31	10	4	8	5,975	2,489	1,126
1970	31	15	4	8	8,102	3,090	1,404
1972	31	18	4	9	9,857	5,015	1,404

NOTE: The UN Fund for Drug Abuse Control (UNFDAC), which does not appear in this table, had seven staff members in 1973.

aOnly a very small part of this section's work is devoted to alcohol. However, alcohol does not constitute such a distinctive work area that we can specify the proportion of resources allocated to it.

tariat service for drug matters. The increase in its resources as measured by manpower during the League days was negligible, but when the division began its work in 1947 there was a marked expansion of the unit. Although descriptions of work organization indicate that the two WHO units concerned have at their disposal the services of other departments not specifically concerned with drugs, their resources seem limited indeed when seen in relation to the other units in the table. There was an increase in manpower in INCB secretariat staffing in the late 1960s; INCB officials attribute this to increased workload brought about by the conclusion of new treaties (Greenfield and Dittert, interviews). As far as the Mental Health Unit of WHO is concerned, it should be remembered that alcoholism represents only a small part of the unit's work program, whereas drug matters are the only concern of the other organs. Thus the actual resources available for work in the field of alcoholism are even more limited than the table indicates. In fact, at no time has there been a single person in the unit whose entire time is devoted to alcohol work.

The table shows that manpower resources for work related to drug control have not increased at the same rate as manpower for the activities of UN, WHO, and ILO as a whole; the pace has been slower. This could mean that in proportion to overall increase that of drug control's claim on the total resources of the UN and WHO, as determined by the priorities of these organizations, has been relatively slight.

As has already been mentioned, the development of budgetary resources over time closely follows that of manpower, as indeed it must when the bulk of the budget goes into salaries (see Woodcock, 1974: 312, 313). However, to provide some idea of the size of expenditures involved, table 4.2 gives the 1972 budget estimates of the institutions under review.

Quite clearly, drug programs do not have a very important role in the activities of the international agencies. Drug dependence and mental health activities together represent about 0.2 percent of the total WHO budget, while the proportion of the UN's budget allocated to drug control is just under 0.6 percent. WHO, the Division, and the INCB Secretariat do, however, have access to other sources of income. Voluntary funds, for instance, are used to finance some of WHO's projects, while the creation of the UN Fund for Drug Abuse Control (UNFDAC) has meant an increase in headquarters' resources all round.

TABLE 4.2
Budget Estimates of Key Drug Control Organs, 1972

	U.S. Dollars
Commission on Narcotic Drugs	150,000[a]*
Division of Narcotic Drugs	621,000[a]*
INCB and Secretariat	421,000[a]
WHO Drug Dependence Unit	52,742[b]
WHO Expert Committee	14,100[b]
WHO Mental Health Unit	106,600[b]
United Nations	207,721,500[a]
WHO	83,001,400[c]**
ILO	71,503,000[d]

SOURCES: [a]General Assembly Off. Rec. 26th, Supp. 6 A/
8406 *Gross Expenditure under Regular Budget.*
[b]WHO Off. Rec., 187 *Proposed Regular Program
and Budget Estimates for 1972* (1970)
[c]WHO Off. Rec., 195 *Report of the Executive
Board*, 48th session (1971)
[d]ILO: 56th, 1971 Report II *Draft Program and
Budget* (1972–73)

NOTE: *These figures represent regular budget financing,
which provides such costs as secretariat salaries, conference expenses, and general "housekeeping costs." In
1960 a "continuing program" of technical cooperation in
drug control was set up which had financial backing from
the regular budget of $60,000 (increased to $75,000 in
1961 and $100,000 in 1971) per year.

**Additionally, approximately $50 million are made
available through other international sources, including
voluntary contributions.

Before we proceed to consider how these resources are used,
and what specific tasks are performed by these bodies in pursuit
of their goals and by virtue of their terms of reference, we must
point, albeit arbitrarily, to the distinction between the policy-
making, supervisory, and advisory bodies and what is generally
referred to as the international civil service, although it must be
stressed that in practice any dichotomy between them is false.
Between the extreme of obvious policy and obvious implementation (or administration, or the "carrying out of orders") is a
wide no-man's-land in which the departmental orientation, the
advice of the expert, the personal views of the top officials all have
a part to play. The essence of a secretariat is its continuity and

durability: it is always there. True, its action derives from rules laid down by others, in treaties, resolutions, and the like, but the decisions or policy statements which trickle through the machinery often have to be interpreted, and it is usually the international civil servant who interprets them and puts them into effect according to his judgment about the intent of the decision, or the objectives to be pursued, or the right tactics to follow. Moreover, the officials are often involved in the earlier stages of the decision process when alternative plans and actions are being formulated (for example, when alternative drafts of a treaty are being worded), so that here, as well as later, the secretariat has a role. In 1938, for example, the Opium Advisory Committee asked its secretariat to prepare a draft of the main articles of a future convention for limiting opium cultivation. This was done by the Opium Section with the help of the Legal Section of the League, and very few changes were made by the Committee in the document (Pastuhov, 1945: 27). It is also well known that all the UN drug treaties enacted between 1946 and 1971 were drafted primarily by Adolf Lande, a former secretariat staff member. During the days of the League of Nations, the secretariat often determined what actions were to be taken by the governing bodies (Pastuhov, 1943: 1). As time passed, the relative importance of the civil servant increased; this was said to have been the case with the League of Nations (Ranshofen-Wertheimer, 1945: 393). Yet the work of the secretariat is to a high degree centered around the meetings of the policy-making, supervisory, or advisory bodies. Usually, only the professional staff members in the higher ranks of each department attend these meetings, and their participation affords an opportunity for individual maneuvering and influence. Compared to earlier years, the duration of the meetings of the INCB and the Commission has decreased. Although this might have been paralleled by an increase in efficiency, it is possible that the tendency towards shorter meetings will add to the relative importance of the civil servant.

The international civil servant maintains contact with those higher up in the UN hierarchy, and consultation occurs between the drug secretariats and such other UN offices as that of the Legal Adviser. But these are not frequent occurrences and we will not dwell on them; instead, we turn now to the more or less routine work which is being done by the agencies under review.

5   WHO

> The Expert Committee, which had begun its work seventeen years earlier, [is] today concerned not only with measures to prevent the abuse of drugs, but also with other problems connected with drug dependence and abuse, more particularly the sociological implications of drug dependence.
>
> H. Halbach, to the Commission (1966)

We will begin with a consideration of the place of alcohol and other psychoactive drugs in WHO's program. The low priority given to matters of alcoholism and drug dependence compared to other concerns, is illustrated by table 5.1, the compilation of which was based on the annual reports of the WHO director-general to the World Health Assembly and the UN. The table shows that while the space given to "Pharmacology and Toxicology" (which embraces "Drug Efficacy and Safety," "Pharmaceuticals," "Drug Monitoring," and the like) in the reports has increased over the last twenty years, signifying its growing importance, that occupied by "Drug Dependence" has remained largely constant. It is significant that in 1965 the amount of space allotted to "Pharmacology and Toxicology" was double that in 1960, while that given to "Drug Dependence" was halved. This coincides with the increased involvement of WHO in the promotion of drug safety in the face of drug-screening shortcomings which the thalidomide tragedy revealed. During the fifteenth World Health Assembly in 1962 a resolution was approved which requested that a study be made of the feasibility of WHO developing a program for the formulation of standards for drug evaluation, the exchange of information on drug safety

66

TABLE 5.1
Space Occupied by Drug Matters in WHO Director-General's Reports to the World Health Assembly and UN

Year covered by report	Number of pages						No. of entries in index	
	Total	General review	Pharmacology & toxicology	Drug dependence	Mental health	Alcoholism	Drug dependence	Alcoholism
1950	202	81	–	1.5	2.0	0.0		
1955	241	67	4.0	1.0	1.0	0.0	3	3
1960	224	54	2.5	1.0	0.5	0.0	1	–
1965	244	87	5.5	0.5	1.0	0.0	3	2
1970	305	118	6.0	1.0	2.0	0.5	8	2
1971	401	184	7.0	1.5	3.5	1.0	11	5

NOTE: The figure 0.0 indicates that the subject is mentioned but takes up less than half a page. In 1950 no index was provided, and "drug dependence" was not part of a larger section. The structure of the report was in many ways different from that of other years. "Drug dependence" is used here as a heading although the actual terms used in the reports were: "addiction producing drugs" (1950), "drugs liable to produce addiction" (1955), "addiction producing drugs" (1960), and "drug dependence and drug abuse" (1965). Although the Division of "Pharmacology and Toxicology" was not established until 1966, this rubric is used for the entire period under review. The original headings covered by the rubric were: "international conventions, agreements and regulations of health" (1950), "drugs and other therapeutic substances" (1955), "biology and pharmacology" (1960 and 1965). For 1955 and 1960 the chapter "Co-operation with Other Organizations" has been included in the figure for "General review" for the sake of comparability. The headings for "Mental health" were: "mental well-being" (1950), "mental health and public health service" (1955). Although the space for "alcoholism" was limited in 1955, the paragraph was much more substantial than in later years. In the 1970s, "alcohol" and "drug dependence" were generally mixed; thus the index entries would often refer to the same page. It was difficult to compile comparable figures for the pre-WHO years (i.e. during the time of the League of Nations Health Committee) as the reports were then of activities between sessions and not by year. In 1972 the mental health section came under the Division of Non-communicable Diseases, which was originally the Division of Health Protection and Promotion.

and efficacy, for rapid reporting of adverse reactions to drugs. (For the thalidomide story see Sjöström and Nilsson, 1972).

Alcohol is briefly touched upon in these reports. In the last two years there has been greater overlap between the contents of "Alcohol" and "Drug Dependence," and therefore the apparent increase shown in the table is somewhat exaggerated.

Evidence for the relative lack of importance attached to this field can also be found by looking at the projects which have been undertaken by WHO and at the extent to which the Assembly and the executive board have adopted resolutions and made decisions in connection with drug dependence. As far as programs are concerned, the records reveal a modest range. In 1955 it was decided to embark upon a survey of alcohol problems in Europe, but by 1957 this was no longer listed as a project. Two "Drug Dependence" projects were mentioned for 1970 and 1971—one was, in fact, the convening of a working group; the other proposed the evaluation of the treatment of drug addicts in Hong Kong. In 1971 "alcohol" and "drug dependence" were jointly cited in reference to consultations on "National Responses to Problems of Alcohol and Drug Dependence" and an interregional training course—a seminar traveling to three European countries.

As for decisions reported in the *WHO Handbook of Resolutions and Decisions of the World Health Assembly and the Executive Board* covering the period 1948–70: alcoholism was featured four times but only during the period from 1948 to 1952, whereas twenty-three decisions were registered in relation to "Drug Dependence," divided into three categories—expert committees' decisions made between 1948 and 1953; control measures for psychotropic substances, 1965–70; and international conventions, 1948–66 (WHO Handbook of Resolutions and Decisions, 1971).

Historical descriptions of WHO's activities point in the same direction. In a paper on the mental health program of WHO from 1949 to 1972 (MH/72.4) little more than half a page out of a total of twenty is given to "dependence on alcohol and other drugs." And whereas alcohol and other psychoactive drugs were not given differential emphasis in a history of the first ten years of WHO, more attention was paid to the other drugs in the sequel—"The Second Ten Years." But even here attention to psychoactive drug-use problems was overshadowed by that paid to evaluation for safety and efficiency. (*The First Ten Years of WHO* [1958]; *The Second Ten Years of WHO* [1968].

These documents do not reflect the entire work program of the departments under review. In addition to the activities mentioned, the Mental Health Unit is, according to the annual report for 1971, working on a glossary of psychiatric illnesses, featuring, among other items, alcoholism and drug dependence. The corresponding text on the Drug Dependence Unit does not say much about concrete activities and is more a description of an approach to the program. There are statements of principles on the multiple causation of drug dependence, on control measures based upon the limitation of availability and the limitation of demand through education and treatment, and on the importance of increasing knowledge of the causes and consequences of drug dependence. The Vienna Protocol is also mentioned.

The work of WHO is characterized by the use of a variety of competences; expert committees and scientific and study groups are regularly convened, and consultants are called upon, to deliberate on a particular topic. The most prestigious of these are the expert committees, which are composed of individuals appointed by the director-general of WHO. At least in the area which concerns us, WHO has usually followed the advice of the head of the Drug Dependence Unit in selecting these individuals. These experts are not representatives of their governments but serve in their personal capacity. Expert-committee members are selected from WHO's expert advisory panels, which are subject-oriented lists of individual experts who contribute information by correspondence or reports on matters falling within their particular fields. Appointment to a panel is usually for a period of five years, and here WHO seeks the approval of the respective governments. In early 1969, 29 persons were listed on the Drug Expert Panel and 129 on the Mental Health Panel (EB 43/WP 2). Nearly half of the former were drawn from the U.S. and the U.K. (12), whereas world-wide representation is better reflected on the Mental Health Panel. Selection of expert-committee members is not confined to the corresponding expert panels but may be made from other panels. Expert committees usually comprise no more than ten members. They are convened to consider specific topics, and their reports serve as guides for governments and for action in WHO. As alcohol expert committees will be dealt with later (chapter 12), we will confine our remarks here to the Drug Dependence Expert Committee.

The Drug Dependence Expert Committee shoulders the main burden of WHO's obligations under the international drug treaties. In the League days, the Health Committee assisted in determining what substances were to be placed under the control schedules, but since WHO's inception this function has been performed by the Drug Dependence Expert Committee. Although we refer to this body as though it were a standing committee, its composition, in fact, varies from year to year and it is not to be compared with the permanent organs of the UN. The committee is in a unique position on account of its role under WHO's treaty obligations. In January 1952 the WHO executive board decided that all the reports of the expert committees (which are published) should bear the disclaimer "This report ... does not necessarily represent the decisions or the stated policy of the World Health Organization" (EB 9/R 74). Thereafter, this disclaimer can be found on the covers of front pages of the reports of all the expert committees except those of the Drug Dependence Committee. However, in the latter's report published in 1973 this disclaimer appears for the first time. The explanation for this may lie in a divergence of views between the director-general of WHO and the experts with regard to the Vienna Convention. The changing character of the committee may be another reason for the change.

The committee has met almost every year; during the period from 1949 to 1972 it met nineteen times. The committee convenes for a week at WHO headquarters in Geneva, and during that time a report is prepared for publication. As this requires much advance preparation, the organizers of the meeting in the secretariat usually undertake negotiations for the appointment of a chairman and a rapporteur ahead of time, so that the officers can be elected at the committee's first meeting.

So as to provide some clues to the work of the committees, an effort was made to classify all the recommendations which they have made since 1949 (see table 5.2). Before making any inferences from the figures, a word of caution is in order. It is not always clear from the reports what constitutes a recommendation by the committee, and recommendations are not always immediately distinguishable from expressions of opinions and advice. At the same time, we have noticed that the term "recommendation"

TABLE 5.2
Recommendations by WHO Expert Committee on Drug Dependence, 1949–72

Year of meeting	Number of recommendations	Procontrol recommendations with reference to international treaties	Similar recommendation without reference to treaties	Recommendations endorsing exclusions from international control	Other recommendations	Government notifications
1949	9	5	1		3	3
1950	10	2	2		6	2
1952	9	6	2		1	1
1953	6	4		1	1	4
1954	9	6	2		1	8
1955	10	6		3	1	8
1956	2	2				2
1957	7	7				7
1958	7	4	2	1		6
1959	8	8				8
1960	12	7	1	4		9
1961	9	4		5		8
1963	4	2		2		3
1965	4	2			2	2
1966	4	3		1		4
1968	1	1				1
1969	2		2			2
1970	2	1			1	1
1972	2	2				2
Total	117	72	12	17	16	81

NOTE: All expert committee reports are published in the WHO technical report series, except for the first one, which appears in WHO Official Records 1949, 19:29–34. Where two or more governments have notified the same drug, this is counted as one notification only.

has been used with care and with the connotation that it is to be transmitted to the UN secretary-general, that is, the Division of Narcotic Drugs in practice. Our tabulation is therefore based on statements which bear these two attributes and which may be regarded strictly as recommendations; those which give rise to uncertainty are omitted. The results which we obtain do not therefore correspond to an earlier claim regarding how frequently the expert committee has recommended controls; for instance, it was said that the committee had recommended subjecting amphetamines to control in four reports (Cameron, 1971). Although views have been expressed by the committee on these occasions, they did not amount to general policy; moreover, no clear opinion was transmitted to the UN as a recommendation by the committee. This reinforces our belief that the impact of the committee on the development of controls is slighter than is generally supposed. Another shortcoming of the table is that it does not reflect changes in orientation; the first time Dale Cameron served as secretary to the expert committee, the ordering of the contents of its report was altered and the passages dealing with drug control notifications came at the end of the report instead of at the beginning. This may reflect a shift away from WHO's earlier orientation, which was towards "the drug or agent of addiction" rather than towards the individual or his environment (see Cameron, 1971: 145). Finally, one should not be misled by the figures in the table representing the number of control recommendations into thinking that the committee was procontrol. The committee has discussed some drugs (such as barbiturates) without making accompanying recommendations for control. Thus the areas untouched by recommendations must be borne in mind when noting those marked by them.

There have been 117 recommendations. Most of these were for the inclusion of a specific drug in one control schedule or another by application of the relevant provisions of the existing conventions. In addition, similar recommendations have been made without treaty paragraphs being invoked. Some recommendations were for the acceptance of goverment notifications for the exclusion of a drug from international control; others advocated changing the status, or degree of control, of a drug. The number of other recommendations is relatively small, and the majority of them was made in the first two years. Government notifications provide the bulk of the committee's drug classification work. Following a decrease in the number of notifications, a significant decrease in the total number of recommendations occurred in 1963. However, it should be noted that at the beginning many recommendations were made which were not instigated by notifications.

The largest number of notifications (about 40 percent), stems from the U.S.; France and the U.K. are next, and the three countries together account for about two-thirds of all notifications. That the total number has diminished is due to at least two developments. First, in recent years there has been less readiness to propose for international control, new drugs that are not yet, or not likely to be, marketed. Secondly, pharmaceutical research aimed at developing substitutes for morphine without addiction liability has become far less intense, discouraged by the failure of earlier efforts. This leads inevitably to a reduction in the number of recommendations, since the Committee has been engaged mostly in evaluating drugs of the morphine type.

Although these circumstances explain the decrease in recommendations in recent years, the impression gained from a comparison of the reports is that, on balance, the committee's recommendations for placing new drugs under international control have tended to be sparing and to lag behind actual events. Barbiturates and amphetamines, for example, were discussed for years before a clear position endorsing international control emerged in the committee. There has been little interest in relating scientific knowledge to social purpose, and little discussion (at least insofar as can be judged from the reports) of the principles of drug control. Even given the fact that, during the first two years, heroin and its therapeutic use engaged much of the committee's attention, and statements relating to definitions and research were, contrary to later practice, framed as recommendations, the committee seems to have been more prone to controls in earlier years than later.

That slight attention has been paid to issues involving principles may have to do with the fact that the expertise of the committee has lain predominantly in the field of pharmacology. The fact that WHO governmental representatives and professional secretariat members are preponderantly medical doctors may also have a bearing on the selection of members and, indirectly, on the nature of the decisions reached. One notes that of the representatives in two WHO meetings in 1967 (the executive board and the World Health Assembly) over 70 percent and 65 percent, respectively, were physicians (Cox and Jacobson, 1973: 196).

6 The International Narcotics Control Board

> The Board has continued to show a narrow conception of
> its duties. The completion of incomplete and problematic
> statistics will never solve the problem.
>> A. E. Blanco, in an Anti-Opium Information
>> Bureau communiqué (1930)

Describing the activities of the INCB is, on the one hand, a relatively easy task and, on the other, one beset by difficulties. The ease is due to the fact that the Board has clear-cut duties and that much of its output is in the form of publications; by studying these one can learn a great deal about the nature of its work. The difficulties arise from the Board's use of secrecy. The need for secrecy is stipulated by the international legislation under which the Board operates and is understandable in view of the necessity to treat as confidential the information supplied to it by individual governments. But "official secrecy," as it operates in bureaucracies (see Gerth and Mills, 1948) has a way of expanding the area it covers. Thus the minutes and agendas of INCB meetings and its communications with governments have all become classified material. A written request we made to the INCB for access to the minutes of the PCB and DSB, from their inception up to 1942, was turned down. An idea of how "closed" the area of participation in information-sharing is can be gathered from the following incidents.

During the plenipotentiary conference to consider amendments to the Single Convention, the chief British delegate, Peter Beedle, observed that, although the reports of the Board were becoming increasingly important because of the information they gave on the illicit traffic, "the source of information remained a mystery," and this he considered "unsatisfactory and anomalous in a world where co-ordination and dialogue were the order of the day" (E/CONF.63/C.1/SR.4, 1972). As this delegate was also for some time a representative to and chairman of the Commission on Narcotic Drugs, his statement implies an information gap between the two bodies.

Earlier too, the Board had not shared its information with the Advisory Opium Committee, as is evidenced by the following letter from its first president, Leonard Lyall, to the chairman of the Committee:

The Board was further informed that the Advisory Committee would probably ask the Board to communicate to it the annual estimates for the year 1930 that it will receive from the various governments.... The Board, anxious as it is to oblige the Advisory Committee in every way, considered this question carefully, but came to the conclusion that these forms are confidential, and that the Board would therefore scarcely be justified in communicating them even to the Advisory Committee, without the consent of the Governments concerned (Letter from L. A. Lyall to C. Fotitch: OC 1093 1 XI, 1929).

This predilection for confidentiality imposes a limitation on any attempt to assess the work of the Board. The limitation is probably not so very serious when it is only a question of describing the statistical work of the Board, but, as one of its own vice-presidents pointed out, the Board is not merely a body "for the mechanical recording of statistics; a computer could fulfil that role" (CND: 24th, 1971: 170). It makes decisions with regard to these statistics, and, if there are treaty violations, it can recommend sanctions against the government concerned (see Appendix B). We see only one aspect of how the Board exercises control, but we can only conjecture with regard to the other—that which is generally referred to as its semijudicial function. It is thus difficult to determine to what extent the Board has fully used or underused its powers, or to what extent it has kept strictly to the performance of its obligations under the treaties. The Board has interpreted the scope of its functions as widely as it could, and it has appeared more willing of late to take stands on matters of policy. Its 1972 report is a good example of the recent readiness to venture opinions on the circumstances and social consequences of drug use. In doing so, it runs the risk of laying itself open to criticism and pressure—criticism from those better versed in such matters, and pressure from those countries wishing to convert others to their point of view.

The Board is in session twice a year and its annual meeting-time amounts to about a month. Previously, it had met more frequently, and the pattern of meetings was such that not only did the PCB and DSB hold joint meetings (in addition to separate ones) but even their own individual meetings overlapped in time. Indeed there was increasing personal union, in that several people were simultaneously DSB and PCB members. Although arguments have been advanced in favor of having separate bodies (Eisenlohr, 1934), few would deny today that merging the two was an improvement on the old system. There has also been some disagreement over the frequency with which the Board should meet. The Board is in favor of more frequent meetings; when the secretary-general's Committee on the Reorganization of the Secretariat recommended that the Board should only meet once a year, the Board pointed out that not only was it necessary to meet twice a year but that a third meeting might well be called for from time to time (INCB, 1969). A factor which may have contributed to a diminished need for so many meetings is the accumulating experience of the Secretariat. The Board's sessions are an opportunity for more intense contact between its members and the Secretariat staff; probably because of the smallness of the two bodies, the relationship seems to be closer here than for corresponding groups in other parts of the drug control apparatus.

One of the main tasks at these meetings is the inspection of advance estimates furnished by governments of their drug requirements for the following year. For this purpose the Board has a subcommittee which meets before the full Board meets. This subcommittee in fact performs to a large extent the job of the earlier Supervisory Body. In its plenary sessions the Board discusses what eventually becomes the contents of its publications.

The main output of the Board consists of four documents: a basic annual report and three separate publications containing mostly quantitative data.

Of these three publications, the first we will consider is the annual statement of the *Estimate of World Requirements of Narcotic Drugs and Estimates of World Production of Opium.*

The main purpose of the estimates is to limit the manufacture of and trade in drugs to legitimate requirements. The estimates are based on governmental estimates given in advance and are tabulated by country, by drug, and by type of use. The categories of use are: domestic consumption for medical and scientific purposes; utilization for the manufacture of other substances; maintenance of reserve stocks.

Governments are required to state the method used for determining their figures, especially if they are found to be significantly higher than those of previous years. Some countries fail to provide the Board with their estimates of requirements, and in these cases the Board determines them itself. The Board may have reason, sometimes, to challenge the validity of the governmental estimates, and this can give rise to extensive correspondence with the governments concerned. The provision for governments to submit supplementary estimates adds flexibility to the system but creates considerable additional work for the secretariat. The supplementary estimates are published four times a year as addenda to the original statement of estimates. The outcome of the Board's correspondence with governments is difficult to assess without a systematic study of its contents, which, for reasons already mentioned, we did not find possible.

The crucial question underlying the application of the estimates system is, by what criteria are medical requirements determined? The Board is faced with this question when it is not able to relate the figures it receives to the method claimed to have been used to arrive at them. For the consumption estimate the Board offers a formula to be followed by governments; for the other categories no method can be uniformly used in all countries, since conditions vary widely. The search for criteria of medical need goes back to the time of the League of Nations, when a subcommittee of the Advisory Committee and Health Committee grappled for a time with this question. Initially, it was suggested that calculations of requirements should be based on a rate of 600 milligrams of raw opium per inhabitant per year. Subsequently, the subcommittee adopted a norm of 450 milligrams; consumption above this level was to be considered not only unnecessary but also harmful, and consumption below it was to be an indication that part of the population was being deprived (CH 264, 1924). There seemed to have been some recognition of the relativity of this norm, for it was conceded that it applied only to European countries. It was estimated that, at 450 milligrams of opium per capita, the world's legitimate requirements would amount to 720 tons annually. Interestingly enough, the U.S. Congress had, in a resolution of 1923, declared that 100 tons would satisfy the annual medical and scientific needs of the world (Buell, 1925).

Uncertain and arbitrary as the criteria must be, the system was not unworkable, and the Drug Supervisory Body was able to tell which governments had overestimated their needs. In the Commission also, a resolution had been passed to discourage overestimation, the extent of which was reckoned at 25 percent for morphine and 54 percent for cocaine (CND: 9th, 1954). Moreover, the Drug Supervisory Body was able to observe that estimates were often merely a reflection of sales projections. In its 1960 report it expressed surprise that "the criteria on which some governments base their estimates should have been dictated solely by prospects of sales" (DSB, 1960: 9).

Further criteria were elaborated, based on such measurements as the number of hospital beds, the number of doctors, dentists, and veterinarians in each country. WHO was approached for its advice. The Drug Dependence Unit to which this question was referred presented its conclusions in a paper entitled "Variations in Legal Narcotics Consumption as between Countries and Underlying Factors" (WHO/APD/INT/22, 1961). According to this paper the criteria used did not yield figures that reflected actual needs.

In fact, it is evident that the key factor in determining medical requirements is actual use. The Board, too, has observed that the majority of countries claimed to base their estimates on consumption in previous years, even though the estimates and the use figures did not always tally (INCB/Estimates, 1970: vii). Deciding which comes first is very much in the nature of deciding between "the chicken and the egg," although one might also see the usefulness of the estimates system as an "educational device" (Halbach, interview) that impels countries to follow more critically the level of their drug consumption. On the other hand, it is also likely that, instead of doing that, some countries merely fall back on consumption levels of previous years and produce an estimate based on those without further enquiry.

Although a full evaluation of the estimates system is not possible without considering the other statistical work of the Board and the interventions it has made, it does seem as if the Board has had to adjust to changes in medical practice without being able to question them. A case in point is the therapeutic use of cannabis in several European countries during the 1960s. Another illustration is provided by trends in the level of demand for medical purposes for certain drugs, as shown in table 6.1. We see from this table that the estimated requirements for pethidine and codeine have all risen over time while those for heroin have fallen. The increase in morphine is accounted for by the increased demand for codeine, for whose manufacture most of the morphine produced is used. Methadone requirements show a different trend. It will be recalled that when heroin was first developed it was greeted as a welcome substitute and cure for morphine addiction. Now methadone is used in treating opiate dependence, and since 1969 an increase of nearly 100 percent in its rate of production has been reported by the Board: of the total increase, the share of the U.S. rose from 41 percent in 1967 to 84 percent in 1970 (INCB/Statistics, 1970). The acceptance of methadone maintenance represents such a deviation from earlier policies which favored abstinence—the conference which adopted the Single Convention, for instance, urged the setting up of facilities for treatment "in a hospital institution having a drug-free atmosphere" (Resolution II)—that one wonders what the international reaction might have been if methadone had been introduced on a large scale by any country other than the U.S.

These changes make it difficult to determine what in fact constitutes medical need, nonmedical need, and quasi-medical need. What conclusion is one to draw from the fact that India, with a population of 550 million, anticipated using eight times as much opium for medical purposes during 1971 as the United States, which had a population that year of 205 million, whereas total requirements of U.S. citizens for codeine and pethidine for that same year were, respectively, twice and fifteen times those of India's? Is the acceptance (implied by approved estimates) of the increase in the use of codeine justified, when the WHO Expert Committee had pronounced it an addiction-producing drug (WHO/EC DD, 1958) and cases of its use intravenously and in high oral doses had been reported (CND: 24th, 1971)?

TABLE 6.1
Estimated World Requirements (in kgs) of Morphine, Heroin, Methadone, Pethidine and Codeine, 1935–71

	1935	1939	1950	1955	1960	1965	1970	1971	1972a
Morphine	9,021	54,883	96,985	105,589	128,484	163,796	207,158	202,623	252,149
Heroin	1,103	885	843	259	103	115	144	112	111
Methadone	–	–	1,694	900	908	478	1,385	3,035	2,570
Pethidine	–	–	8,198	17,927	19,185	25,505	27,823	28,418	26,283
Codeine	25,560	36,388	90,597	99,065	115,187	140,423	217,393	256,259	262,512

SOURCE: DSB/INCB reports.

aThese figures will be increased by the supplementary estimates.

The second part of the statement of estimates relates to estimates of opium production, which are tabulated by country, and within each country by region and area. Estimated amounts of opium to be harvested and area of cultivation are given, as is the average moisture content of the opium to be harvested. The same difficulties must attend the assessment of these estimates as of those already discussed, but because the number of countries is limited to those complying with the 1953 Opium Protocol, this exercise is more manageable. Opium producers often protest that these estimates are at best a rough guess since variations in weather and other physical conditions can greatly affect the size of the crop.

The Board also publishes an annual report entitled *Statistics on Narcotic Drugs*. This contains nine statistical tables and, in recent years, some comment and analysis of the data presented. These tables provide a picture of the consecutive stages of the legal trade in drugs—from agricultural production to manufacture to export/import, consumption, and stocks. Data relating to these stages are taken from returns from governments, and control is exercised through checking whether the returns from an exporting country correspond, for example, to those of the importing country. In addition, the publication contains information on seizures.

The third addendum to the Board's annual report is the *Comparative Statement of Estimates and Statistics* which is a balance sheet showing whether the amounts available have been accounted for and whether each country has stayed within the limits set by its estimates. This way, the Board exerts "control" by showing that the supply of drugs in a country does not exceed its estimated requirements. If this limit has been exceeded, the Board can intervene by asking the country concerned to take steps to remedy the situation. The effectiveness of this kind of control depends on a number of factors: one is the quality of the returns received by the Board and another is the way the estimates have been made up. If the estimates were merely figures adjusted to former levels of production or importation and consumption, then comparing them with the contemporary statistics would seem to be a superfluous exercise. All that the Board is doing then is simply repeating what the governments themselves have already done, if, in fact, governments draw up their estimates on the basis of prior consumption. Often the estimates are not even adaptations; they are repetitions of the previous year's data without account being taken of any changes which may have occurred (INCB, 1968). But if the estimates are not just the statistics in another guise, then the situation is, of course, different; control will have been exercised not only over whether consignments of drugs keep within the estimates of their intended destinations but also indirectly over drug consumption in the general population, overprescribing of drugs by physicians, and so on. If the Board does question the estimates submitted to it and if the governments concerned do then modify them accordingly, with consequent changes in production or import, then this form of indirect control will to some extent have been applied. It is clear, nevertheless, that the basis of the Board's supervision is in seeing that, in any given country, the legal supply of drugs is not so abundant that it can spill over into the illicit market. How large or small the supply should be depends on how much medicine the country's government decides is needed by its citizens, and often this depends on how much medicine is being taken to begin with.* In some countries addicts or drug-dependent persons are included in the category of medicine-takers while in others they are not.

In summary, the Board's statistical output consists of estimates of requirements, data on the licit movement of drugs, and comparisons between estimates and utilization—all of which are based on government reports. The history of the Board is in a sense a history of constant struggle for better cooperation from national authorities and for a higher quality in their returns. Sometimes the level of precision expected from governments is extremely high, as when, for example, the Yugoslavian government was asked by the Board in 1972 to explain a failure to report five milligrams of LSD (E/CN,7/SR.688). In its annual reports the Board often refers to the need for an improvement in governmental reporting. In its 1947 report, the Board defined three criteria for measuring the adequacy of the statistical reporting system:

    —the number of countries collaborating;
    —the number of returns (each country has to complete ten per year);
    —the quality of the statistics.

* The term "medicine" is used here with the same limited application as the term "drugs" (see Introduction).

The Board's reports regularly give the yearly percentages of total returns received compared to the number expected. Some of these are given below:

Year covered by statistics	1947	1950	1955	1965	1970	1971
% returns received	80	88	92	90	94	92

The figure for 1971 represents 867 returns out of a total of 948 due. Despite the high rate of returns, the limitations of the three measures are evident, given the lack of criteria for estimating production, trade, or medical need.

Many countries do not submit their estimates of requirements, and in these cases the Board establishes them. In 1935 the Board established estimates for 48 countries and received estimates from 123. In 1972 the corresponding numbers were 14 and 174. It is noteworthy that estimates of drug needs for all China had been provided by the Nationalist government in Taiwan.

The last publication to be considered is the Board's main annual report on its work, to which the reports already discussed are supplements. The report contains comments on the working of the system of statistical returns, but there seems to be a tendency in recent years for these to become a less important feature of the report. More attention is being paid to the kind of issues that are discussed by the World Health Organization and the Commission.

The report is one of the media used by the Board to exert moral pressure, and it therefore contains many appeals, declarations, and expressions of approval and disapproval, as the case may be. Because it provides valuable insight into the values and beliefs which underlie the Board's approach to the problem with which it deals, and so as to convey the "feel" of the report's phraseology and style, we will briefly review one issue—that for 1971, the last available at the time of writing this chapter.*

The report begins with a listing of the eleven Board members (see Appendix B), accompanied by details of their academic and professional qualifications. The personal data are considerably

* The 1972 report, which has appeared since this section was written, will be referred to in subsequent chapters.

fuller than those given for the individuals serving the WHO expert committees and the Commission on Narcotic Drugs in their respective publications, and the rationale for this must lie in the need to stress the independence and high caliber of the INCB members. The report proceeds to a survey of the general world drug situation, and the tone here is alarmist: a "virtual epidemic" of "drug abuse" (p. 8) is said to have occurred. The report then goes on to review the current state of international control, and "problem countries" in the Middle East, South East Asia, and the Andean region are specially mentioned. This is followed by another review of the general situation, this time by class of drug—the opiates, cannabis, the coca leaf, and cocaine. In an earlier chapter the report states that "so long as demand persists (and there is reason to fear that it will in fact expand), production will inevitably rise, in one place or another, to meet it" (p. 20). A subsequent chapter states what the Board thinks should be done to curtail demand; from this one learns that the Board's concept of "demand" is, in fact, no less narrow than the earlier notion that it is a question of curing addicts and deterring would-be users. The measures proposed entail the identification and treatment of "individual cases of addiction which may be redeemable"; checking "the epidemic spread" by "protecting" the "individuals or groups particularly at risk"; and the limitation of "deterioration in severe and relapsing cases" (p. 28–29). The report concludes that

humanity is facing a world crisis: a crisis which is portrayed in the spectacular growth of drug abuse; in the revival of the evil in countries where firm action seemed to have succeeded in checking it; in the emergence of new channels of illicit traffic; in the appearance in law-respecting countries of group defiance of the law . . . (p. 34).

There is no lack of drama in these polemics. They also show a certain insularity; a failure to see things in their proper proportions. One's own area of concern is seen as the all-important one, claiming more attention than can reasonably be assigned. Its seriousness is played up in terms which go beyond the immediate circumstances in a way which is likely to distort judgment.

Finally, some observations on the members of the Board. The conditions of appointment laid down by the Single Convention are "competence, impartiality and disinterestedness." However, it is doubtful whether actual practice adheres to these strict standards. The Board is not a "pure" apolitical body because governments will not allow it to be. An illustration of this is provided by the German declaration at a League Council meeting in 1927 that German ratification of the 1925 convention would be contingent on a German expert becoming a PCB member (Council, 6 December 1927). Although a requirement of appointment has been that a person in government service should relinquish his position on appointment to the Board, one of the members, Marcel Granier-Doyeux, is, in fact, simultaneously an ambassador and an INCB vice-president. One would also have thought that Harry Greenfield's close connections with the British-American Tobacco Company were not altogether compatible with his position as president of the Board, given the Board's goal of combating drug dependence, and the dependence factor in, and health damages of, cigarette smoking.

We have discussed the Board at some length without considering the secretariat. This is not to imply the latter's insignificance. On the contrary, most of the work which goes into the preparation of the published reports is carried out by the staff members, but as this forms the bulk of the secretariat's work program, (E/4463), it is not necessary to explore its activities in greater detail.

7   The Commission on Narcotic Drugs and the Division

> The proceedings of the Opium Committee and still more
> of the conferences which it organized, were the scene of
> violent language and hasty action to a degree unknown
> among other organs of the League.
>
> F. P. Walters, *A History of the League of Nations*

If, as Walters observed, the Advisory Opium Committee members were not given to restraint in their debates, the same cannot be said of their successors in the UN Commission on Narcotic Drugs, many of whom are practitioners of elegant diplomacy. Yet in many other respects the two organs do resemble each other; the fundamental control problems remain the same, as do the dimensions of conflicting interests. These interests are still active, but practical considerations, such as the sheer number of states which have been added, dictate that disputes do not too frequently frustrate all action. Indeed, attempts to settle most disputes are probably made by interested (or aggrieved) parties outside the formal meeting. Hadwen and Kaufmann observe (1962):

most UN decisions are settled by informal negotiating processes outside the formal meetings.... The UN visitor, therefore, hears, except in cases of major conflict, the public explanation of what has been agreed privately.

The membership of the Commission has been enlarged along with the general increase in the membership of the UN. From an organ of fifteen member states, the Commission has developed

into one with a membership of thirty states. The composition of
the Commission is determined both with a view to the subject of
its concern and by the political considerations of the overall
membership policy of the UN itself, which purports to exclude
states which are not "peace-loving." The original criteria for
selecting members—that there should be adequate representation
of those countries which are drug producers or manufacturers, or
are victims of the illicit traffic—reflected the functionalist
approach, while political factors were clearly operating, for
instance, in the decision of the Commission in 1946 to exclude
from the then existing drug treaties "the Franco Government in
Spain for so long as this Government is in power" (E/168). The
increase in the membership from fifteen to twenty-one in 1961
was part of a general expansion of the functional commissions of
ECOSOC to make room for the increased membership of the UN.
This was also the case with the increase from twenty-one to
twenty-four members in 1967. However, the honor of having
belonged to the original fifteen is to a large extent preserved in a
kind of "gentlemen's club" which has evolved with the continual
renewal of contact between the same delegates attending the
yearly sessions of the Commission over the years (Lowes, 1966:
163 and 181). The Commission's membership is further discussed
in Appendix C.

The duration of the regular sessions of the Commission has
been quite stable but their frequency has been reduced by
ECOSOC in 1969 from once every year to once every other year.
That 153 individuals representing 51 states and 17 international
organizations participated in the 1971 session gives an indication
of the size of the present meetings. For every session the
Commission elects a chairman, two vice-chairmen, and a rapporteur, and these constitute the Bureau. Those elected to the Bureau
function until the next session, and what this means in formal
terms is that the chairman performs such functions as signing
letters, accepting proposals for agenda items for the next meeting,
and playing a mediating role between consecutive sessions. These
office-bearers succeed each other. Thus the rapporteur of the
previous session becomes the second vice-chairman of the subsequent session, while the erstwhile second vice-chairman becomes
first vice-chairman. The first vice-chairman of the last session in
turn becomes this session's chairman. In addition there is a

standing committee composed of the Bureau and the chairmen of previous sessions. The meetings of the Narcotics Commission, like most UN meetings, are an occasion for consultation between participants, for the special views of the various agencies and organizational units to be aired, and for arriving at some recommendations. To some extent these activities are bound to be contained within the framework of custom, styles of action, and precedents which have been set through the years and which have become the very basis of the Commission's operations. They are circumscribed, too, by the range of information or choice of emphasis offered in memoranda prepared by the secretariat and circulated among delegations.

The views and concerns of the Commission are best reflected in the resolutions it drafts and adopts. With this in mind, we have systematically analyzed the contents of all the resolutions appearing in the report of each session of the Commission to ECOSOC, from its first to its twenty-third session, on the assumption that this is a means of studying not only the priorities, preoccupations, and activities of the Commission but also its roles relative to other bodies or agencies. Moreover, by studying the resolutions for the entire period of the Commission's existence, it may be possible to see what changes have occurred in the type of issues with which it has been concerned and the kind of approach it has adopted towards them.

A limitation of this analysis is that it is based entirely on resolutions as they finally come to be worded and ignores those features of the text which have been dropped or modified through successive drafts. Thus the resolutions analyzed represent only the resultant of all the positions which have been taken during the debate on the question at issue. Furthermore, a resolution which goes on record as a Commission decision does not necessarily have the support of all its members, as can readily be seen from the voting pattern on resolutions. We have not, however, studied voting behavior because the breakdown of votes is not always on record.

Nevertheless, resolutions do focus and express the collective will; they reflect the issues which receive the attention of the Commission and the majority response to them. We assume that every drug issue of a politically significant nature will be covered by at least one resolution, and that the number of resolutions addressed to a particular problem area signifies either its perceived importance, or its persistence and intractability, or that because of its political sensitivity only pressure cumulatively applied by way of repetitive resolutions is thought to have any effect. The form of the resolutions has undergone some changes over time, but generally speaking it depends on the addressee to whom it is directed. A typical resolution begins with a number of paragraphs in which previous UN materials, pronouncements, or decisions are cited, the subject matter is introduced, the background is sketched, and tone set. Following the preambular paragraphs are the operative paragraphs which make recommendations or express attitudes or call for particular actions to be taken both within or outside the UN system.

In Appendix C we have tabulated, for the years from 1946 to 1971, the number of resolutions which have been passed by the Commission and their breakdown by year and type. The scheme of classification underlying the table requires a few words of explanation. First, only those expressions which the Commission itself calls resolutions are included; in the first few years of the Commission's existence resolutions were interspersed among similar statements not specifically called resolutions. These are excluded from our list. In later years, however, resolutions were clearly and separately enumerated in the reports. Other changes are apparent; similar statements about forthcoming meetings may be formulated as resolutions in some cases and made in ordinary terms in others. However, there has been sufficient consistency over the years to allow comparison. In Appendix C we have enumerated those resolutions which specifically refer to a country or region on the one hand, and to a drug or group of drugs on the other. Each resolution is assigned to either or both of these categories. Because of multiple assignment—for example, a resolution which names a drug and a country in its text will be assigned to both categories—the total frequency counts do not equal the total number of resolutions. To be counted at all among the drug-specific categories, a resolution has to contain the name of a drug or group of drugs. The name of a drug many be omitted because of the low level of the Commission's concern with it or because of a deliberate broadening of the terms in which the resolution is cast. Indeed, resolutions touching national interests are seldom passed without a substantial dilution of their original contents.

There are altogether 159 resolutions for the period from 1946 to 1971. Roughly a fifth of the total resolutions adopted mention a country or region and more than half are drug-specific. The country-specific resolutions are more evenly distributed among the years than the drug-specific ones. We see that a marked increase in the number of resolutions occurred in 1954 and a less marked decrease from about 1961. It seems reasonable therefore to compare the periods 1946–53, 1954–62, and 1963–71.

In table 7.1 the resolutions are classified by type of drug and region for each of the three periods mentioned above. The period from 1954 to 1962 strikes one immediately as the golden era of

TABLE 7.1
Analysis of Commission Resolutions, 1946–71

| | Frequency of Resolutions | | | |
	1946–53	1954–62	1963–71	Total
Region				
Andean region	5	1	2	8
Middle East	–	9	4	13
Far East	5	–	3	8
Others[a]	2	4	–	6
Total number of region-specific resolutions	12	14	9	35
Drug or drug group				
Coca, cocaine	6	4	2	12
Opium	14	20	2	36
Heroin, morphine	1	6	–	7
Cannabis	–	9	4	13
"Synthetics" of morphine type	4	9	1	14
Psychotropics	–	4	4	8
Others[b]	–	3	4	7
Total number of drug-specific resolutions	25	47[c]	17	89[c]
Total number of resolutions	38	93	28	159

[a]1946–53—Germany, Mexico; 1954–62—India, Morocco, Latin America, Germany.

[b]1954–62—ketobemidone, khat, codeine; 1963–71—two each on khat and LSD.

[c]Because of multiple assignment, this figure is not the sum of the figures in the column.

resolutions. Resolutions were less frequent in the last period than in the first although the latter covers fewer years. As for the regions, there are curious differences. The Commission appears to have been quite concerned with the Andean region and the Far East in the first period and almost not at all in the second period, during which interest is focused on the Middle East, where it has continued to hover. Although not shown in the table, Peru is the most frequently mentioned among individual countries.

One notes that almost all resolutions in the regional category refer or are addressed to the producers of "natural" classical narcotics (that is, to the developing countries); industrialized producing countries hardly ever feature. In 1946 Japan and Germany—two countries from which there was much illicit diversion—were the countries addressed. The tendency to designate as problem countries only the weak ones—in this instance the Third World states or those defeated in war—is also noticeable elsewhere (see chapter 10).

As far as the frequency of drug types is concerned, opium gets predominant attention, representing over 40 percent of the total number of references to drug types. The dominance disappears in the third period. Cannabis began to figure in resolutions when its prohibition was being considered. The interest in coca leaf/cocaine has lingered but has declined compared to earlier years. During the second period "new synthetics" commanded much attention. "Psychotropics" appear for the first time in the 1954–62 period and khat and LSD between 1963 and 1971.

We had intended also, originally, to analyze the resolutions in terms of the kind of action prescribed by them, the level of action called for (such as national or international), and the international bodies (such as FAO or INCB) addressed. But we abandoned this exercise because the texts of the resolutions are often too vague to allow clear-cut classification. If the directives contained in resolutions form the basis of the secretariat's work, tremendous problems of interpretation must occur. Many resolutions are restatements of general concern and exhortations to countries to adhere to treaties. In fact, most resolutions are addressed to governments, requesting or urging them to take action on a particular issue. Many of the resolutions of the second period enlist the help of the specialized agencies, especially WHO and FAO, to provide technical assistance to countries.

It is noteworthy that the spate of resolutions occurring in the second period coincides with the tenure of Gilbert Yates as director of the Division of Narcotic Drugs. We are told by members of the Division that the subsequent fall in number was in response to an indication by ECOSOC (to which the resolutions are ultimately submitted) that it did not have the time to deal with so many. Whatever the reason, the coincidence leads to the inference that the Secretariat has a hand in the drafting of resolutions. In fact many resolutions originate from the Division, and before submitting a draft resolution to the Commission delegation members would often hold consultations over the wording of the text with secretariat members.

We have seen in Chapter 4 that the resources of the Division greatly overshadow those of the other drug units. But this does not reflect its prestige or reputation within the UN. In the League days, too, the reputation of the Opium Section was relatively low compared with other sections of the organization, partly because its staff members were recruited from among the ranks of the diplomats available in Geneva at the time, and employment was offered to them more as a reward for past services than in expectation of their making contributions to future action (Pastuhov, 1943: 14).

An idea of the range of official duties performed by the Division and the structuring of manpower around them may be gained from table 7.2 below. This gives the projected program components of the Division's work and their corresponding man-month requirements at the two levels into which the UN Secretariat is divided, the professional and the general service, for the years 1972 and 1968, the latter year being the first for which such a breakdown is available.

The table suggests that although 1972 shows an increase over 1968 in terms of professional manpower requirements and a decrease in the man-month requirements of the consultant category, the period between those years is marked by relative stability. The formal definition and organization of tasks remain the same, as do the manpower requirements of the general service category. The latter fact is somewhat surprising given the increase in the proportion of professional manpower requirements and seems to suggest that either a great deal of routine work is being carried out by the professional staff or that the output of the

TABLE 7.2
Program Components of the Division of Narcotic Drugs, 1968 and 1972.

Program components	Man-months required (professionals)	
	1968	1972
Scientific research on cannabis, opium, and other substances which engender dependence	48	60
Studies on opium, cannabis, coca leaf, and synthetic narcotics	14	–
Studies on psychotropic substances not under international control	12	15
Studies and other work related to substances under control including advice on treaty matters and changes in the scope of control, action to secure universal participation	12	12
Replacement of illicit or uncontrolled production of narcotic raw materials	–	18
Work related to drug addiction	14	12
Work related to illicit traffic in drugs	7	12
Work related to national laws and regulations	14	12
Liaison with other international bodies	12	12
Outposting of officers	12	24
Technical cooperation	16	12
Program formulation and management	4	18
Preparation, servicing, and follow-up of the annual sessions of the Commission and of the Council	16	–
Annual reports of governments	14	12
Information activities, including preparation of the *Bulletin*	9	9
TOTAL	204	228
Additional man-months		
General service category	168	168
Consultants	17	6

SOURCES: UN documents E/4793 and E/4463.

professionals is not sufficiently large to warrant additional sup-porting services from the lower category.

The items of work listed correspond to the headings of the Division's report to the Commission: National Laws and Regula-tions, Illicit Traffic, Drug Addiction, and so on. It appears that work is assigned to professionals on the basis of well-established subject sectors which in turn reflect the kinds of information which treaty provisions require that countries supply to the secretary-general. Thus many of the program components relate to the collection, analysis (usually for trends), and reporting of information given to the secretariats by governments under their treaty obligations. This information is often quite inadequate. It is also unreliable; this is bound to be the case when, for example, prevalence of use is established on the basis of returns from governments that give "abusive consumption" data without the term being defined. A discussion between representatives at the twenty-fourth session of the Commission is illustrative. Vaille of France argued for the retention of the term "multiple addiction" in a draft resolution on cannabis because, he said, "the Secretary-General's note on drug abuse (E/CN.7/534) contained a number of tables which gave data on the abuse of cannabis in association with other narcotic and psychotropic drugs." The U.K. represen-tative (Stewart) questioned the applicability of the term "multiple addiction" to cannabis use, and pointed out that "the informa-tion supplied by his own Government concerning cannabis users was based on criminal convictions for the possession of the drug, which in itself constituted no proof of addiction" (E/CN. 7/SR. 716:11). A further illustration of the inaccuracy of such reporting is provided by a cross-national study of prevalence, based on UN data, which showed that by such a measure developing countries had more drug problems than developed ones (Blum, 1969: 174, 175). It is evident from the last two sessions of the Commission (CND:24th, 1971; 25th, 1973) that the questionnaires used for such reporting are in need of overhauling, and this is in fact being attempted.

The paucity of information in the national annual reports to the UN may be illustrated by reference to the contents of the 1971 returns under the heading "drug abuse" (on conditions in 1970). A systematic study of these reveals the limited value of the information given. The reports are on the whole brief, the most laconic being those submitted by Nauru, Western Samoa, and Sweden. National conditions are depicted on the basis of observations (for example, on "drug addicts") made by official agencies, law enforcement authorities, and medical practitioners; none of the data are based on scientific studies carried out on representative population samples. Some of the information given is not without quaintness: Honduras, for example, reports that it has two addicts and provides their names, while Monaco admits to only one, an eighty-five-year-old woman who takes drugs in her whisky. However, the more sophisticated statistical tables given by such countries as Canada, the U.S., and West Germany are no less heuristic and bear little relation to the figures yielded by investigations carried out by researchers in these countries. Burma, on the other hand, strikes an honest note when it remarks that it is "very difficult to get a correct estimate of opium addicts, and it is feared that actual figures may be more"—a summing-up which may be generalized to all countries. All this is complicated by the lack of standardized terminology: for example, while the U.S. reports no "cannabis addicts," West Germany does (346 among those taking one drug only). As far as implementing international obligations is concerned, Burma again demonstrates an important point when it reports that "attempts are being made with some success to bring Kokang area under effective administrative control"; and, "The question of extension of narcotic laws to the area east of Salween river is also under consideration by the Government." These remarks highlight a situation typical of a number of developing countries, namely, the insecure foothold which central government control has in the areas of drug production. The reports on international trade indicate a lack of articulation between import and export controls. A number of countries complain that copies of export authorizations sent to governments of importing countries have not been returned. The U.S. reports 107 instances of such omissions, the U.K. 362 (representing 25 percent of all authorizations), Belgium 73 and so on. Israel states that it has yet to receive the copies which it reported as missing for the years 1965–69. The Netherlands maintains "that, in fact, the issue of import licences by the authorities of importing countries renders superfluous any check on the part of the exporting countries as to possible exceeding of the estimate for those countries, and that such a check can be carried out only by the International Narcotics Control Board."

Some countries include comments on the international system in their reports. For instance, Thailand reports that at the UN Training and Consultative Course held at the Parusakawau Palace in Bangkok, a series of lectures "of enduring interest on narcotic control" was given by four European UN officials. The Republic of Korea expresses great appreciation for the information bulletin of the UN Narcotics Division, which was found to benefit the government policies.

An important item of the program is what is referred to as scientific research being carried out by the UN Laboratory. Set up in 1955, the Laboratory was an outcome of a number of resolutions adopted by ECOSOC (1959 II C [VII]; 246 F [IX]) and the General Assembly (834 [IX]). The program for which it was established was the development of chemical methods for the determination of the geographical origin of opium. This was considered to be of great value in identifying the sources of illicit traffic. Chemical tests for this purpose have been developed based on comparing the analytical data for seized opium with data for opium samples of known origins. It is said that, where adequate numbers of authenticated samples are available from a country or region, it is possible to determine whether a seizure stemmed from that country. Nevertheless, geographical origin of seized opium has remained a matter of much contention in the Commission (see chapter 15). Obviously, since the opium poppy does not respect national borders, it is not possible to decide, on the basis of such tests, whether a sample of seized opium has come from a particular country if that country was one of several contiguous opium-growing countries. The determination of the origin of opium is now considered to be of lesser importance in view of the changing patterns in the illicit traffic within recent years. Opium now travels lesser distances in the illicit traffic because the morphine base (which is much easier and more profitable to smuggle) is being extracted from the opium nearer the place of production of the opium (Braenden, interview), and priority is now given, on the Commission's instructions, to other projects (E/CN.7/537, 1971: 26). The Commission had decided that "research on opium had reached an advanced stage, and that methods developed for the determination of the origin of opium were very satisfactory." The view was expressed that the Laboratory should devote more attention to cannabis research and to "other drugs of interest to the Commission" (CND. 20th, 1965: 33).

In 1959 a cannabis research program was initiated the purpose of which was, again, the identification of samples as a step towards countering illicit traffic (Commission resolution 8 [XIV]). More recently, interest was expressed in research on the development of tests for the detection of cannabis users that can be employed in cases of automobile accidents in a way similar to that of blood tests for alcohol. However, it is clear that most of the work is done by collaborating scientists in various countries, the resources of the Laboratory being sufficient for little beyond maintaining a "reference" sample of cannabis which can be sent to collaborating scientists on request. Such collaboration adds to the status of the Laboratory.

The activities of the Laboratory are not confined to research alone. It maintains a scientific literature collection and periodically issues the *List of Narcotic Drugs under International Control*. It also provides training, initially in methods for determining opium origin but now on a broader basis, to holders of fellowships awarded to chemists from developing countries under the UN technical assistance scheme.

The Laboratory was founded for an activity which, according to its director, is now obsolete. While events have demanded a reformulation of objectives, it is difficult to discern what these are from Commission discussions. Research interest has been lodged in areas relevant to law enforcement, and this choice is likely to have long-term effects on future research priorities.

One of the Division's most important functions is the provision of information. A vehicle of information dissemination is the *Bulletin on Narcotic Drugs* which was created by a resolution adopted by the Commission in 1948. The *Bulletin* is not only a scientific journal, it also conveys much information on the activities of the international drug control bodies. In fact such material constitutes about half of the *Bulletin*'s contents, the rest being largely made up of solicited articles. Few articles submitted for publication are rejected, for the number received is not high (Sotiroff, Khan, interviews). Authors are often drawn from those with whom the Division has direct contact, such as those attend-

ing UN meetings. Moreover, representatives at the Commission
sessions may suggest writers or submit articles, so that the risk of
papers appearing in the *Bulletin* with views very divergent from
those of the Commission members is rather small. Nevertheless,
room for disagreement existed, as the following incident shows.

At the twentieth session of the Commission, Harry Anslinger of
the U.S. delegation, in connection with the publication of a paper
by Dr. Oswald Moraes Andrade entitled "The Criminogenic
Action of Cannabis and Narcotics" (*16*, 4), raised the question of
the policy followed by the secretariat in its selection of articles:
"no article," said Anslinger, "had done so much harm to the
Commission's work. . . . It was difficult to see how such a study
could have been accepted, since everything published in that field
by or under the auspices of the UN was diametrically opposed to
the thesis developed in the article" (E/CN.7/SR 538). He continued to say that

the purpose of the Bulletin should be to educate the public, not to
give it arms with which to fight the policy advocated by the
Commission. Certain groups in the US were already using the
article in an attempt to obtain legal authorization for the use of
marihuana. In the circumstances, he would like to know how the
Secretariat envisaged its functions as the organ responsible for
the publication of the Bulletin.

In the discussion which followed, Mabileau of France and
Curran of Canada supported this view, the latter suggesting that
an editorial committee be formed of members of the Commission
to select the articles for publication. The secretariat was defended
by the representatives of the United Kingdom and Yugoslavia.
The latter (Nicolić) recalled that in the past an article contributed
by the U.S. had been published in which a negative attitude had
been taken towards the Single Convention despite the fact that
ECOSOC had urged the ratification of the treaty. Green of the
United Kingdom thought that

It was clearly very embarrassing for a government when an article
appearing in a UN publication was quoted against it. . . . He
personally did not know what the aims of the Bulletin were. . . .
Reference had been made to the view of the Commission. But the
Commission did not always have a single view and it was difficult
to decide at what point a minority view should be regarded.

Sotiroff of the secretariat replied as follows:

It was not easy to find interesting articles, particularly as authors
had to be drawn from as many regions as possible . . . the articles
appearing in the Bulletin were usually obtained through official
channels and often through representatives of the various
countries in the Commission itself. The article to which reference
had been made had been received from the representative of the
country from which the author had come and had been signed by
the latter. The Secretariat did not have a special editorial group
for the Bulletin . . . The great majority of articles were in keeping
with the general views expressed by the Commission though
occasionally that was not so. The Secretariat was of course, ready
to follow the instructions the Commission cared to give it
concerning the choice of the articles.

It was finally decided that the *Bulletin* should continue to be
edited by the Division in consultation with the representatives of
WHO and PCB, but if it was considered that a matter of policy,
whether administrative or legal, was involved the articles in
question should be referred to the officers of the Commission for
a second opinion. In the event of the officers being equally
divided in their views, the article should not be published.

These are nonetheless exceptional cases, and the editors do not
on the whole feel any constraint beyond the occasional need to
exercise some care in their selection of articles for publication.

We subjected the content of the *Bulletin* to systematic analysis,
and the results are given in the table in Appendix D. All issues of
the *Bulletin* from 1949 to 1971 were analyzed. In order to obtain a
rough impression of the changes over time, we divided the span of
years under review into two periods. The periods are unequal in
duration because issues were slimmer in the earlier period, and
the cut-off point was chosen so as to balance this fact. The
method used in compiling the figures is explained in a footnote to
the table.

The table shows the dominance of the basic sciences category
throughout the entire period. This dominance was less marked,
however, in the later period, when articles in the medical and
social sciences categories became more frequent. In this the
Bulletin reflects the general multidisciplinary trend. The breakdown of articles by drug shows, as did our earlier analysis of the
Commission's resolutions, the prominence of the opiates. It is
noteworthy that there were almost twice as many "drug-specific"

articles in the earlier period than in the later one, whereas the total number of cannabis articles doubled after 1961.

The figures for the country or regional settings of articles show that the United States is the best covered of all the countries which have been featured in the *Bulletin*. The largest increase in frequency over the years is that observed for the United Kingdom. Surprisingly, the Middle East has not been featured much in the years since 1962 despite the attention which Iran, Turkey, and Lebanon have received in discussions in the Commission and among INCB members. The explanation for this is suggested by the preponderance of North American and Western European contributors to the *Bulletin*. In fact, of the articles classified, 59 percent in the earlier period and 66 percent in the later period were written by authors from North America or Western Europe. In general, and as confirmed by Sotiroff in the interview touched upon earlier, articles on special geographical areas are written by authors from those areas. This explains the parallel changes in frequency over time between geographical setting and author background for India and the United Kingdom. However, there are instances where the authors from a particular area are fewer than articles on that area. This is true for Latin America, for Asia excluding India, and for Africa. This suggests that authors from Western countries do write about non-Western countries. However, the opposite is not the case; that is, articles on Western countries are not written by Asians, Africans, or Latin Americans.

The statistics so far discussed do not, of course, represent criteria for an assessment of the quality of the *Bulletin*. For this we must turn to a study made by the UN Joint Inspection Unit (JIU) of the publications and documentation of the UN. The JIU found that while the *Bulletin* had a good index and was promptly issued, a "User Survey" in which UN officials and subscribers were asked to rate the *Bulletin* on a scale of "Very Useful," "Useful," and "Not Useful" gave it a fairly low rating (JIU/REP/ 7/18, 1971). Commenting on the JIU report, the director of the Division said that the negative views expressed were at variance with the opinion of the Commission. Far from thinking, as the JIU did, that the *Bulletin* should be "significantly changed or merged with other publications," the Commission was considering wider coverage and distribution with possible support from the UN Fund for Drug Abuse Control. It was claimed, moreover, that there were other indications of its usefulness, such as the fact that it has frequently been referred to in articles published in other drug journals, notably the *International Journal of the Addictions* and the *British Medical Journal* (Letter, 26 October 1971).

Apart from the *Bulletin*, the Division has one other periodical publication: the *Information Letter*, which is distributed gratis to about nine thousand readers and is financed by UNFDAC. The contents include notices of drug seizures, meetings on drug matters, programs of the Division, news on treaty adherences and contributions to UNFDAC, and resumés of the contents of the latest issue of the *Bulletin on Narcotics*. The earlier issues carried short descriptions of the internationally controlled drugs. But, apart from occasional commentary, news rather than appraisal is the chief feature of the publication.

8 Interrelations between Control Bodies

The Advisory Committee would continue to work on [the illicit traffic], which was [a task] peculiarly its own, even if it handed over some part of its functions to the Permanent Central Board.... Life was dear to the Committee and it would not abandon it lightly.

Opium Advisory Committee (1929)

So far, we have dealt with the key organs singly. But to understand the workings of the control apparatus, we must consider the relationship of these organs to each other. On the surface, and as is impressed upon one by the tone of their own reports, harmony and mutual respect prevail.

Anyone familiar with the literature on organizations will know that such a picture is deceptive. Organizations typically seek to expand, and such expansions often take the form of increasing claims over areas of responsibility, with subsequent invasion of the territories of other departments. Competition for resources and recognition reaches a point of conflict, accentuated on occasion by differences of opinion on a particular issue, or even by personal antagonism among top-level officials. History tells us that these have always been features of organizational life. Observable behavior has many causes, only some of which are determined by the role of the organ as officially prescribed, for example, in its terms of reference. The less rational elements figure importantly but are less susceptible to description. We are thus confined to a few concrete illustrations of the nature of the interrelations between the drug control bodies.

It has generally been acknowledged that the creation of the Board by the 1925 treaty followed from the loss of confidence in the Advisory Committee, whose narrow representation was subjected to heavy criticism. The creation of the Board injected a certain uneasiness into the Advisory Committee, and a much debated issue in its meetings was the precise relation of the Board to the League and the role of the secretariat of the Board. During one meeting, the decision was taken, by six votes to four, that the Board's secretariat should be part of the League. The votes were an indication of the extent to which opinions were divided on this question (OAC Minutes: 6th, 1924). That it was still not completely resolved in 1927 is suggested by the following statement in the minutes of the session held that year: "As regards the criticism directed against the Central Board, it was pointed out that the Board formed part of the machinery of the League" (OAC Minutes: 10th, 1927).

The Committee certainly felt threatened by the new Board and was at pains to guard the boundaries of its field of activity against capture by the Board. A traditional "gray area" was that of illicit traffic, in relation to which both the Committee and the Board had certain duties. For the Board to obtain early access to the data transmitted to the Committee by governments, its president had to write to the chairman of the Committee; but the Board put up barriers of red tape to discourage requests for information from the Committee. The excerpt of the letter from L. A. Lyall, the Board's first president, to Constantin Fotitch of the Committee, which we quoted in chapter 6, portrays the distance at which the Board held the Committee. A discussion by the Advisory Committee at its twelfth session of its relationship to the Board is revealing. The Portuguese representative, de Vasconcellos, said that:

It would ... be a curious way to show friendly co-operation if the Central Board began its work by deciding to prevent the Advisory Committee from examining statistics which were absolutely indispensable to it. This would amount to lopping off a limb and the Committee could not submit to such an operation.

The Japanese representative, Sato, said:

In regard to [the] observation that to deprive the Advisory Committee of one of its most important duties, the examination

of the annual statistics meant suicide for the Advisory Committee,
[he] could not agree . . . the question of the illicit traffic was still
before the Committee. (OAC: 12th, 1929: 23, 25).

The question of a joint secretariat of the Commission and the
Board has attracted much debate. But, before discussing this
question, we must mention another feature of the total set of
relations. This is what is generally referred to as the "technical
independence" of the Board. It has sometimes been claimed that
the INCB and its secretariat have an existence independent of the
UN. The legal basis for this claim is said to lie in the fact that the
INCB's predecessors, the PCB and the DSB, existed before the
UN itself existed, having been brought into life by special treaties,
and that the INCB is likewise a "treaty organ." The following
provisions in the Single Convention are invoked as supporting
the argument:

— the expenses of the INCB are to be borne by the UN and
by parties not members of the UN;

—the INCB elects its own president and other officers and
adopts its own rules of procedure;

— ECOSOC, in consultation with the INCB, is to make
arrangements to ensure the full technical independence of
the INCB.

It would appear that this independence precludes the integration
of the secretariats of the INCB and the Commission, or of the
organs themselves.

On the other hand, arguments can be advanced against such an
interpretation. Between parties to the Single Convention, the
treaty, upon coming into force, terminates earlier narcotics
treaties, except the 1936 Convention. Legally, the INCB is a
creature of the Single Convention and it is to the "International
Narcotics Control Board provided in the Single Convention"
which the Vienna Convention refers in its first article. Furthermore, the Board is given through the Single Convention the
functions of the PCB and the DSB with respect to the states which
are parties to the earlier drug treaties but not to the Single
Convention. Also, the provisions relating to expenses (article 6)
and UN secretariat services (article 16) are the same for the INCB
and the Commission. The latter article does not spell out the way
in which these services are to be provided, although the administrative arrangements agreed to between the secretary-general and

the PCB and endorsed by ECOSOC specify that the latter has to be consulted before budgetary and personnel decisions are taken. There is no legal impediment to having a single secretariat of the Commission and the Board and, indeed, the Division of Narcotic Drugs had proposed that such an arrangement be considered. "The agreement between the Secretary-General and the Board, intended to ensure its technical independence" could provide, the Division suggested, "for consultation of the Board in regard to the appointment and removal of members of the [single] secretariat" (E/CN.7/AC.3/Rev.1).

The General Assembly was also in favor of a joint secretariat. Its Fifth Committee's view on the subject was that "in as much as both units had been housed since 1955 in the European Office, it appeared illogical and wasteful to maintain the existing separate arrangements" (A/4336, 1959). However, the Commission itself was against unification (E/3010/Rev.1), as was the Board, naturally. How the Board's insistence on keeping its secretariat separate from the Division has affected relations between the Division and the Board secretariat may only be surmised. It seems that personal factors are involved to a high degree in the whole question. When he was a staff member of the Division, Adolf Lande argued convincingly in favor of a single secretariat. However, when he was appointed secretary of the Board, his arguments were equally convincing in the other direction.

At the conference to amend the Single Convention in 1972, there was a debate on the role of the Board vis-à-vis the Commission—whether advisory, subordinate or otherwise. The balance of participation in decision-making by the drug control bodies eventually agreed to was one struck between attempts to vest the INCB with greater authority and independence on the one hand, and efforts to attenuate its influence on the other. The latter activity characterized the position of both the drug producing countries and the Soviet bloc, whose attitude was a mixture of opposition in principle, defence of sovereignty, and resistance to supranationalism. The USSR delegate at the conference was quick to point to the turnabout in the position of those countries which, during the drafting of the Vienna Convention, had opposed all proposals designed to enhance the power of the Board. Manufacturing countries generally tend to be in favor of strengthening the Board when it is a question of controlling opium production at source, but not so when "psychotropics" are involved.

Another source of conflict lies in the fact that WHO has been authorized by the treaties to recommend whether or not a drug should be placed under international control. Although the final decision rests with the Commission, there is little room, in fact, for decisions contrary to what WHO has recommended. Since the decisions on the control status of drugs have to be based on the findings of WHO as to whether, for instance, a substance "is liable to similar abuse and productive of similar ill effects as the drugs in Schedule I or Schedule II or is convertible into a drug," WHO virtually decides what type of control should be applied to a particular drug. There are misgivings on the part of the Division's officials about the competence of WHO, an organization in which the medical profession predominates, to decide about matters into which social and economic factors enter to such a large degree. Different perceptions of the boundaries of each other's competence have affected personal relations between the members of the secretariats of the organs concerned.

Mutual criticism is implied in the following interchange between the representatives of the Commission and WHO during the discussion of a WHO Expert Committee report containing remarks on the treatment of drug dependence through methadone maintenance (WHO/EC DD, 1965; 343):

Beedle (U.K. delegate on the Commission) said that: "It was also curious, having regard to the short duration of the Expert Committee's meeting, that it should have attempted to make such a generalized comment on so important a subject.... The Expert Committee should have adopted a more detached approach, instead of expressing enthusiasm, admittedly tempered with some caution, for the treatment methods described. The same criticisms applied to the last paragraph of the section, dealing with community-oriented treatment; that was a very broad subject to be disposed of in four sentences, particularly since the Committee concluded by approving a broad philosophy."

Halbach (WHO representative) said that: "... all the conclusions of the medical profession must be reached on a strictly ethical and scientific basis. On the other hand, many members of the Commission represented law enforcement organs, which had their own particular objectives and methods; this was the source of the Commission's difficulty in understanding the intentions of the Expert Committee in drafting section six of its report. The Commission tended to concentrate on the possible effect of that section on the general public, whereas scientists were concerned exclusively with facts" (E/CN.7/SR.537: 5-6).

A similar question may arise in relation to the INCB's confirmation or establishment of government estimates of yearly medical requirements. WHO may perceive itself as a more competent body to handle this question and, as we have seen, WHO has, in fact, lent its assistance to the Board in connection with this task. Within WHO itself, diverse role-perceptions exist between different units; for example, alcohol is traditionally approached from a psychiatric viewpoint and the other drugs from a predominantly pharmacological one.

Perception of one's own role is intimately linked to definitions of competence. At the Shanghai conference, for instance, a vote taken on the competence of the conference to discuss "medical aspects of the opium question" was narrowly defeated, seven votes to six, the latter cast mainly by countries which had in their delegations people with medical qualifications. The INCB has always been particularly concerned to underline its status as a treaty organ with fixed duties and its inability to do more or less, as the case may be, than what is laid down in the treaties. The WHO Expert Committee has gone beyond its original role as a classifier of drugs for international control.

Despite disagreements over the boundaries of each other's provinces, the drug control organs and particularly their secretariats do collaborate to a marked extent. Their interaction occurs at several levels. They attend each other's meetings, and they meet at conferences convened by other UN bodies or by groups outside the UN system. They travel abroad on missions together (see table 8.1). It is interesting to note how frequently INTERPOL has accompanied the Division on its missions: though peripheral to the key drug control machinery, INTERPOL has done this with greater frequency than even the Board and WHO. This is an indication of the importance of police matters in the business of these missions.

Relations between the key organs have been affected by the creation of the UN Fund for Drug Abuse Control, which, because of its unstructured position in the total system and its relatively brief history, we have so far discussed only in the context of other topics.

TABLE 8.1
Interorganizational Contact on Missions, 1960–71

Missions to	Division	WHO (Drug Dependence Unit)	PCB/ DSB INCB	INTER-POL	FAO
Bangkok	x	x		x	x
Rio de Janeiro	x	x		x	
Middle East (1st)	x	x			
(2d)	x	x			
Lima (1st)	x	x			x
(2d)	x	x		x	
(3d)	x				
Addis Ababa (1st)	x	x	x	x	
(2d)	x			x	
Tokyo	x	x	x	x	
Manila	x			x	
Lagos	x			x	
Teheran	x	x		x	
New Delhi	x	x	x	x	
Far East	x	x			
Beirut	x	x	x	x	
Africa (1st)	x		x	x	
(2d)	x		x	x	
Mexico	x	x	x	x	
South East Asia	x		x		
East Africa	x		x	x	
Iran	x	x			

UNFDAC was established as a special trust fund for the purpose of securing "priority attention to urgent drug problems" without diminishing the resources of other programs, especially the United Nations Development Programme (UNDP) (GE.72–17024, 1972). It was managed, in the initial year of its existence, by a personal representative of the secretary-general, who, assisted by three special consultants, had exclusive responsibility for the approval of projects financed by the Fund. The Division was given responsibilities for planning and executing programs, but the cooperation of other international organizations was repeatedly stressed. An interagency meeting of all the organizations concerned, in July 1971, endorsed "a system-wide approach to the global problem of drug abuse." The actual programs to be undertaken were outlined in a "Plan for Concerted Action against Drug Abuse" (E/CN.7/538) prepared by the Division. The immense list of projects which this plan contained was later subjected to much criticism by the Commission: not only did the estimated cost of the projects go far beyond the resources then available, there were no concrete suggestions as to the order of priorities (CND:24th, 1971: 88).

Difficulties were encountered soon after the Fund went into operation. Some of these were financial, but others had to do with the lack of coordination between the various involved agencies and the duplication of efforts which ensued. That it has not been possible to avoid the overlapping of efforts is evident from the resolution drafted at the Commission's twenty-fifth session (1973), enjoining the Division to study the coordination problem and ways of resolving it (E/CN.7/L.354). Two years after the Fund's establishment, the UN secretary-general decided on a new organizational structure for it vis-à-vis the other drug organs (See figure 8.1). As yet, no one has been permanently appointed to the post of executive director of the Fund, although the director of the Division is currently acting in that capacity, taking over from the secretary-general's personal representative the overall management of the Fund.

The establishment of the Fund has led other agencies hitherto uninvolved in drug matters, such as ILO and UNESCO, to stake their claims to drug control responsibilities, competence, and resources with consequent competition for business. Although the readiness of other agencies to interpret their mandates to include action on drugs as a result of the sudden availability of funds can lead to a broadening of the base on which present policy rests, it can also aggravate the difficulties of work coordination. Because the priorities for action adopted by the Fund are determined by the preferences of the contributing nations, the Commission, in spite of its being the policy-making organ, has had relatively little say in the setting up of programs financed by the Fund.

Interaction with the outside world is illustrated by table 8.2, which lists, among other organizations, the nongovernmental organizations (NGOs) which are represented at the sessions of the Commission on Narcotic Drugs. These represent diverse interests and are recognized pressure groups whose consultative status gives them facilites for lobbying. Their marked increase in number over the years is an indication of the growing attraction which the drug area holds for different interest groups in society.

FIGURE 8.1

Organizational Structure and Relations of UNFDAC

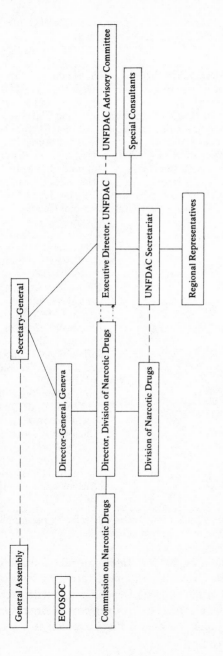

—————— Administrative connections

– – – – Policy-making, cooperation, advice, consultation

Division of Narcotic Drugs
1. Regular functions
2. Technical evaluation and advice to Director, UNFDAC, re project proposals
3. Consultation and cooperation with UNFDAC and INCB secretariats
4. Executing agency for projects assigned

UNFDAC Secretariat
1. Receipt and referral of project proposals
2. Approval of projects
3. Decisions as to executing agencies
4. Follow-up and monitoring of projects
5. Evaluation of performance
6. Fund-raising

SOURCE: UN document GE.73–2039, 1973

TABLE 8.2
Organizations Represented at Sessions of the Commission on Narcotic Drugs 1950, 1960, 1971 (other than the key drug control organs)

1950	1960	1971
International Criminal Police Commission (2) UN Commission of Enquiry on the Coca Leaf (1)	International Civil Aviation Organization (1) Permanent Anti-Narcotics Bureau of the League of Arab States (1) International Criminal Police Organization (INTERPOL) (1) International Federation of Women Lawyers (2)	International Labor Organization (ILO) (1) UN Educational, Scientific and Cultural Organization (UNESCO) (1) Food and Agricultural Organization (FAO) (1) International Arab Narcotics Bureau of the League of Arab States (1) Customs Cooperation Council (1) UN Fund for Drug Abuse Control (5) UN Development program (UNDP) (1) UN Conference on Trade and Development (UNCTAD) (1) League of Red Cross Societies (2) International Criminal Police Organization (INTERPOL) (3) International Federation of Women Lawyers (1) World Young Women's Christian Association (2) Friends World Committee for Consultation (1) International Council on Alcohol and Addictions (ICAA) (1)

NOTE: The numbers after the names of organizations refer to the number of representatives from the organization concerned.

Apart from the attendance by the International Council on Alcohol and Addictions (ICAA) at the more recent meetings of the WHO Expert Committee on Drug Dependence, participation of non-UN groups in the meetings of the drug control organs has been limited to the public sessions of the Commission.

9   The Pattern of Power

It would be wrong to deduce from the gap of six years
between the ... last meeting of the ... Advisory Committee and the first meeting of the Commission that the
new body started everything afresh. In fact it is rather
striking to note that a number of people at present
engaged in the work of the Commission, as well as in the
Division ... had also worked in the same field during
the period of the League of Nations.
"Twenty Years of Narcotics Control under the
United Nations," *Bulletin on Narcotics*, (1966)

A description of international drug control will
be incomplete if it does not go beyond the surface activity to take
a look at what happens behind the scenes. The facade of common
goals presented by the records of the international bodies is
deceptive. The assertion of national interests by individual countries is usually cloaked in the language of diplomacy, and the way
in which decisions are formulated is typically vague and sometimes deliberately inexplicit. Although these decisions are often a
compromise between conflicting interests, the more powerful
individuals and countries can better make their wills felt in both
the formulation and interpretation of the decisions. The limits of
action in the drug field are, like in many other fields, set by the
lines of political relationships prevailing in the world at large.

A Note on Power

The concept of power is necessary to an understanding of all
international systems. We discuss it here without any intention of
making a contribution to the extensive social science literature on
the subject. Indeed, we will draw from this literature, and use
what others have written to elucidate those aspects of the system
which we are attempting to describe and to which this concept is
particularly pertinent.

113

Power denotes the capacity to produce intended results; one speaks about power when its possession or exercise makes a difference in the behavior or situation of others. Paradoxically enough, when one has power one does not always have to wield it; objects behave without coercion in accordance with the expectations of those having power (Russell, 1937; Jansson, 1964). As soon as one begins to consider the exercise of power by different groups or nations, one is faced with the fact that power relationships are diffuse and arise from the combined action of a number of actors on several fronts. In the case of international drug control such fronts consist of diplomatic activity, mass media, and international organizations. Johan Galtung's discussion of power in his book on the European Economic Community (1973) is helpful, and we will use it as a framework in which to organize our own discussion of the relations between states in the international drug control apparatus.

Galtung distinguishes between types and channels of power. There is the "ideological" power channeled by culture and the international transmission of ideas. There is also the exercise of "renumerative" power by the promise of rewards through trade and economic concessions. Finally, there is the excercise of "punitive" power by, at the extreme, the threat of military force. In the drug control field, power is exerted both by the threat of sanctions—a means akin to the last category of punitive power—and by the promise of reward.

In identifying the sources of power Galtung distinguishes between resources and structural power. The former relates to knowledge, money, people, size, and military capability. The latter, structural power, is an equally important concept to which the notions of exploitation, fragmentation, and penetration belong. The notion of "exploitation" needs no clarification. Fragmentation, or "divide and rule," is the concept implicit in the statement by the UN secretary-general, Kurt Waldheim, that bilateral agreements may harm the UN system (*Dagens Nyheter,* 9 May 1973). That the scientific elite of a developing country is mainly trained in the West or at least in institutions modeled on those of the West is an illustration of the phenomenon of penetration. It is this phenomenon which nullifies the UN principle of equitable geographical representation, especially where it applies to the selection of members for bodies like the expert committees. If the "experts" from developing countries are drawn from the Westernized elite, then the so-called equitable geographical representation achieved is merely formal.

Key Countries

One way of discerning the pattern of power is by measuring the degree to which various countries are represented in the membership of the key organs. Countries which are represented in an organization will have greater opportunity for exercising influence over the policy of that organization than countries which are not represented, and the duration of their representation will determine how consistently they can wield that influence. Thus both access and continuity are necessary for the deployment of power. In order to identify the more influential countries in the international drug control arena, we arrived at a set of criteria by which to rank countries. These criteria were based on the duration of the country's membership in the key organs, the size of their delegations—since multiple action depends on manpower capability—and the frequency with which its representatives were elected to office in the Commission, since this confers some power of decision and implies recognition on the part of others. Thus, for every country we counted the number of years over the period 1921 to 1971 that it had been a member of the Opium Advisory Committee, the Commission, the Drug Supervisory Body, the Permanent Central Board, or the INCB, and the number of times it had been represented in the WHO Expert Committee and in the Bureau (that is, among the officers of the Committee and the Commission). This yielded eight criteria on which countries can be rated. As it is impossible to justify whatever cut-off point is used, we arbitrarily drew a line after the top eight countries and defined as influential all those which, on at least one measure, can be relegated to one of the eight topmost positions. Table 9.1 displays the countries and their respective scores on each of the criteria mentioned. In cases where the ninth and tenth countries have the same score as the eighth, they too are included in the table.

Twenty-one countries appear in table 9.1. It is apparent that wide differences exist between them as to the duration of participation in the system and as to the number of criteria which are met. If, however, we consider as influential only those countries which satisfy at least four criteria, on the assumption that a

TABLE 9.1
Influential Countries in International Drug Control, 1921–71

Country	Advisory Committee/Narcotics Commission					Years of membership in DSB	Years of membership in PCB/INCB	Times represented in WHO DD Expert Committee
	Years of membership		Years of membership in Bureau		Number of delegates			
	AC	CND	AC	CND	CND			
U.K.	20	26	6	8	45	12	44	18
U.S.a	(18)	26	–	6	128	22	44	24
France	20	26	10	9	72	16	37	2
India	20	26	3	9	48	6	36	6
Yugoslavia	19	26	3	7	32	8	26	–
Turkey	7	26	–	6	76	10	18	1
Brazil	–	7	–	–	14	10	15	7
Japan	20	10	1	2	30	–	14	–
Egypt	11	26	1	4	57	2	11	12
Greece	3	3	–	–	5	10	10	6
Switzerland	16	6	8	5	41	20	10	–
Chinab	20	24	–	4	56	–	8	–
Netherlands	20	11	7	1	15	–	4	–
Austria	9	3	3	–	3	–	–	–
Belgium	11	–	–	–	–	–	–	9
Canada	7	26	–	10	57	10	–	–
Iran	7	26	–	4	44	–	–	–
Poland	11	13	3	2	19	–	–	–
Spain	11	–	3	–	–	–	–	6
Sweden	3	4	–	–	25	–	–	12
USSR	–	26	–	2	54	–	–	7

aThe U.S., not being a member of the League, could not be elected to the bureau. We have used parentheses to indicate its observer status.

bTaiwan after 1949.

country which can pursue its interests in only one of the several bodies will be a less active force than one whose presence is more pervasive, then we arrive at the following results. The U.S., the U.K., France, and India qualify for inclusion among the "elite" on the basis of seven criteria, Yugoslavia and Turkey on the basis of five, and Switzerland and Canada on the basis of four.

These eight may be considered the key countries in international drug control. They are of course by no means equal in their degree of influence upon the system. Clearly, in terms of the weight of the indices in table 9.1, the U.S. predominates. It is also noteworthy that countries which might be expected to be influential on the basis of the stratification of power in the world at large do not appear to be so in the drug area: the USSR, for instance, is conspicuously absent.

The absence of the USSR from among the top influential countries requires some comment. As historical continuity is a criterion in our definition of key countries and the USSR, being a latecomer to the system, was not present for the entire period, this does, to some extent, explain its apparently minor role in the international drug control context. Yet, despite the USSR's not having been active in policy-making, a study of the proceedings of the two last drug conferences—the Vienna Conference and the conference to consider amendments to the Single Convention— clearly reveals that it and other socialist countries have played a decisive role in the treaty-making process. The case of the USSR reveals a limitation in our analysis of power, which may have been unduly confined to participation in the the drug control organs. The USSR's role may be said to be that of a countervailing power or a "vetoer," somewhat analogous to that of the U.K. during the League period, when it consistently exercised a countervailing power to U.S. initiatives and set the limits of action. One of the USSR's main concerns has been to ensure that limitations are not placed by treaty provisions on the exercise of its national sovereignty, by binding it to accept inspections, sanctions, arbitration, and the like. It has therefore constantly voted against the inclusion of such measures in international action, although its general stand is one of providing support for pro-control initiatives. That the USSR has not been more of an initiator itself may be a consequence of its assertion that it has no significant drug problem.* Also, consistent with its socialist ideology, the USSR expresses more interest in general socio-economic change than in programs specifically focused on such symptoms of social malfunctioning as drug addiction.

Key Persons

But influence is wielded by states through individuals, and a policy never emerges without having gone through the process of formulation, discussion, and amendment, a process which is carried on by individuals. Thus attempts at locating the sources of power must take account of persons also. Individuals may derive much of their influence from the positions they occupy and the status of the countries they represent, but personal forcefulness can enhance it. However, to extract from the international drug control system those who may be considered influential requires somewhat different criteria from the set used to identify the key countries.

We looked at the composition of the national delegations to each of the sessions of the key bodies throughout the period from 1921 to 1971. The names of those persons who figured in them repeatedly were noted. The heads of the various secretariat units were also noted. The list of people thus derived represent those who have had most opportunity for excercising influence: they constitute our key persons. Inclusion among this group presupposes that a person has

—participated in at least 10 sessions of the Advisory Committee or the Commission; or at least four times in the Bureau;

—been reelected at least once to the DSB and PCB or the INCB, and has held office for six years at a minimum;

—served at least three times on the WHO Drug Dependence Expert Committee;

—headed one of the following secretariats for a minimum of five years: the Division, the Board secretariat, the WHO

* See, for example, its report to the UN for 1971 (NAR/AR.96/1971), which states that: "As in previous years, drug addiction is not a public health problem. As has been stated earlier, this is due primarily to the general social and economic conditions prevailing in the Soviet Union and to the special measures generally taken by the Soviet Government. In the Soviet Union there is no unemployment whatsoever. Special measures taken by the Government constantly raise the population's economic and cultural level of living. All this serves to prevent the spread of addiction."

Drug Dependence Unit; or, if such a position has been held for less than five years, the person concerned has occupied other positions in the secretariat for a sufficiently long period to make up for the deficiency.

These criteria are, of course, all arbitrary, but they do yield a group of persons which covers all those who might be termed influential, if other criteria, based on what can be gleaned from the literature and from our interviews, are applied. Where a person has participated in more than one organ, this was noted in the tabulation (see Appendix E).

Altogether seventy names from twenty-eight countries appear in the list. Their distribution by organ and nationality is shown in table 9.2. It will be seen that the Committee/Commission accounts for more than one-third of the names. This is a consequence of its size and age. The distribution of names among the three other bodies is fairly even. Altogether, thirteen people have been represented in various combinations of two or three bodies. Thus five people, for example, have at different times been members of the INCB as well as representatives of their governments on the Commission, and three have been Commission representatives as well as members of the WHO Expert Committee. Insofar as distribution by country is concerned, the eight key countries earlier identified account for forty-two names and the top four countries for twenty-eight. The U.K. and the U.S. have nine and eight respectively; Switzerland has six; France has five; India has four; and Canada has three. The other two key countries, Yugoslavia and Turkey, have two each. When countries are compared as to what influential positions they have occupied, it is noteworthy that only the U.S., the U.K., and Switzerland have had influential nationals in all the bodies concerned; that no national of France or India has held a leading position in the international civil service; and that no French person has been a leading figure in the WHO Expert Committee.*

An attempt was made to gather information on these seventy persons in terms of previous occupation and training or disciplinary background. Our sources of information on the

---

* It is interesting to note in this connection that the U.K. has consistently had more nationals occupying positions in WHO's professional secretariat than any other country (Cox and Jacobson, 1973: 211).

TABLE 9.2
Distribution of Key Persons by Organ and Nationality, 1921-71

	AC/ CND	PCB INCB	WHO	ICSc	CND INCB	CND WHO	INCB WHO	INCB ICS	CND INCB WHO	Total
Austria	1									1
Belgium	1		1							2
Brazil		1								1
Canada	2				1					3
China	2									2
Egypt	1	1								2
France	2	2			1					5
Germanya				2	1					3
Greece							1			1
India	1	1	1		1					4
Iran		1								1
Italy	1	1		1						3
Japan		1	1							2
Mexico	1									1
Netherlands	2									2
Peru			1							1
Poland						1				1
Portugal	2									2
Siamb	1									1
Spain			1							1
Sweden			1	1						2
Switzerland	1		1	2			1		1	6
Turkey	1	1								2
U.K.	2	2	1	3	1					9
Uruguay	1									1
U.S.	2	1	1	2		1		1		8
USSR						1				1
Yugoslavia	1							1		2
Total	25	12	9	11	5	3	2	2	1	70

aFederal Republic of Germany after World War II.
bNow Thailand.
cThe nationality of some international civil servants has been difficult to determine. P. O. Wolff, who at some point acquired Argentinian nationality, is a case in point.

individuals concerned are given in Appendix E. Because of lacunae in the data, any interpretation of the figures given below must be subject to the following reservations. The first of these is that data on persons serving on WHO expert committees and the Board are more complete than those on Commission representatives. This may have inflated the ratio of pharmacologists/ chemists to other categories in the breakdown of persons by disciplinary background. Second, as the personal information provided by the official reports is itself selected (see chapter 6), using them as sources may have lent a slight distortion to the results. Third, it was not possible to analyze the professional training of some persons simply because they appear to have had no higher education. This was true of some of the international civil servants. As was pointed out by the Bertrand study on UN personnel questions (Bertrand, 1971), the practice of promoting general-service staff nearing the end of their careers to the professional category has led to the exclusion of university graduates from the professional ranks, and is a major factor in the aging of the Secretariat.

The distribution of key persons by their occupations in their respective home countries when they entered the international drug control scene is given below.

Health and welfare	13
Police	4
University and research	19
Revenue, commerce	9
Diplomatic service	13
International civil service	2
Civil service (general)	5
	65

Information on training and disciplinary background was available for just under two-thirds of the group. The breakdown is as follows:

Pharmacology, pharmacy* or chemistry	24
Medicine and psychiatry	7
Law	7
History	1
Accounting	1
Navy	1
No specialized training	3
	44

* Some pharmacologists are also doctors of medicine but are placed in the pharmacology category if this is their field of specialization and main activity.

The first category, "health and welfare," covers all those working in the field of public health, including civil servants employed by ministries or departments of health. The category "university and research" includes all academic positions. In the last category are placed those civil servants whom we were unable to assign to any particular category. Even given the reservations mentioned earlier, the preponderance of pharmacologists is striking. They account for the bulk of the "university and research" category in the previous listing.

In an earlier chapter we referred to a "gentlemen's club" of nations, nations which have had a long-standing stake in the system. But we have been told also of the informal existence of a gentlemen's club made up of persons. Our attention has been directed to the fact that, prior to the official opening of a Commission session, a small group of such persons meets in Geneva to settle, in advance, some of the issues which are expected to crop up at the coming session.

Can the membership list of a club such as this be established? To do so one would need a more rigorous definition of key people. We therefore required that fifteen years of activity in the Committee/Commission, the Board, or WHO be a minimum condition of inclusion in the key person category, while retaining in that category all the civil servants and those who have occupied a combination of positions. Two persons (Chodzko and Carrière) were borderline cases, but their eligibility for the category is enhanced by the fact that they were also prominent members of the Health Committee, in spite of the omission of this body from key-country considerations and in spite of its not being systematically subjected to the key-person tests. In figure 9.1, the service span of those who satisfied the above conditions is charted. The names are arranged in groups by country. We observe from the chart that six of the names thus derived belong to the U.S., five to the U.K., four to Switzerland, three each to France, India, and Germany, and two to Yugoslavia, all other countries having claim to only one name each. Of the eight key countries, only Turkey, by this measure, has no key person.

A pattern emerges. During the 1920s, Delevingne, the British assistant under-secretary of state, and Bourgois, the French diplomat, were clearly the leading personalities. Dame Rachel Crowdy was also from the U.K. This is consistent with the fact

FIGURE 9.1 *The Gentlemen's Club*

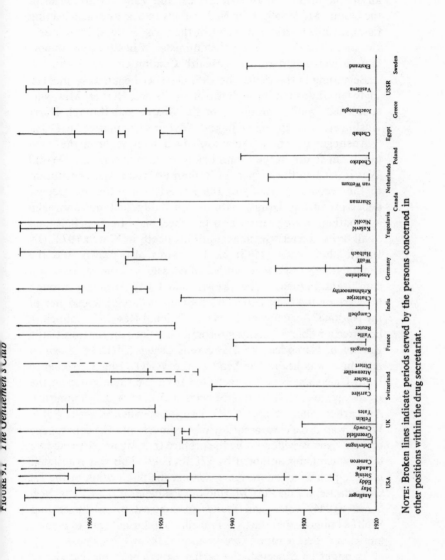

NOTE: Broken lines indicate periods served by the persons concerned in other positions within the drug secretariat.

that the League was predominantly English-French. Campbell, an official of the Indian civil service, and Van Wettum, head of the Opium Monopoly of the Netherlands Indies, were also leading figures, while Carrière, director of the Swiss Federal Health Service and Chodzko, former Polish minister of health, were important in connection with the Health Committee.

Beginning in the 1930s, the U.S. presence began to be increasingly felt. It was felt through two of its citizens, Herbert May, who succeeded Lyall as president of the Board, and through Harry Anslinger, who appeared in the Advisory Committee in 1933.

Anslinger is generally acknowledged to have been the most dominant figure in the Commission for many years after World War II. He had the support of Nathan Eddy, a major contributor to the recommendations of the Expert Committee on Dependence-producing Drugs, with which Eddy had an unbroken association, having served as a member, and often as chairman, at all of its nineteen sessions, until his death in March 1973 (UN Information Letter, 1973: 5). Eddy was also drawn into the Commission's work on a number of occasions in the capacity of a consultant. In the U.S., he was associated with Anslinger through his work on the Committee on Problems of Drug Dependence of the National Academy of Sciences–National Research Council, a body responsible for making recommendations on controls to the Bureau of Narcotics and Dangerous Drugs (BNDD), of which Anslinger was head. The head of the WHO Drug Dependence Unit, Dale Cameron, was recruited from the same group in the Academy; indeed, he had once been chairman of the Committee. An earlier chief of the WHO Drug Dependence Unit, Pablo Wolff, was also a close associate of Anslinger, and the congruence of their views is evidenced by the preface that Anslinger wrote to a book on cannabis authored by Wolff (1949). This was translated into English as a countermove against the publication of the La Guardia Report on the "Marihuana Problem in the City of New York" (1944) which had found, in contrast to Anslinger and Wolff's opinion, that the use of marihuana did not lead to mental and moral degeneration (see chapter 13).

As might be expected, the earlier experiences and careers of many of the leading figures had a direct bearing on their subsequent activity in the drug control field. Understanding of the system would benefit from more intimate knowledge of these figures rather than mere acquaintance with their nationality, professional background, and previous occupation. It is significant, for example, that Don Ugo Theodoli, secretary of the Board in the 1930s, was an "old China hand," while Lyall, prior to his retirement in Geneva and his appointment to the Board, served for forty-one years in the Chinese maritime customs. One can assume that their experiences gave them added insight into the Chinese drug problem and the Chinese point of view. It is also likely that their earlier experiences made them more appreciative of the difficulties arising from cultural differences between countries. It is beyond the scope of this study to give detailed information on all the leading personalities, but to illustrate the usefulness of such information we give below a selected sample of biographical sketches.

Otto Anselmino (1873-1955) studied pharmacology and food chemistry at the University of Heidelberg, and taught at the Universities of Greifswald and Berlin. From 1908, he was a scientific assistant at the Imperial Health Office (Kaiserliches Gesundheitsamt) in Berlin. Later, he was appointed senior government counselor in the Health Department of the Reich. He was dismissed in 1934 and from that year onwards, until 1938, worked in the pharmaceutical firm of Goekecke in Berlin. He was an active participant in the work of the Advisory Opium Committee between 1922 and 1934, and one of his more important contributions was the writing of a document entitled *ABC of Narcotic Drugs* much consulted by the Committee.

Harry J. Anslinger was born in 1892 in Altoona, Pennsylvania. The earlier years of his career were spent in the State Department, working in consular posts in Holland, Germany, Venezuela, and the Bahamas. He was assigned to the latter to find a way of stopping the smuggling of rum into the U.S. In 1926 he became chief of the Foreign Control Section of the Alcohol Prohibition Unit in the Department of the Treasury and in the same year represented the U.S. at international conferences on smuggling. In 1929 he became an assistant commissioner for prohibition—"a thankless and impossible assignment," as he later put it (Anslinger and Oursler, 1961). When Levi Nutt, the head of the Federal Bureau of Narcotics lost his job (members of his family were found to have dubious connections with a liquor and narcotics racketeer), Anslinger was promoted to head the Narcotics Division temporarily. Within a few months he was appointed the first Federal Commissioner of Narcotics. The prevailing climate being intensely hostile to opiate addiction and pushers at the time, Anslinger enjoyed much political and public support during his tenure in this office.

Gaston Bourgois (1874–1955) was educated at the École Polytechnique in France. He was successively an officer in the artillery and the navy, an interpreter of Far Eastern languages, and finally settled for a career in the French diplomatic service. His interest in mathematics, coupled with his knowledge of Japanese (which he presumably perfected during his tenure as naval attaché in Japan), allowed him to become a specialist in Japanese mathematics. Unlike the other figures whose biographies are sketched here, Bourgois's earlier experiences were in fields remote from drug control. However, he was obviously a man of diverse interests and took to narcotics control work, it would appear, with as much ease as he had to the navy and Japanese mathematics.

Herbert May (1877–1966) was born in Philadelphia and obtained his LL.B. from the New York Law School. His father, according to Anslinger (*Bulletin on Narcotics 15*,2 [1963]:1–7), had started a "highly successful business venture in the drug trade"; by 1928 the "May building in Pittsburgh was the executive center for a number of drugstores." When he returned to the U.S. after traveling abroad in Europe for two years, May went into partnership in the family drug business and remained there for eighteen years, dealing with legal matters and public relations. He held a number of public appointments, including that of deputy food administrator for Western Pennsylvania in 1917. After retirement at the early age of forty-five he became active in the Foreign Policy Association, particularly in its Opium Research Committee. Because of the U.S.'s dissatisfaction with the 1925 Conference, the Committee had wanted a study carried out to clarify the situation, and May had been chosen to do the study. He spent several months in the Middle East and the Far East doing this, and when his report was published, it "created a great stir." One of the suggestions it contained was for "the limitation and control of opium production as basis for the abolition of opium smoking."

In the earlier years, U.S. and League relations had been poor.

The U.S. had, for instance, refused to participate in the nominations for the Board. But although the League's invitation had been sharply rebuffed by Secretary Kellogg in 1928, this did not deter the League from electing an American—May himself—to the Board (Fleming, 1938:229). May had been nominated by the New Zealand government, which had been asked to do so—so as to circumvent the obstacle posed by the nonmembership of the U.S. in the League—by a group of "public spirited Americans who were anxious to have one of their countrymen on the Board."

One of May's foremost contributions, according to Anslinger, was the original proposal to place under control in advance all substances which might, because of their chemical structure, be suspected of addiction liability. As May himself had put it: "the accused should not be acquitted unless proven innocent." These ideas came to be embodied in article 11 of the 1931 Convention.

Colonel C. H. L. Sharman was born in 1881 in England. We are told by Anslinger (*Bulletin on Narcotics 11*,4 [1959]:1-4), that Sharman, when watching Queen Victoria's Diamond Jubilee, was so captivated by the Royal Canadian Mounted Police that in 1898 he left England for Canada and joined the Mounties at Regina, Saskatchewan. He later fought in the Boer War and in the First World War. After his return to civilian life, he joined the Canadian Narcotics Service and was appointed its chief in 1927. Sharman was one of Anslinger's staunchest supporters: in fact, he and Anslinger "saw eye to eye in most problems and collaborated very closely both in and outside the [Advisory Opium] Committee and later on the Commission" (Renborg, 1964:10).

Pablo Wolff was born in Berlin in 1894. At the University of Berlin, where he obtained his degrees of Doctor of Medicine and Doctor of Philosophy, he specialized in pharmacology. He decided to go into exile when the national socialist regime came to power in Germany (*Bulletin on Narcotics 10*,1 [1958]:39). In Geneva, to which he emigrated, he became a regular contributor to the *Journal Suisse de Médecine*. He also carried out missions and studies for the League of Nations and for national governments, particularly the U.S. government. In 1939 he went to Argentina on a League mission and remained there until 1948, working in close liaison with the Argentine health authorities. In 1949 he came into WHO and headed the Drug Addiction Unit there until 1954. Wolff had fought in the First World War as an officer in the German army and had been gassed; thus for years he was a sick man. He died soon after he left WHO, in 1957.

Sir Malcolm Delevingne (1868-1950), the British deputy under-secretary of state, was a classics scholar at Trinity College, Oxford. He entered the British Home Office in 1892 and repre-sented the U.K. at a series of important international conferences. He was one of the main architects of the League system of drug control, particularly as embodied in the conventions of 1925 and 1931. Among the grand old men of the League, Delevingne was, according to Renborg (1964), undoubtedly the most remarkable of all. Renborg recalls him as having "a sharp brain in a small body," and as often being very irritable at meetings, not being a person who suffered fools gladly. The following incident during the 1931 conference has been recounted by Renborg as being typical of the man. When the conference refused to entertain the Advisory Committee's draft providing for a monopoly on world manufacture for the manufacturing countries under a quota system (which he had a hand in formulating), Delevingne took offence and withdrew from the proceedings. However, he sat through all the meetings hidden behind the London *Times*. Once when the conference encountered difficulties and turned to him for advice, Delevingne replied with a curt "Certainly not." Imme-diately afterwards the Canadian delegate, Colonel Sharman, who was sitting behind Delevingne, was heard to say, "Sir Malcolm, your attitude would be much more convincing if you did not read your London *Times* upside down." After his retirement in 1932, Delevingne held a number of public appointments at home, including membership in the Council of the Pharmaceutical Society and in the Royal Commission on Safety in Coal Mines.

As one might expect from looking at the professional and occupational distribution data, civil servants—whether diplo-mats, law enforcement officers, or health administrators—are strongly represented in the foregoing sample of biographical sketches. More important to note are the personal friendships of these individuals and their relations to the drug industry.

The primary source of influence is nevertheless nations rather than persons. Only those individuals who are acceptable to their governments are chosen to represent them, and individuals often

become influential because they represent influential governments.

The Standpoints of Key Countries and Persons

Many an international decision is the result of negotiations
between countries on different levels of power and asserting
different viewpoints. We will briefly consider the kind of standpoints and beliefs which characterize our key countries and
persons.

France has traditionally been in favor of strict controls. Its
leading spokesman, Vaille, believes strongly in the "dangers" of
cannabis. The draft resolution which he introduced at the 1971
session of the Commission on "Abuse of Cannabis and Multiple
Drug Abuse" exemplifies his view on the subject. The resolution
"protested against" the statement that cannabis was not a drug of
addiction; it referred to demonstration by scientific research of its
association with the use of "other narcotic drugs" and its
tendency to lead to the use of hallucinogens and other drugs; and
it asked for "forceful application" of control measures by governments. When the U.K. delegate queried the research alluded to,
and expressed doubts as to whether he could propose a resolution
to ECOSOC which was based on scientific work whose conclusions he was called upon to accept on faith, Vaille said that "the
Commission was a technical commission composed of experts; as
such, it should be able to take a decision about what it wished to
propose to the Council." He proposed that the text should read:
"Bearing in mind that apart from the great dangers of the use of
cannabis as such, which has been demonstrated in a number of
scientific studies ..." (E/CN.7/SR.716). He was not averse
either, at least where cannabis was concerned, to the predeter-
mination of research findings by notions held beforehand. Allu-
ding to a Commission request to the secretariat to prepare a study
on the medico-social aspects of cannabis use, he pointed out that
such a study would be an extremely important one, for "it would
draw attention to the medical and social dangers of cannabis and
would explain the reasons for its having been placed under
international control by the narcotics treaties" (E/CN.7/SR.714).
On another occasion he observed that "drug addicts are normally
both liars and active proselytizers" (E/CONF.63/C.2/SR.6). The
French are also noticeably procontrol where "psychotropics"

under the Vienna Convention are concerned. Although France is a fairly large exporter of drugs, a significant proportion of its national pharmaceutical output is produced by companies mainly controlled by foreign (American, German, and Swiss) interests. Its pharmaceutical industry has, by tradition, developed from small-scale production in laboratories attached to pharmacies rather than in association with the chemical industry, as was the case in Germany. These structural origins have prevented the industry from becoming a powerful multinational enterprise. Moreover, the attitude of the French government has provoked the following criticism from a committee set up to report to the Ministry of Industrial and Scientific Development and the Ministry of Public Health on problems of the pharmaceutical industry:

Drug manufacture today has all the earmarks of an industry. The Committee is sorry to say that this statement has not yet penetrated all minds and that pharmaceutical issues are dealt with more in terms of social and budgetary concerns than in their industrial and economic aspects (Report, July 1972).

The United Kingdom delegation has, as a reading of the records of discussions will show, usually argued for regulation rather than prohibition. At home, the U.K. has continued to allow the use of heroin by addicts and in medical practice. The British have also shown sympathy for the Indian stand on cannabis, which is tied to its sanction of cannabis use in medicine. India's position on opium has understandably been one of opposition to increased controls over licit production. It has always held, for example, that the drawing up of estimates of cultivation and production was merely an academic exercise, for the vagaries of weather make it impossible to organize opium production to meet predetermined targets. Another facet of India's position is a strong stand against synthetic drugs, which found expression, for instance, in Vienna in 1971, in arguments for control over the "psychotropic substances." Switzerland derives its position from two sources: from being the host country of the European office of the UN and of many of the specialized agencies, and from the importance of its chemical industry. Before the war, it was highly negative towards control; its current position still seems to serve the interests of Swiss drug manufacturers (see chapters 15 and 16). Turkey is a traditional opium producer and a major source of contraband opium; it has come under much discussion in the international forum, but its actual influence is probably less than that of the other countries. The Yugoslavian influence is wielded by two individuals, one of whom —Nikolić—is a veteran in the Commission and noted for his frequent interventions. Opium production is now less important in Yugoslavia than it used to be, economic conditions having diverted the interest in this activity to other modes of employment (see chapter 14). Nevertheless, Yugoslavia often joins countries like India in arguing for controls over the manufacture of synthetic drugs to be as stringent as those over production of raw materials.

One conclusion which can be drawn here is that the drug control system is characterized by widely varying levels of influence and participation. Divergence and conflict in the styles and interests of the different key countries have been touched upon and will be further explored later. But when all is said and done, it remains true that more is invested in the system by way of effort, people, and, as will be seen later, money by the United States than by any other nation in the world community. Its influence is preeminent, and in the next chapter we will explore it in greater detail.

10   The United States—
the Principal Force

Any government whose leaders participate in or protect
the activities of those who contribute to our drug problem should know that the President of the United States
is required by statute to suspend all American economic
and military assistance to such a regime, and I shall not
hesitate to comply with that law where there are any
violations.
> Richard Nixon, in an address to a State Depart-
> ment-Sponsored Narcotics Coordinators
> Conference (1972)

As has been indicated in the historical review
and in the previous chapter, the United States has occupied a
leading role in the international drug control field. Interestingly
enough, this role was assumed before the U.S. gained "superpower" status after World War II. In this chapter, the international drug policy of the U.S. will be further elaborated and
related to the concept of power discussed earlier. Our task has
been made considerably lighter by the fact that there are recent
historical accounts of the earlier phases of U.S. drug policy
(Musto, 1973; Taylor, 1969). The period since 1946 is less
well-covered, however, although books and papers of a polemical
character exist. The recent appearance of these materials is an
indication of the topicality of the drug issue and of the fact that
the objectives and means of both domestic and international drug
control are being questioned. Disagreements have sometimes
been so intense that the defense of a particular policy has entailed
the use of censorship. In 1961, for example, a representative of
the U.S. Federal Bureau of Narcotics visited a publisher in
order to discourage the publication of a book by a committee
appointed by the American Medical Association and the American Bar Association containing views contrary to the official one

(Lindesmith, 1965: 246). Similarly, during the 1970s leaders of the National Institute of Health "found themselves unemployed" because of the views they expressed on the cannabis issue at Senate committee hearings (Lanouette, 1972: 170).

That views in the U.S. are divided probably makes it more difficult for its representatives to put across an official view in the international arena. Although U.S. policy has shown considerable consistency over the years, it is nonetheless probable that the changing domestic situation has influenced the motives behind the policy and the strength with which it is sustained. And when domestic problems prove intractable, to show that something has been achieved on the international level may become a political necessity, especially if the problem is seen to have originated from outside the country. The following statement by Richard Nixon in a message to Congress on 14 July 1969 illustrates the tendency to see the U.S. drug problem in this light:

Most of the illicit narcotics and high-potency marihuana consumed in the United States is produced abroad and clandestinely imported. I have directed the Secretary of State and the Attorney General to explore avenues of cooperation with foreign governments to stop the projection of this contraband at its source.

The frequent use of the term "victim country" to describe the U.S. in Senate hearings as well as in the international organizations is a further illustration.

It would be naive to suppose that the drug issue was something outside the world of politics. If the U.S. defines the drug issue as an important one, then the resources of the U.S. will guarantee that its importance is recognized beyond the domestic setting. The channels of power described by Galtung will be employed to this effect. Thus part of our analysis will be concerned with the variations in the importance attached to the drug issue by the U.S. government over the years.

The link between moves made by the U.S. in the area of international narcotics control and its overall foreign policy is well documented by Taylor's thorough study. He suggests that from the American point of view the period until World War II may be divided into three phases. During the first phase, the U.S. took the initiative to foster international cooperation in the drug field; it was the moving force behind both the Shanghai Commission and the Hague Conference. The U.S. interest in the opium question may be understood against the background of its China policy. Taylor writes (1969: 329):

As is well known, the object of American policy with reference to China was the establishment and preservation of a strong, stable and prosperous nation which would be able to resist the encroachments of foreign powers and at the same time provide opportunities for mutually profitable commercial relations with the West. As the opium habit was believed to be largely responsible for the political, social and economic degeneration of China, its suppression was considered indispensable to China's revivification and to the development of her commercial potential.

The fight against opium in China was not independent of economic interests; in assisting China in its effort to ban opium, the U.S. was siding with China against Western European commercial interests, particularly those maintained by the Anglo-Indian trade. However, it will be remembered that before the Shanghai Commission the U.S. had already developed "a comparatively large addict population, probably 250,000" (Musto, 1973:5), and that the problem in the Philippines was of considerable concern, particularly to Bishop Brent, who was to become the chairman of the Shanghai Commission. All these factors contributed to the fact that during this first phase the U.S. became the leading country in international drug control. Yet, not all of its proposals were accepted in Shanghai and The Hague, although some of the fundamental principles it espoused were established, such as the requirement to prevent the export of opium products to countries prohibiting their entry.

The second phase delimited by Taylor is that covered by the 1920s. The U.S. stand in the international scene was affected by its domestic legislation and by the outcome of internal conflicts on how to interpret the new legislation. Of considerable importance, for instance, was the declaration of the U.S. Supreme Court that maintenance of addiction, with some exceptions, was illegal. Doctors who prescribed doses of narcotics for addicts were threatened with prosecution (Musto, 1973). The American principles of drug control could not, however, be effectively sold to the international control agency—the Advisory Committee of the League—of which the U.S. was not a member. Because the

State Department refused to recognize the transfer of the administration of the Hague Covention from the Netherlands government to the League, cooperation in the drug field between the Advisory Committee and the U.S. was difficult to establish. When the U.S. attended the meeting of the Committee for the first time, its chief delegate, Stephen Porter, showed little understanding of the League system: not only did he try to secure the secretary-general's acceptance of the U.S. proposals, believing that they would thereby be binding on member states, he also proposed that a new committee be set up composed of five U.S. delegates and five League ones (Taylor, 1969: 162-63). The arrival of the American delegation was "unexpected and almost unannounced." It surprised Geneva and "galvanized the Advisory Committee immediately" (Fleming, 1938: 224). The League's policy had been based on the hypothesis that the drug traffic would have to be stamped out by degrees, but Porter came fortified with a resolution of Congress which he himself had sponsored and which stated that "the effective control of these drugs can be obtained only by limiting the production thereof to the quantity required for strictly medicinal and scientific purposes, thus eradicating the source or root of the present conditions." To meet this objective, the president should ask Great Britain, Persia, and Turkey to limit opium production and make a similar request to Peru, Bolivia, and the Netherlands in regard to coca leaves (Buell, 1925: 75-76).

Although American influence was at its lowest ebb during this period, many of the proposals for reform came from the U.S. Taylor (1969: 330) describes the tenets of the U.S. position as follows:

(1) The United States regarded the use of opium and other narcotic substances for other than strictly medical and scientific purposes as a moral and social evil.

(2) As a corollary, the United States concluded that the only legitimate transactions in these drugs, from production to consumption, were those designed to meet medical and scientific needs.

(3) The United States maintained that the basic solution to the drug problem lay in limiting the production of raw materials to the quantities necessary to fill the world's legitimate requirements.

These principles were presented by the U.S. delegation to the Geneva conferences of 1924-25. The failure of the delegation to secure the agreement of other countries to these principles led it to withdraw from the conference. The delegation was actually bound by instructions prescribed by a resolution of Congress of 15 May 1924 which appropriated $40,000 for the delegation's expenses, "Provided that the representatives of the United States shall sign no agreement which does not fulfill the conditions necessary for the suppression of the habit-forming narcotic drug traffic." Commenting on the U.S. withdrawal later, the Dutch delegate said: "such a conference is doomed to failure if any one of the parties has imperative orders to impose its will upon the others under pain of leaving the conference " (Buell, 1925: 100, 112).

During the second Geneva conference, the U.S. proposed that the manufacture and distribution of heroin be prohibited. Although this item was not on the agenda, no one queried its presentation. Simultaneously, the U.S. delegation moved that the conference consider the limitation of raw opium and coca leaves. The Indian representative objected on the grounds that the adoption of the American proposal would entail the prohibition of internal consumption of opium and moved to rule the motion out of order, since the conference agenda was restricted to considerations of controls over production *for export*. The U.S. delegate's reply was: "there is nothing peculiarly sacred about an agenda." When, later, further protests were made, Porter said: "There is no reason why this conference cannot reach agreement and allow those three or four nations that do not feel that they can agree ... to make reservations. Then we can all be good and neighborly and try to help them solve their problems" (Buell, 1925: 102-5).

Dissatisfaction with the League was a reason for American support of the Permanent Central Opium Board, which the U.S. regarded as "completely independent from the League, and as fulfilling a function which the United States [regarded] as necessary" (Hubbard, 1937). The development of a new supervisory organ had been an old American proposal (Taylor, 1969: 86). Although the Board's members were supposed to be experts serving in their personal capacity and independent of their governments, its American chairman, Herbert May, maintained informal contact with the U.S. State Department and the appropriate federal agencies during his term in office (Musto, 1973: 203-4; Taylor, 1969: 261-63). The third international drug organ, the Drug Supervisory Body, was set up by the convention of 1931, largely because of American insistence on its inclusion in the convention (Hubbard, 1937: 368).

The third phase covered the 1930s. By modifying its attitude towards the League, the U.S. was able to regain its leadership. Limitation of manufacture was achieved, and here the U.S. was more fortunate than other drug-producing countries in having no serious opposition within the country. The American drug producers were, in fact, in favor of the control of manufacture because this would bring their European competitors under the same system of regulations as themselves (Taylor, 1969: 243). Taylor observed that many features of the 1931 convention were similar to American legislation (Taylor, 1969: 253). The estimates system, the creation of the DSB, and the inclusion of codeine under control all bore marks of U.S. initiative.

During this phase, Harry Anslinger enters the picture. In the 1920s domestic controls in the U.S. were exercised by the Bureau of Prohibition, which enforced alcohol prohibition as well as narcotics laws. Anslinger contributed to bilateral agreements aimed at curbing illicit alcohol traffic. In 1928, when much of the earlier support for prohibition began to wane, Anslinger proposed a way whereby the prohibition campaign might be saved: he suggested criminalization of liquor purchase and a harsh criminal policy (Musto, 1973: 211). Anslinger's proposal elicited no response, but he transferred many of his views to narcotics control when he became Commissioner of the Federal Bureau of Narcotics, established in 1930. In fact, Anslinger had always felt that "the most effective way of gaining public compliance with a law regulating a dangerous drug was a policy of high fines and severe mandatory prison sentences for first convictions" (Musto, 1973: 212).

However, Anslinger was careful to avoid conflict with federal judges, who were angered on behalf of the indicted citizens, and with the medical profession, which had been harassed by the agents of the Bureau (Musto, 1973: 213, 319). Organizational expansion and public support of the Bureau were later ensured through the assumption of new responsibilities under the famous

Marihuana Tax Act of 1937 (Dickson, 1968). Cannabis control
had, in fact, already been envisaged in an earlier draft of the
Harrison Act, but had been resisted by the producers and by the
American Medical Association.

On the international scene, U.S. initiative brought about
another conference—the one which concluded the 1936 Convention for the suppression of illicit traffic. This was a subject
"particularly favored" by Anslinger—the strengthening of
criminal penalties for drug trafficking (King, 1972: 214). In an
action reminiscent of the 1925 conference, the U.S. delegation
walked out of the conference, dissatisfied with the treaty's limited
coverage. In a note to the secretary-general of the League,
explanations were given in detail as to why the U.S. withheld its
signature from the 1936 Convention. Among them were the
following (Hubbard, 1937: 370):

. . . the stipulations of the Convention do not tend in any
increasing measure effectively to prevent or adequately to punish
the illicit traffic.

. . . we regard the Convention inadequate in so far as cannabis is
concerned.

Taylor's study ends at 1939. No equally thorough study of the
sequel exists. Nonetheless, we will attempt to sketch the main
developments which have occurred since then. We will deal with
the Anslinger era, which lasted almost three decades, and with the
period of hectic U.S. foreign policy starting in the late 1960s.

During World War II, six members from the League drug
section moved to Washington on the invitation of the U.S.
government. In conferences with representatives of allied countries
the U.S. secured their agreement to abolish opium monopolies in
territories liberated from Japan; in Japan itself the MacArthur
regime introduced a Japanese Harrison Act after the war (King,
1972: 215-16). The U.S. probably thought it to be in its own
interest to have the control organs based in America, for it
attempted to have the UN Narcotics Division, which had moved to
Geneva, returned to New York "where the full force of wide public
opinion can be brought to bear on the fight against illicit narcotics
traffic" (King, 1972: 144). The Board was able to carry on after war
broke out because, in the words of Herbert May, then president of
the Supervisory Body, "I persuaded the State Department to allow

me to operate from Washington.... There being no League of Nations funds available to set up the office, two American foundations donated the necessary money" (*Bulletin on Narcotics* 15 2 [1963]:5).

As we saw earlier, U.S. nationals have been among the key persons in all the international drug control organs. During the period under review, the domestic problems of the U.S. were beginning to determine its stance on international control, and thus the morally based internationalism of the early days was transformed into a policy of ordinary self-interest. There has, in fact, always been an interweaving of domestic and international motives. Hamilton Wright and Stephen Porter had tried, for example, to enforce domestic legislation in time to underline the seriousness of U.S. intentions at international meetings and thereby increase their capacity to influence international decisions; at the same time, they used international obligations as an argument for domestic legislation. This strategy was further elaborated by Anslinger. The following episode provides an illustration of the domestic-international link. In a Bureau of Narcotics publication, vigorous arguments were leveled against ambulatory treatment. By way of support, reference was made to the prestigious domestic organ, the National Academy of Science-National Research Council, which had asserted that "ambulatory treatment of addiction is impossible." There was also a reference to a resolution of ECOSOC which expressed appreciation of WHO's assistance and recommended "that, in the treatment of drug addiction, methods of ambulatory treatment and open clinics are not advisable" (Bureau of Narcotics, n.d. [1958?]: vii.-ix.). The reference seems to be to a WHO Expert Committee statement in October 1955, that "ambulatory treatment was not advisable." It will be remembered that the drug dependence committee of the Academy did the Bureau's drug classification work and that both Anslinger and Nathan Eddy had been on the committee. It will also be remembered that Eddy was probably the most influential WHO expert committee member. Considering these interconnections and the likelihood that Anslinger was the initiator of the resolution referred to, it would appear that some of the recommendations of international bodies were a reflection of domestic preoccupations in the U.S. It may not be immediately obvious to an outsider that pharmacological expertise does not necessarily imply knowledge of the efficacy of various types of treatment. It certainly does not imply knowledge of the efficacy of ambulatory treatment in societies other than the U.S. The ready generalization from the U.S. situation to the rest of the world also appears to have occurred in the case of cannabis control; there was also a close parallel between the earlier views expressed by WHO on cannabis and the official U.S. position on this drug (see chapter 13).

The conclusions of the WHO expert committee were largely based on the work of the Lexington Hospital in Kentucky, on which the Academy's recommendations were often based. This is clearly acknowledged in the following statement in a Drug Supervisory Body report:

as long ago as its first meeting in January 1949, the WHO Expert Committee on Addiction-Producing Drugs had noted the addiction-producing properties of several synthetic drugs. . . . For its conclusions, the Committee relied then, as it has done ever since, on the observations of the research workers at the Lexington Hospital, the scientific value of which is indisputable (DSB, 1961: xi).

In the Commission, in contrast to the recriminatory criticisms of the American position by the League Advisory Committee, an increased acceptance of U.S. views on opium production is evident. Extreme as the following expression of these views may seem, a number of representatives, "in particular those of Canada and France," had "warmly supported" them when they were articulated by Anslinger at the 1965 session of the Commission:

(Anslinger stated that) . . . in the next decade it might well be possible to achieve international agreement on the complete abolition of all legal opium production. Even now, many opium derivatives could be replaced by synthetics, and most, if not all, medical requirements could be met without producing and stockpiling opium. . . . When it had been demonstrated, as was to be expected within the next few years, that opium was not essential for medical purposes, the United States would give very favourable consideration to discussions leading to an international agreement which would abolish legal opium production entirely (CND: 20th, 1965: 14).

It is the acceptance of these premises which the search for synthetic alternatives to opiates of natural origin—a task in which WHO has continued to be involved—implies. Although these views were expressed in 1965, the Nixon administration was still espousing them in 1973, as is shown by its response to the shortage of morphine for the manufacture of codeine in the U.S., brought about by the Indian opium crop failure in that year. Contending that codeine and morphine are replaceable by synthetics, the Nixon administration is said to have threatened not to release morphine and its derivatives from the U.S. strategic reserve stockpile, seeing this as an opportunity to curtail all world opium production. That many other Western countries share these assumptions to some degree may be inferred from their support of the U.S. proposals to amend the Single Convention, the effect of which would have been to place further constraints on licit opium production. The position of the British on these amendments was, for instance, a very long way away from that held in 1925, when their representative, Viscount Cecil, criticized the American proposals to the Geneva conference for the sole reason that they could not be accomplished (Records, Second Geneva Conference, 1925, 21st meeting).

It is an openly acknowledged fact that the U.S. has applied pressure on countries not at all, or not particularly, preoccupied by drug problems to adhere to treaties or to enforce drug laws. "Problem countries" in U.S. terms are also problem countries in the eyes of the INCB, in whose reports they are frequently enumerated. Instead of coming under international discussion for its apparent mismanagement of its drug problems, the U.S. is often applauded for all its efforts. Such applause is most marked in the Board's reports (for example, INCB, 1972: 27). In contrast, it is invariably the developing countries, rather than the rich consuming countries, which are taken to task, albeit gently, for their inability to enforce controls.

Anslinger retired from his office in 1962 but continued to represent the U.S. at the Commission until 1970. The recent period of hectic activity in international drug control is intimately linked to the Nixon administration's overall diplomatic activity abroad. Indicative of the importance attached to the drug issue is the appointment of a Cabinet Committee on International Narcotics Control in June 1971 and the inclusion of the item of drug traffic control in negotiations at a high political level, such as those between Nixon and Pompidou (U.S. Senate, 1972: 5), and between U.S. Secretary of State William Rogers and Chairman Ne Win of Burma (Gross, 1972). In fact, President Nixon elevated international drug control to a "foreign-policy level of high priority" (Gross, 1972). When a "superpower" exhibits this degree of involvement, there is unlikely to be much resistance or unresponsiveness on the part of countries appealed to for support unless such support is contrary to national interests. Generally speaking, cooperation with the U.S. in drug control matters does not conflict in any significant way with the interests of other Western countries, and it is therefore readily provided.

Without going into details, one might note that in the domestic setting an increasingly critical attitude towards the traditional U.S. policy has developed, at least insofar as criminal sanctions and marihuana are concerned (see, for instance, the report of the National Commission on Marihuana and Drug Abuse, 1972), and this internal dissension may weaken the U.S. position in the international forum. Yet, heavy resources have continued to be committed to the Bureau of Narcotics, which was transferred in 1969 to the Department of Justice and was renamed the Bureau of Narcotics and Dangerous Drugs (BNDD).* The manpower resources of the Bureau have increased from less than 400 employees in the 1930s and less than 450 during Anslinger's period to 1,200 employees in 1971, representing a markedly higher rate of expansion than the pace characteristic of the earlier period (data from BNDD). Of course, BNDD had responsibility only for some sectors of narcotics control. A precise estimate of the total U.S. expenditures on "drug abuse control" is difficult to establish, but government spending in fiscal year 1972 has been calculated to be between $417 and $601 million. Of the former figure, treatment and education account for nearly $200, enforcement for $126, research for $50, and education for $42 million (Goldberg and De Long, 1972: 302-4). Compared to these figures, the budgets of the international narcotics control agencies look small indeed; in fact, even the budget of a world organization like WHO appears meager when measured against the U.S. drug control expenditures. The expansion of U.S. establishments for

* Since then the BNDD has been dissolved, and in July 1973 a new organization—the Drug Enforcement Administration (DEA)—was established under the attorney general to "carry out the following anti-drug functions": all BNDD's functions, the functions of the Bureau of Customs pertaining to drug investigations and intelligence, all the functions of the Office for Drug Abuse Law Enforcement and of the office of National Narcotics Intelligence.

law enforcement is accompanied by a reformulation of the objectives of U.S. international efforts. The primary objective has been identified as the reduction of the illicit flow of narcotics and dangerous drugs into the United States (see Kinney et al., 1972). This is in some contrast to its earlier crusade against drugs on behalf of other countries, particularly China.

To reach this goal there was a marked increase in the despatch of BNDD (DEA) agents abroad. During the Anslinger era, BNDD agents worked abroad on a limited scale for reasons explained by Anslinger in a letter to Senator Dirksen on 10 April 1959:

Our work is confined to the international, national, and wholesale illicit traffic. We have only five men in Europe because that is all we can use at the present time. We can work only in countries where we are invited and in some areas the matter of placing a man has delicate overtones.

In 1962, however, the assistant secretary of the treasury, James Reed, assigned enforcement responsibilities to the Bureau for all foreign areas. And by 1965 the Bureau had ten offices abroad and fourteen agents in Europe.

The above is only one indication of the hectic drug control activity abroad. In addition, the U.S. has developed a Narcotic Control Action Plan (the contents of which we have not been able to discover) for each of fifty-nine countries (see table 10.1). The plans are intended to cover most areas of the world except large parts of Africa, Australia, China, the USSR, and some other socialist countries.

U.S. diplomacy has resulted in thirty bilateral drug treaties. In addition, every U.S. mission has had to designate a drug control coordinator (U.S. Senate, 1972: 66). The table shows a progressive increase in the number of foreign offices, which now total forty-seven spread over thity-five countries. Uppermost among the countries hosting U.S. agents are Mexico, which has fifteen; France, eleven and Thailand, ten. It is also noteworthy that for Europe the number of bilateral treaties exceeds the number of offices, whereas for all other areas the opposite is true. In some instances (such as the Turkish opium ban), it is clear that the U.S. has paid for the action it has asked to be taken; there are probably other instances where one suspects that the threat of withdrawing foreign aid has been used to secure cooperation in U.S. efforts to interdict the drug traffic (U.S. Senate, 1972: 19).

TABLE 10.1
United States' Plans, Bilateral Agreements, and Foreign Offices for Narcotics Control, 1972

Region and country	Narcotics control action plans	Bilateral agreements relating to drug control	BNDD foreign district offices
Africa			
Morocco	x		x
Algeria	x		
Tunisia	x		
Libya	x		
Near East and South Asia			
Afghanistan	x		x
India	x	x	x
Iran	x		x
Lebanon	x		x
Pakistan	x		x
Turkey	x	x	x
Nepal	x		
Ceylon	x		
Israel	x		x
Greece	x	x	
Egypt	x	x	
Latin America			
Mexico	x	x	x
Panama	x		x
Colombia	x		x
Bolivia	x	x	x
Chile	x		
Paraguay	x		x
Peru	x		x
Jamaica	x		x
Argentina	x		x
Brazil	x		x
Equador	x	x	x
Uruguay	x		
Venezuela	x		x
Guyana	x		
Barbados	x		
Bahamas	x		
Netherlands Antilles	x		
Cuba		x	

Region and country	Narcotics control action plans	Bilateral agreements relating to drug control	BNDD foreign district offices
Europe			
France	x	x	x
Germany	x	x	x
Italy	x	x	x
Yugoslavia	x	x	
Bulgaria	x		
Rumania	x	x	
Austria	x	x	
Spain	x	x	x
England	x	x	x
Denmark	x	x	
Sweden	x		
Czechoslo- vakia	x	x	
Hungary	x		
Switzerland	x	x	
Belgium	x	x	x
Canada	x	x	x
Netherlands		x	
Poland		x	
Portugal		x	
East Africa and Pacific			
Burma	x		
Cambodia	x	x	x
Laos	x	x	x
Philippines	x		x
Thailand	x	x	x
Indonesia	x		
Vietnam	x	x	x
Hong Kong	x		x
Singapore	x		x
Korea	x		x
Malaysia	x		x
Taiwan		x	
Japan		x	x
Total number of countries	59	30	35

SOURCE: United States Senate, Committee on Foreign Relations. Hearing 27 June 1972. *Protocol amending the Single Convention on Narcotic Drugs*, 1972: 66, 60, 9. (Countries are grouped as in the document, p. 66).

Moreover, not only does the American government train narcotics officers in Afghanistan, but BNDD sent its staff to supplement UN personnel on missions to developing countries to provide law enforcement training courses (see chapter 15).

It is against the background of U.S. domination that two recent developments, the establishment of the UN Fund for Drug Abuse Control (UNFDAC) and the amendment of the Single Convention, must be seen.

An idea which has gained much currency in the international forum is that some countries have not met their treaty obligations and have allowed illicit opium production to occur less through lack of goodwill than through lack of resources to control such production. The idea has come to be accepted that the treaty system has to be supplemented by technical assistance. The drawback to this strategy is that the majority of the potential recipients of technical assistance accord drug control a low priority. Thus, initially, the machinery established for UN aid in drug control was underused (E/3077). For the UN's assistance-financing body to be paying for drug control activities, when its primary concern is with national economic development, with which a drug program may even be at odds, is clearly incongruous. The need for other financial arrangements has led to the creation of UNFDAC. More than the theoretically mandatory contributions to the UN budget, the voluntary contributions to the Fund ensure a financial basis for UN activity in a field with which electoral concern, notably in the U.S., is clearly great.

The U.S. proposal to amend the Single Convention represents a renewed attempt to control opium production at the source. One of the objectives of the original U.S. proposals was to strengthen the Single Convention and give more power to the INCB. To secure support for its proposals, the U.S. government held consultations with a large number of countries and invited would-be cosponsors of its proposals to a private meeting in Geneva prior to the conference which was to consider the amendments. When the amendments were put before the conference, they consisted of a package of consensus proposals jointly made by Denmark, the Federal Republic of Germany, Finland, France, Ghana, Italy, Norway, Sweden, the U.K., and Uruguay.

The conflict of interest was so intense at the conference that the instrument eventually adopted was a much watered-down affair. The U.S. delegation nevertheless held the conference to be a great success. As was explicit in the reactions sampled in the delegates' lounge in the UN building in Geneva (always a better place for this purpose than the conference hall), most delegates believed that the initiative of the U.S. was prompted in any event by an impending presidential election, that it was a vehicle for immediate political gains, and that, therefore, the weakness of the protocol was of less importance than the number of accessions it was likely to acquire.

This last phase of U.S. activity may be viewed in terms of the power concepts elaborated by Galtung. Support for U.S. policy on the part of other nations is won by the deployment of resources; its extensive network of bilateral agreements may lead to "fragmentation," and the accommodation of other countries to U.S. views is secured through the use of "remunerative" or "punitive" measures—for example, by giving or withdrawing aid. The ability to persuade depends on the availability of expertise and technical knowledge. The U.S. clearly leads the world in the extent of investment in drug research. We saw earlier that American writers contribute preponderantly to the UN *Bulletin on Narcotics*. And it is apparent from the sources used in our own study that international drug control has been more widely and more thoroughly studied in the U.S. than in any other country. Access to knowledge by administrators can mean increased possibilities of advancing the U.S. point of view.

To demonstrate the extent of American influence on the international drug control system, we have summarized in table 10.2 those features of the control system which have come about or have been sustained through U.S. efforts, or which are concomitants or logical outcomes of U.S. drug policy. Some of these features will be dealt with in more detail later.

U.S. ascendancy in the international drug control sphere is probably indicative of its position in all areas of concern in the UN. This has to do with the fact that it is the largest contributor by far to the UN budget. The system of a single vote for all UN members in the Assembly is, in fact, untenable in practice when one nation contributes about 30 percent of the budget. The U.S.

government has been accused of skepticism towards the UN—the last place it is said to which U.S. decision-makers would turn where anything touching U.S. interests is concerned (Alger, 1973). It is our feeling that this attitude towards the UN has had a bearing on the increasing resort to bilateral arrangements outside the UN system. The American position of power is buttressed by a number of other factors. For the other nations, not a great deal is at stake in the drug control arena, and accommodation to U.S. wishes is more readily made than is the case elsewhere. The infusion of American funds into drug programs and the general elevation of the status of drug affairs in the UN are welcomed by the Secretariat, for they provide the means for organizational expansion and activity.

TABLE 10.2
Features of the International Drug Control System Attributable to U.S. Influence

Goals of control	Limitation of production to medical and scientific needs
	Prohibition of drugs not medically indispensable
	Prevention of export of drugs to countries prohibiting their entry
Means	Crop substitution programs
	Statistical data collection
	Criminal policy
Control apparatus	Creation of PCB and DSB
	Additional power to INCB
	Creation of UNDFAC
Drugs controlled	Heroin prohibition
	Cannabis prohibition
	LSD prohibition
	Evaluation of dependence-producing drugs by experts
Initiation of conferences	Shanghai, 1909
	Hague, 1912
	Geneva, 1924
	Illicit traffic, 1936
	Amending the Single Convention, 1972

11   Pressure Groups

Official representatives of manufacturing countries are
frequently seen in earnest conversation with representatives of manufacturers, or the actual manufacturers
themselves, whom they, presumably, consult as to the
best, quickest, and most equitable means of limiting
manufacture.

A. E. Blanco, on the Limitation Conference of
1931, in an Anti-Opium Information Bureau
Communiqué.

An account of the international drug control
system merely in terms of the influence of individual countries
and persons can be seriously misleading. The activity of interest
groups can have a significant influence on the decisions reached
by governments and in international negotiations and must
therefore be considered.

Formal access to the UN by interest groups is gained by
becoming accredited as nongovernmental organizations (NGOs).
NGOs have a statutory basis under the UN charter whereas under
the League convenant they fell outside the constitutional framework and were therefore of an informal nature. Under the UN
arrangement* formal consultation is virtually limited to
ECOSOC and its area of competence. On the other hand, the
form of consultation followed by the League with other international bodies ranged across the entire compass of the League's
interest areas. The influence of NGOs on UN activities has

* The criteria for selection of NGO candidates include the relevance of the
candidate's activities to those of ECOSOC; the conformity of its aims and
purposes with those of the UN Charter; the representative nature of the candidate
within its particular field of interest, and authority to speak for its members.
National organizations would not normally be eligible unless' there was no
international organization in that particular field or unless the national organization had special experience.

declined over the years (Skjelsbaek, 1973), although their number has steadily increased. For example, it has risen from 216 in 1962 to 419 in 1970 (*Yearbook of the UN*, 1970: 622).

NGOs represent a great variety of interests, which in turn vary considerably in form, intensity, and scope. These interests can be classified in a number of ways but for our purpose we may distinguish between three broad categories. The first category is exemplified by religious, temperance, and antiopium movements. The second comprises professional interests, such as those of lawyers, doctors, and scientists, while the third embraces the field of industry and commerce. From the historical point of view of international drug control it is the first and third categories which are of particular interest; the first because it is from among its members that pressure for increased controls has mainly come, and the third because it includes the interests of the economy which these controls are intended to regulate. The second group has emerged as an important factor more recently and will be seen in action later in connection with the Vienna treaty (chapter 16).

What influence any of these groups has had on decision-making in international organizations is difficult to measure. To say that influence has been exercised one must be able to demonstrate that the decisions, orientations, and opinions of the targets of influence have been changed from what they would have been in the absence of influence. On the other hand, success or failure to bring about an outcome does not necessarily imply the presence or absence of influence: pressure group activity may shift the probability of an outcome without perceptibly bringing about the desired outcome.

In the absence of adequate measures of influence, one is reduced to describing attempts at, rather than the effects of, influence. Only rarely can one conclude, as Pickard does, in reference to the nonratification of the various pre-1914 international agreements on such matters as the protection of women, child welfare, the opium traffic, obscene publications, and slavery, that:

circumspect pressures from various organs of the League, plus the less prudent pressures permitted NGOs, notably national NGOs, effected the requisite ratifications in double-quick time.

He further notes that, while the NGO contribution in the above cases was clear, "there are doubtless other instances, less definable and measurable ... where the NGO impact has also been effective" (Pickard, 1965: 47).

As pressure groups, by definition, work outside the system they seek to influence and as their efforts are difficult to describe, it is inevitable that our discussion will leave out a great deal. In what follows, we will be mainly concerned with two key groups— the antidrug manufacture lobby and the drug suppliers.

Earlier we saw that procontrol groups have worked hard throughout history to interest governments and international organizations in instituting controls over opium and alcohol. The temperance groups, as will be seen in the next chapter, gained little headway beyond Anglo-Saxon and Scandinavian countries. In contrast, it was the antiopium missionaries in the Far East who exercised the greatest influence in shaping American public opinion and in inducing the U.S. to play a leading role in the international effort against the opium trade (Taylor, 1969: 29-30).

After international opium controls were well underway, perhaps the most important, and certainly the most persistent, pressure for control over drug manufacture was that exerted by the Anti-Opium Information Bureau, a one-man operation set up by A. E. Blanco, who, it will be remembered, had once been with the League's Opium Traffic Section. Blanco fervently believed that the solution to the drug problem lay in the limitation of manufacture to the amount sufficient to fulfill medical needs, and it is clear from the numerous communiqués he released to the press, the Advisory Committee and other League organs, inveighing against the Committee, that he was highly suspicious of the motives of the members of the Committee, when they rejected plan after plan put before them for controlling drug traffic. His press releases, according to Renborg (1964), "caused great irritation to the older members of the Committee." Taylor notes that (1969:227) "Because of the glare of publicity which it directed towards the Opium Advisory Committee and other agencies of the League concerned with the drug question, the Bureau was not uninfluential."

Blanco was the author of the "Scheme of Stipulated Supply," designed to control manufactured drugs. Under the plan, each country was to state in advance its requirements of each narcotic drug and to stipulate the country from which it would purchase these requirements. The plan was presented to the Advisory Committee by a private American citizen, C. K. Crane, through the medium of the U.S. State Department. Blanco had to resort to this roundabout way of bringing the scheme before the attention of the Advisory Committee because his own attempt to introduce it through the secretariat had failed. The Committee rejected Blanco's plan (OAC: 12th, 1929: 288), but its rejection so incensed the consuming countries that they voiced their protests to the League Assembly, which then stepped in to call for action to limit manufacture and for the enlargement of the Committee to include nonproducing countries.

The scheme was presented as an alternative to a plan devised by the manufacturing countries of the Advisory Opium Committee in a private meeting in London in 1931. Their plan was based on a quota system whereby drug manufacture would be divided between the existing manufacturing countries. The system was open to the criticism that it would perpetuate the privileged positions of these countries and secure for them a monopoly of the drug industry (Pastuhov, 1945). Eisenlohr notes that Blanco was part of the opposition which finally demolished the quota system (Eisenlohr, 1934: 275).

In the League days, the fact that the furtherance of industrial interests was government sponsored (in the sense that it was often the interest of their national drug industries which the Advisory Committee members served rather than the avowed interests of the Committee) obviated the need for private pharmaceutical pressure-group activity. Unlike attempts to influence decisions in domestic politics, influence at the international level could occur without any activity on the international stage by the interest group concerned. At the Hague conference in 1912, the country most responsible for the dilution of a resolution on manufactured drugs was Germany, which was a major manufacturer of opium derivatives and which had a virtual monopoly of cocaine production. Its chemical industry had exerted much pressure on the German government not to attend the conference; thus the German delegation "was out to scuttle any strong measures that might jeopardize the favoured position of their manufacturers" (Taylor, 1969: 102).

While it is only relatively recently that commercial interests in pharmaceuticals have become visibly active at an international level in the drug control field, lobbying efforts by physicians and pharmacists at the domestic level have had a long history (see Musto, 1973). Vested interests in the alcohol field have also long been represented by such NGOs as the Permanent International Committee on Wine Growing, the International Committee on the Trade in Wines, Ales, Ciders, Spirituous Liquors and Kindred Industries, and the International Union of the Development of Grape-Cure Resorts and the Consumption of Grapes (White, 1951). As there has been no real attempt at international control of alcohol, the efforts of these groups can hardly have been tested.

International pharmaceutical associations were already active during the League period. Interest was shown, for example, in the 1924 Geneva Opium Conference by the International Pharmaceutical Federation, which sent a letter to the president of the conference asking that favorable note be taken of the recommendations which the Federation had arrived at during its meeting in Paris in November 1924. Some of these recommendations read as follows:

... it will be necessary that the law regulating the traffic in narcotics in the different countries shall not impose upon pharmacists administrative provisions which might prove a source of worry and annoyance and hinder them in the conduct of their business, while not proving effective to prevent drugtakers from obtaining these substances by fraud or from persons less conscientious than the pharmacists.

... the prohibition to supply these medicaments to customers without a medical prescription should not, however, prevent the sale of medicaments containing so small a quantity that there can be no question of abuse. It is not necessary to demand more than is laid down in Article 14(b) and (c) of the Opium Convention.

Provisions regulating the sale of narcotics in pharmacies, and any registers and lists that may be prescribed, should be as simple as possible and drawn up in agreement with the pharmaceutical profession before being enforced (Records, Second Opium Conference, 1925:332).

More recently, shared interests among pharmaceutical manufacturers have led them to form such joint organizations as the Groupement International de l'Industrie Pharmaceutique des Pays

de la Communauté Economique Européenne (GIIP), established
in 1959, and the Pharmaceutical Industries Association in the
European Free Trade Area (PIA). In 1968 these groups, together
with their counterparts in the U.S. and Canada, formed the
International Federation of Pharmaceutical Manufacturers
Associations (IFPMA). IFPMA was admitted as an NGO to
WHO in 1971 (see chapter 12). Individual drug companies appear
to be members of several NGOs simultaneously. This is suggested
by the fact that at the WHO standing committee on nongovernmental organizations which considered IFPMA's admission in
January 1971, the International Pharmaceutical Federation,
another NGO, was represented by a senior member of the
management of the Swiss drug firm CIBA-Geigy who a year later
appeared as an IFPMA representative in the WHO executive
board's listing of NGOs (EB 47 SR 17:275).

Although ECOSOC has been careful about granting status to
profit-making businesses, organizations seeking such status can,
and do, register under nonprofit-making codes and gain admit-
tance nonetheless. While not profit-making in the strict sense,
such organizations may still pursue the furtherance of their
members' commercial interests. On the other hand, a commercial
body may be considered so useful to an organization that the
profit factor is ignored. Pickard offers an example of this: "The
World Health Organization, for example, because of a possible
need for close cooperation with great pharmaceutical businesses,
was careful not to include the non-profit making proviso among
its criteria for the granting of official relations to an NGO"
(Pickard, 1956:43).

Although the acquisition of consultative status gives interest
groups opportunities for lobbying, the additional channel of
informal contacts between their representatives and officials in
the control administration is frequently used. Usually these
contacts are personal and the parties involved have known each
other over a period of time. It is said by some drug industry
personnel that such contacts are cultivated for the advantages
inherent in being able to approach the right official on the right
subject so as to obtain a hearing and express views, rather than to
influence decisions directly. However, the fact that these channels
are informal and operate outside the public forum means that
there is no way of knowing what these views are, or how

persuasively they are being expressed. In contrast, the situation in the League period was clearer. It was officially reported, for instance, that de Vasconcellos, the chairman of the Opium Advisory Committee "had been personally approached by a representative of the Société industrielle de chimie organique of Paris with reference to statements in the Committee's reports that this firm had been implicated in the illicit traffic. The representative was extremely anxious to disprove the charges made against his firm, and offered every facility for a thorough inquiry" (OAC minutes: 15th, 1932:9).

Inclusion of the representatives of private organizations on conference delegations is another familiar practice. A joint report by UNESCO and the International Institute of Administrative Sciences (1951) notes that some governments "notably the U.S., prefer to give certain nonofficial groups the opportunity to express themselves as delegation members. At the San Francisco Conference which created the UN Charter in 1945, representatives of numerous private organizations were invited to act as 'consultants' to the American delegation. For financial reasons this practice was scarcely feasible for overseas governments." Another example is afforded by the U.S. delegation to the International Health Conference, which created WHO in 1946. The representative of the American Medical Association (AMA) was an integral part of the delegation. The AMA was opposed to any action by WHO which might promote "socialized medicine," and thought that the organization should not concern itself with "the care of the sick and the social organization related to the practice of medicine" (Cox and Jacobson, 1973:178). Yet another example is the inclusion in the Swiss delegation to the Vienna Conference in 1971 of the executives of the three largest pharmaceutical companies of Switzerland: Hoffmann-La Roche, CIBA-Geigy, and Sandoz (although they were not listed as such), as well as the inclusion, among U.S. delegates to the 1970 drafting session of the Commission, of a representative of the American Pharmaceutical Manufacturers Association.

A well-known feature of the relation between large-scale private enterprise and national government is the interchange of high-level personnel between the two concerns. Senior civil servants often take up positions on the boards of private companies when they reach retirement age, and in the U.S., especially, the phenomenon of clientalism is well known (Grove, 1962:159). In the drug field one can cite several examples of international civil servants leaving the service to join the pharmaceutical industry, or vice versa. The late Gilbert Yates, a former director of the UN Division of Narcotic Drugs, became the director of the Association of the British Pharmaceutical Industry; Adolf Lande, previously secretary of the INCB, has been connected with the American Pharmeceutical Manufacturers Association; and Hans Halbach, a former chief of the WHO Drug Dependence Unit and director of the Division of Pharmacology and Toxicology, is now employed by the Swiss drug company Hoffmann-La Roche. An earlier example is that of Otto Anselmino, who upon leaving League narcotics control work, became an employee of a German drug firm. Herbert May, one-time president of the Board, was a partner in his father's drug business before he joined the international drug control body.

To what extent the pharmaceutical industry has been able to exercise influence in the drug control area is, of course, an open question. That its interests were a decisive factor throughout the development of the international drug control system is manifest in all the more systematic historical accounts of narcotics control (Eisenlohr, 1934; Musto, 1973; and Taylor, 1969). Moreover, one of the more visible effects of the controls applied during the League period seems to have been to wrest the prominent legitimate pharmaceutical firms from their deep involvement in the illicit trade (see chapter 15).

The effectiveness of the industry's attempts to influence decisions depends on a number of factors. The degree of susceptibility of the targets of influence is obviously one of them. Clearly, the ability to persuade also depends on the persuader's reputation and the resources at his disposal. We indicated in the last chapter that, among other factors, the economic capability of the U.S. has provided it with the basis for intense activity and leadership in the field of drug control. Like countries, pressure groups too are unequal in their resources, power, and access to centers of decision-making. Although such attributes provide a frail basis for an estimation of the power potential of the pharmaceutical industry, we offer below some indicators of the extent of the industry's resources and interests.

Pharmaceuticals are a branch of the larger chemical industry. The chemical industry is a dynamic sector of modern industrial economy; on the average, it has had a growth rate about two-thirds higher than that of the national economy as a whole. Except for the food processing and texile sectors, the chemical industry also expands faster than the average for all manufacturing activities (UNIDO, 1969). The value of world chemical production is given below:

	Million dollars	Dollars per capita
1960	72,281	31.3
1965	112,092	44.2
1970 (forecast)	153,400	55.0

The percentage shares of pharmaceuticals in the overall chemical production are as follows:

	Selected developed countries*	Selected Latin American countries
Early 1950s	9.2	—
Early 1960s	10.5	13.4

Four regional blocs, namely Western Europe, North America, Japan, and Eastern Europe account for 95 percent of the world production of pharmaceuticals. Among the product classes psychotropics rank fifth, and on a world scale this class represents a group of high growth (Woodward, 1973). The three leading exporting countries of pharmaceuticals have been West Germany, the U.S. and Switzerland if one takes sales by branches abroad as an indicator (SOU 1969:24; Breckon, 1972:28). Among the world's ten largest companies in 1965 seven are in the U.S., two are Swiss, and one is Japanese (SOU 1969:42). In addition to the trend towards monopoly, the larger companies have developed, since the Second World War, a "multinational" nature, geared to the extension of markets and reduction of costs through the establishment of subsidiaries in countries providing

* The developed countries indicated are the members of the European Economic Community (including Great Britain), Norway, Poland, Sweden, U.S., and USSR; the Latin American countries are Argentina, Brazil, Chile, Colombia, Mexico, Peru, and Venezuela. (Source: UNIDO Monograph on Industrial Development, No. 8 [1969].)

favorable conditions for this purpose. A high price is usually paid by developing countries for this so-called technology transfer. A study has been reported in Columbia, for example, which calculates that, of the effective returns to the parent corporation of a sample of pharmaceutical firms investigated, overpricing accounted for 82 percent, the remainder being made up of reported profits and royalties (Vaitsos, 1970). The exceptional profitability of the pharmaceutical sector has been noted by a few investigations (Sainsbury, 1967; Monopolies Commission, 1973). It is more profitable, in fact, than industry as a whole. A comparatively large proportion of the profits is spent on drug sales-promotion and research. One also finds small sums being invested in influencing political decisions: Beecham and CIBA-Geigy, for example, donated £ 20,000 and £ 2,000 respectively to the British Conservative party in 1971.

Resources, therefore, may have at least potentially important political consequences, although using them to create influence involves varying degrees of risk, in that the outcome cannot always be guaranteed. For example, the organization under whose auspices this study was undertaken, the International Research Group on Drug Legislation and Programs, and of which we ourselves are members, was partially financed by a group of European drug companies. These companies supported some of the Research Group's work, hoping that "the widest possible dissemination of the knowledge that such a project is being undertaken may delay or impede ratification of the Vienna treaty by a significant number of states" (Letter from CIBA-Geigy executive to chairman of the group, 5 August 1971). Our belief, however, is that such hopes did not influence the final outcome of the group's investigations.

There are conflicting views on the industry's relationship with governmental agencies; one view sees the industry as being encumbered by excessive regulations, and another believes that the industry's power is such as to frustrate any attempt to prevent it from acting entirely in its own self-interest. Some pharmaceutical companies claim to be in favor of controls as such controls would debar their more dubious competitors from the trade. A licensing system would, for instance, create a vested interest of the authorized drug firms in the effective functioning of the control regime which accords them this privilege (Lande, 1970). Nonetheless, the close association of the industry with national governments would lead one to suppose that governments themselves—especially when it comes to a question of export trade and "balance of payments"—take an interest in the protection of industrial interests, and insofar as the individuals involved often assume double roles, private and public, the actual relationships between industrial concerns and the agencies supposed to regulate them are not at all clear to the outsider. Against this background, one would be chary of supporting the view that those affected by governmental regulations should have a say in their planning, since at present this is not made contingent on a public declaration of interests. In the absence of such declarations, there is no opportunity for the public to assess the industry's influence or to decide to what extent government decisions are affected by commercial interests. In many cases the latter do have a say in planning since governments are often anxious to know whether a particular measure will arouse opposition or support, so that by a process of mutual accommodation between the interests involved controversy may be avoided. The private concerns in turn provide technical expertise, contacts, and general support. Again, it is important that these relations be subjected to public appraisal.

Before we conclude this chapter, one last problem must be mentioned. This is the degree to which the practice of medicine is open to the influence of the commercial sector. Studies in Britain and America have all pointed to the importance of pharmaceutical detail-men and drug advertising as sources of information used by physicians in determining the types of medication to prescribe (Worthen, 1973; Wilson et al., 1963). Recognition of this problem has led the Board to state in its 1967 report that: "Commercial advertisment of psychoactive drugs could bring serious danger to public health and should therefore be restricted or if possible prohibited" (PCB/DSB, 1967: 26). A WHO document likewise attributed the excessive consumption of drugs in a number of countries to pharmaceutical advertising (WHO, 1968: 4). In our view these aspects are not irrelevant to international drug control and deserve closer attention and investigation by the intergovernmental agencies.

SUMMARY OF PART II

1. The international drug control system cannot be evalutated on the basis of the writings of insiders alone; there is a need for analysis by outsiders.

2. Conceptions of the drug problem and the definition of the objectives of international control have evolved over the years to culminate in a system aimed at limiting exclusively to medical and scientific purposes the trade in and use of controlled drugs. The goals and means of drug control are dictated by national and bureaucratic interests, the range of feasible options, the place of drug policy in broader social policy, attitudes towards drug control, and the institutional framework of treaty-making.

3. The key international drug control organs are: the Commission on Narcotic Drugs and its secretariat, the UN Division of Narcotic Drugs; the INCB and its secretariat; the Drug Dependence and Mental Health Units of WHO (now merged) and their expert committees.

4. In terms of resources and priority, drug affairs have a low rating in the UN and WHO. The Fund for Drug Abuse Control has, however, sharply increased the resources committed to work on drugs (other than alcohol). The Division has benefited most from the new funds.

5. Although outside experts and political bodies have their share in shaping the control system, the importance of the international civil servant should be recognized. It is generally underestimated because, in accordance with role expectations, his influence is usually played down.

6. All the key organs have their forerunners in the League of Nations. The League's traditions are still strong, and the present system cannot be understood without knowledge of its antecedents.

7. WHO drug-dependence expert committees have been concerned with the evaluation of drugs for control. Their area of interest has widened without a noticeable widening of the range of expertise brought to bear on their work.

8. The INCB's main contribution has been the development of a nearly worldwide statistical reporting system. It is questionable whether the elaborate estimates system the INCB oversees still serves the purpose for which it is intended. In practice, the INCB has exaggerated its independence from governments.

9. The Commission has concentrated mostly on opium/opiates. Its membership has progressively increased but a permanent core group of countries exists.

10. The control system is dominated by the U.S., the U.K., France, India and, to a lesser extent, Yugoslavia, Turkey, and Switzerland. The USSR's presence as a countervailing power is more significant in the treaty-making process than in the operations of the control organs.

11. The most influential country has consistently been the U.S. American influence has shaped the goals of the system, the control apparatus, the range of drugs placed under control, the means used to achieve drug control, and the general international policy. Its superpower status and resources and its own drug problem have contributed to its leading role in the drug field.

12. Pressure groups have had a part in the development of controls: antiopiumists exerted much pressure in the 1930s to bring about increased controls, and during the last decade the pharmaceutical industry has organized itself internationally to enable it to safeguard its interests in the face of international controls.

III   Case Studies

12   Alcohol: Diminishing Control

> When the League of Nations was founded, one question
> of necessity arose in the fighters against alcoholism:
> could not and would not the new international organiza-
> tion, which does not confine itself to political aims but
> displays a beneficent activity in the fields of public
> hygiene and philanthropy, interest itself in the alcohol
> question? . . . Are not alcohol and opium both narcotic
> drugs and cannot their effects be compared? If the
> League of Nations does such splendid work against
> opium why would it not do the same against alcohol?
> > R. Hercod, Proceedings of the International Con-
> > ference against Alcoholism, Geneva, 1925

Prohibition in Africa
         Alcohol became an object of international
control endeavors less through a general acceptance of its danger-
ousness than through its connection with the problem of slavery.
Provisions for the control of arms and liquor were included in the
Brussels General Act of 1889–90, under which colonial powers in
Africa agreed to take measures against the slave trade. This
almost forgotten act has a chapter (6) on "Restrictive Measures
Concerning the Traffic in Spirituous Liquor"; the regulations,
which were valid for all Africa, except for north of latitude 20°N
and south of 22°S latitude, prohibit the importation and manufacture of distilled liquors ("des boissons distillés"). There were
two important exceptions to these strict rules. First, not all areas
were subject to total prohibition, but in the areas outside
prohibition economic control was to be exerted through the
imposition of import and excise duties; second, exceptions were
made for the nonnative population based on the belief that it was
not the liquor as such but the characteristics of the African people
which accounted for the dangerous results of drinking.
        Not only were the signatory powers obliged to take necessary
steps to bar the introduction of liquor to the areas indicated, they

were also called upon by the act to report the measures taken to an office established in Brussels. Revisions of the agreement in terms of progressive increases in the stipulated rate of duty were adopted at conferences held in 1899, 1906, and 1912. New minimum duties were fixed, but more important than these was the introduction of the principle that the duty should vary according to the strength of the spirit.

After the First World War the question of the administration of the German colonies had to be resolved. Under a system of mandates set up by the covenant of the League of Nations, former German territories in Africa were assigned to other colonial powers (called "advanced nations" in the covenant), and these powers were held responsible for their administration "under conditions which will guarantee freedom of conscience or religion, subject only to the maintenance of public order and morals, the prohibition of abuses such as the slave trade, the arms traffic and the liquor traffic" (article 22).

The responsibility placed upon these states for the control of the liquor traffic was further confirmed by a Convention on the Liquor Traffic in Africa which was adopted at St. Germain-en-Laye on 10 September 1919 and which replaced the Brussels General Act referred to earlier. This convention was signed by the U.S., Belgium, the British Empire, France, Italy, Japan, and Portugal. The text of the convention reiterated, in somewhat different wording, the stipulations of the Brussels act. However, the control measures relating to alcohol went somewhat further, as is exemplified by article 2, which reads: "The importation, distribution, sale and possession of trade spirits of every kind and of beverages mixed with these spirits are prohibited." Prohibition of manufacture was covered by another article (5) as were controls over access to distillation apparatus. The tightening of control these provisions represented may have been a reaction to an increased illicit traffic to which earlier control measures had given rise.

The League of Nations supervised the administration of the mandates by the various powers through a Permanent Mandates Commission composed of experts—these were not perceived as government representatives—from the countries concerned. The commission inspected the annual reports of the madatory powers, made observations on the conditions in these territories, and

reported them to the Council of the League. During the first
decade, the illicit liquor traffic was dealt with at length both in
the commission's discussions and in the reports of the mandatory
powers. From 1932 onwards however, very little interest was
shown in either the liquor traffic or in any other aspect of the
alcohol problem, and this may reflect the resignation felt towards
the lack of support for alcohol prohibition in general (it had, for
instance, been repealed in the U.S.). The work of the mandates
commission had been made easier as far as alcohol was concerned
by the fact that the bureau in Brussels had continued its
data-collecting service.

The activities of the Permanent Mandates Commission were
followed with interest by the antialcohol movement, and on
several occasions its members communicated their views to the
commission. The interest in the liquor question in the commission
was probably partially due to the pressures applied by the
antialcohol movement.

To illustrate the kind of ideas expressed at the time, we may
take as an example the following resolution adopted by the
League Council on 18 July 1922:

The Council of the League of Nations conscious of the gravity of
the danger for the native populations of Central Africa arising
from the scourge of alcoholism, recommends that the Mandatory
Powers should do everything in their power that their
administrations should protect the populations from the
above-mentioned danger.

But before the Council adopted this resolution, the mandates
commission had, of course, discussed the liquor problem at some
length. During the second session in 1921, the Portuguese member, d'Andrade, had pressed for the strictest possible control,
using among others the following arguments:

Everyone knew that a native who was addicted to alcohol, when
deprived of spirit, did not hesitate to drink alcohol in any other
form.
   The native must be defended against his natural vice, alcohol.... The abuse of alcohol could only be avoided by prohibition
of import and manufacture of alcoholic liquors both for whites and
for blacks (PMC: 5 October 1921).

The minutes of the commission sessions show that there was

constant disagreement among its members on the degree of
control which was to be exerted. Some of the arguments revolved
around interpretations of the relationship between the covenant
of the League, the St. Germain Convention, and the various rules
governing mandates, and of the intentions behind these documents. One of the difficulties was the definition of such terms as
"trade spirits." Finally, problems arose because of the inequality
of the duties levied by primarily the British and the French
mandate administrations, and these had to be resolved through
negotiations between the two countries.

There were further signs of pressure from the antialcohol
Bureau in Lausanne.* These were discernible in the resolutions
adopted at its international conference in Geneva in early September 1925, at which the mandates commission as well as a
number of governments were represented. Much attention was
given to the colonial question, and on the basis of lengthy reports
from all parts of Africa the conference adopted six resolutions
ranging from expressions of appreciation for the work of the
mandates commission to injunctions to interpret the St. Germain
Convention in the strictest terms. The conference also demanded
that prohibition be applied without distinction as to race (Proceedings, Alcoholism Conference, 1925).

The total effect of these pressures is difficult to gauge. It is true
that they influenced the debates in the mandates commission,
which led the League Council to request further steps to be taken,
with the result that a document on the liquor situation in Africa
was published (L608.M.235.1930.VI). But interest in the liquor
question petered out by the early 1930s, and so far as we are
aware there has been no assessment of this experiment in
internationally supported regional prohibition.

Passivity in the League

The liquor question was, however, brought to the League's
attention through other channels. One of the main problems for
which international cooperation was sought was that of the illicit
traffic. The prohibition-ridden U.S. worked out a series of

* The office of an organization which has undergone several changes of name:
it has been known as the International Temperance Union Against Alcoholism;
International Council on Alcohol and Alcoholism; and, today, International
Council on Alcohol and Addictions (ICAA).

bilateral treaties with, among other countries, Great Britain, Norway, Germany, Denmark, Sweden, Panama, the Netherlands, and France, making it possible for the U.S. to search vessels outside the three-mile limit that were suspected of smuggling. With Canada and Mexico special problems arose from the fact that each had a land border with the U.S., but arrangements were arrived at nonetheless. Because the U.S. was not a member of the League, it had to negotiate on a bilateral basis.

With regard to Finland, which was also attempting total prohibition, the Baltic powers, consisting of eleven governments, adopted a convention in Helsinki in 1925 which dealt with alcohol above a strength of 18 percent by volume. The convention specified the kind of vessels which were authorized to transport liquor, but the effect of this was that the ships of contracting parties registered themselves in nonparty countries and began to sail under Greek or other national flags (Immonen, 1965). This led the Finnish government, particularly, to seek more effective international support. At the alcoholism conference in Geneva referred to earlier, smuggling, like the colonial problems, had been an issue. Inevitably, conflict had arisen between the prohibitionist and the alcohol-producing countries, but in the resolutions adopted the conference enjoined countries to respect each other's control systems and asked for action from the League of Nations (Proceedings, Alcoholism Conference, 1925).

In 1926 the governments of Finland, Poland, and Sweden addressed a proposal to the League that steps be taken to arrive at an international convention on the illicit traffic in liquor and at a thorough international investigation into the alcohol question. This item actually appeared on the agenda of the League Assembly but consideration of it was postponed to the next session. Meanwhile, the foreign ministers of the countries mentioned above and of Belgium, Denmark, and Czechoslovakia submitted a note to the League and its member states supporting the proposal to convene an international conference for the purpose of drawing up an international convention on the liquor traffic. Furthermore they proposed that an Advisory Committee on Alcoholism, analogous to the narcotics control body, be set up.

When the main debate took place in the Second Committee of the Assembly in 1927, it was attended by a person referred to in the minutes as a representative of the French wine growers. The position which he represented lent intensity to the conflict of interests expressed in the debate. The Finnish delegate, Väinö Voionmaa, pointed to the international character of alcoholism, referred to its having been a concern of the Permanent Mandates Commission and the League Committee on Traffic in Women and Children, and proposed that an Advisory Committee on Alcoholism be established. The opposition came predominantly from the French representative, Loucheur, who argued that such a new question could not be discussed without preliminary investigation into whether it was part of the League's activities. He was opposed moreover to the labeling of alcohol as a "dangerous drug." He held that:

> It was essential not to risk causing internal political disturbances in any country by extending the League's activities indefinitely. Certain congresses had even gone so far as to warn people against the use of grape juice. As a defender of France and its wine [he] opposed the abolition of good wine, which brought joy into the lives of the people and from which the French derived many of their sturdy qualities.

Furthermore, he opposed the idea of the League associating with the Bureau in Lausanne.

The French position was supported by Austria, Denmark, Italy, Portugal, Uruguay, and Australia, while Sweden, Hungary, and Belgium aligned themselves with the Finnish view. It was said by the Belgian delegate that, while efforts were being made by the League "to mitigate the evils caused by dangerous drugs used in certain distant countries," "some of its Members seemed hardly inclined to fight with the same energy against the abuses and dangers resulting from the use of dangerous drugs in Europe," which nicely reflected the double standards that were being applied. Great Britain, India, and Switzerland took intermediate positions and recommended the withdrawal of the motion in its present form. The solution which was finally accepted was based on a Finnish proposal and was recorded in the following terms:

> ... considering the difficulties of principle and procedure which have been raised, the signatory delegations, while maintaining the principle of their motion, have decided to withdraw it provisionally, while reserving the right to submit it in another form.

A week later, a new proposal was submitted by Finland, Poland, and Sweden, supported by Belgium, Denmark, and Czechoslovakia, suggesting that an expert committee be convened to study those alcohol-related questions that were under the domain of the League. In September 1928 the Assembly passed this motion on to the Health Committee and the Economic Committee. The latter discussed the question of illicit traffic but considered it to be part of a larger problem. Although the intention behind the motion was thereby diluted, the committee did pass a resolution on 6 June 1930 which held that the flags of member states should not be used on vessels engaging in illicit traffic (Immonen, 1965).

However, the more crucial discussion was the one held in the Health Committee in October 1928. Here, much of the discussion was centered on the wording of the Assembly request, which read as follows:

> ... collect full statistical information regarding alcoholism, considered as a consequence of the abuse of alcohol, giving prominence, *inter alia,* according to the data available, to the deleterious effects of the bad quality of the alcohols consumed ....
> It is understood that this resolution does not refer to wine, beer or cider (A.72.1928).

The British representative expressed dissatisfaction with the exclusion of wine, beer, and cider, observing that a combination of whiskey and soda was no more powerful than these. The Polish delegate thought it impossible to deal only with some varieties of alcohol. However, the wine-producing countries were not interested in taking the matter further than was delimited by the resolution, and the ultimate decision was that the medical director should consult the three countries whose initiative this was, to ascertain their intentions. A further discussion was to take place after this piece of information had been secured (CH Minutes: 13th, 1928). No account was taken of communications sent by various organizations to the League secretary-general supporting the Finnish proposals, presumably because the document containing these (CH 762, 1928) was not made available before the decision was taken. These organizations were: The Latvian "Help the Children" Union at Riga; the National Union of Teachers, London; the National Council of Hungarian Women, Budapest; the Romanian Temperance Society, Bucharest; and the Scottish Temperance Alliance. There were also associations expressing disapproval, namely: the League for the Defence of Individual Liberty, Copenhagen; the Swedish "Abstinence without Prohibition" Association, Stockholm; and the "Arbeitsgemeinschaft der Gaerungsgewerbe," Berlin. The most thorough of the latter category of counterarguments was that of the Danish association, which rejected the formation of a committee of investigation, on grounds of fear that such a committee would be dominated by prohibitionist viewpoints.

It was not until October 1930 that the question was discussed by the Health Committee again. By that time the three countries which had recommended the inclusion of the alcohol question in the program of the League had clarified their position in writing to the medical director (CH 877, 1930). As may be expected, their responses were largely similar. In both the Finnish and Swedish replies proposals were made as to the kind of studies which might profitably be pursued and which would be of value to the health authorities of their respective countries; the Finnish response referred specifically to the relationship between alcohol and cirrhosis of the liver, alcoholism and tuberculosis, use of alcohol and pneumonia, alcoholism and mental diseases, alcoholism and venereal diseases, alcoholism and accidents, and alcoholism and crime.

The discussions in the Health Committee resulted in a limited program which entailed no extensive studies but provided for some services to the three countries concerned. Meager as this concession was, to the French it was still too much. Reservations were also expressed by the Belgian representative, Professor Bordet, who, while not opposing "the suggested procedure ... would urge that any enquiries into alcoholism should be conducted in great secrecy, for, if public opinion felt any doubt that an International Committee of Health Specialists thought that alcohol played no part in the various diseases mentioned, a certain degree of consternation might be caused." Nevertheless, the program was approved after assurances were made that it would not involve too much work. And, with the close of this meeting came the end of the concern of the Health Committee

with alcoholism. No plan was actually submitted to the League
Council for consideration.

Problems of Definition in WHO

In contrast to the League's disinclination to institute alcohol
programs, WHO, when it came into being, was quick to assume
responsibility for alcoholism. In WHO's first assembly in 1948,
alcoholism was recognized as being part of its mental health
work, and, in 1949, when the first Expert Committee on Mental
Health was convened, it dealt with, among a variety of problems,
that of alcoholism and drug addiction. The chairman of this
committee was Menninger of the U.S.; the secretary was G. R.
Hargreaves, chief of the Mental Health Unit, who was British (as
was the rapporteur). The committee held that studies on the
incidence and prevalence of the various types of addiction in
different countries were of high priority and stressed the complex
social, economic, and cultural factors involved. The committee
furthermore believed that:

> although there are many aspects common to the problem of both
> alcoholism and other forms of drug addiction, there are also
> significant differences, and they therefore strongly recommend
> the setting up of two separate specialist sub-committees—one on
> alcoholism and one on drug addiction.

As to the composition of these committees, it was thought that not
only psychiatrists "but also individuals capable of contributing
to the understanding of the social and cultural factors which play
a large role in the epidemiology of these phenomena" were
necessary. Finally, the committee expressed some doubt in regard
to Papaver somniferum (opium) and cannabis as to "whether
control measures alone can ultimately hold the problem in check"
and recommended that a program in preventive medicine be
undertaken.

These views coincided with those of Hargreaves, who was
deeply interested in the alcohol problem and who was to invite E.
M. Jellinek to come to WHO to work as a consultant. Jellinek
came to WHO as the erstwhile head of the world's leading
research institute on alcohol (the Yale Center for Alcohol
Studies), and what he brought to WHO was essentially the benefit

of the knowledge which had been accumulated by the institute. His years in WHO—1950 to 1955—marked a period of intense activity in the field of alcoholism; four expert committees were convened (WHO/EC MH, 1951; 1952; 1954; 1955) and a study group concentrating on statistics was held; international seminars were organized; recommendations on public health measures and treatment were formulated; methods for measuring the extent of the alcoholism problem were developed, and much work was done to clarify key terms and concepts. One may also include among the contributions the sponsoring of a film—*To Your Health*—which was awarded an international prize and which was mentioned with pride in a history of WHO—*The First Ten Years of the WHO* (1958)—with a note of regret that WHO's name was not mentioned in the film. (On the other hand, Jellinek's name was not mentioned in the history!)

We turn now to the work of the expert committees, much of which was concerned with the definition of concepts. The first committee on alcoholism which met in 1950 termed alcoholism a disease and a social problem and was of the opinion that public health authorities had been slow in recognizing the extent and the seriousness of the problem. The committee pointed to the draw-backs of the vague term "chronic alcoholism" and tentatively defined the term "alcohol addiction" as a special and extreme form of alcoholism. During its discussion of these terms the committee referred to another expert committee's report (WHO/EC DD, 1959) which had defined "addiction" at the request of the Commission on Narcotic Drugs.* A new subcommittee to deal with these definitions was recommended, and it is evident that this implied a wish to have a common basis for a joint discussion

* This definition was based on a paper by P. O. Wolff, head of the Drug Dependence Unit (WHO/HFD/19, 5 January 1950), in which he looked back to the 1925 and 1931 conventions which contained references to the "drug habit" and to products "capable of producing addiction" respectively. At the conference which adopted the latter treaty a technical subcommittee had found it impossible to arrive at a satisfactory definition of the term "habit-forming narcotic drug" and had therefore dropped it. Wolff, who participated in this conference, had argued against the use of the expression "habit-forming drugs" on the grounds that the concept of "habit" is widely used to describe behavior which has nothing to do with pharmacological effect. Accordingly the Expert Committee on Habit-forming Drugs was renamed the Expert Committee on Drugs Liable to Produce Addiction. It might also bear noting that in his paper Wolff very clearly underlined the difference between opiate, cocaine, and cannabis addiction.

of addiction to alcohol and other drugs. At its eighth session the executive board of WHO acknowledged the report of the committee as a basis for future action and supported its recommendations.

The question of definitions recurred in the next meeting (1951) on alcoholism which attempted to define alcoholism and "excessive drinking." The following year, the Expert Committee on Drugs Liable to Produce Addiction concluded that:

there are some drugs whose pharmacological action is intermediate in kind and degree between the two groups already delineated so that compulsive craving, dependence and addiction can develop in those individuals whose psychological make-up is the determining factor but pharmacological action plays a significant role. In some instances individual and sociological damage may develop, but since the incidence of the damage is not general, the type and degree of control of drugs of this group are better left at present to national consideration (WHO/EC DD, 1952).

The committee had evidently been thinking of alcohol and barbiturates, although this was not explicitly stated; the expert committees on alcoholism had come very close to regarding alcohol as an addiction-producing drug, and, as this did not at all fit in with the view of the Drug Dependence Unit of WHO or of the UN narcotics control bodies, some distinguishing marks had to be found to justify its exclusion from international control. The committee acknowledged that barbiturates had addiction potential yet did not see them as deserving control, whereas coca-chewing, which *was* an object of international control, was seen as coming "so closely to the characteristics of addiction . . . that it must be defined and treated as addiction, in spite of the occasional absence of some of its characteristics."

This position acquires more meaning when viewed against the conclusions of the Commission of Inquiry on the Coca Leaf, which had returned from Peru and Bolivia and reported their findings to the Commission on Narcotic Drugs (1950). Some of these findings had implicitly struck at the premises upon which international coca leaf control was based. In the Narcotics Commission the query was raised as to whether coca-leaf-chewing was an addiction, as opposed to an economic and social problem (CND: 6th, 1951). Wolff himself was both "surprised" by and disappointed with these conclusions, being in favor of stricter controls in this area (Wolff, 1952). In contriving to fit coca-leaf-chewing into their addiction model so as to vindicate its position in the international treaty system, the expert committee members were allowing considerations of control policy, as opposed to purely pharmacological ones, to enter into their scientific judgments. Moreover, the Commission of Inquiry had observed that coca-leaf-chewing in the Andes was intertwined with heavy alcohol use, which was as much of a "social, economic and criminological problem" as the chewing (Report of Inquiry, 1950:31), but this observation was entirely ignored.

The following two expert committees on alcoholism continued with the discussion of definitions, accepting the view that alcohol was somewhere between the addiction-producing and habit-forming drugs, but dwelling upon differences in addiction characteristics and how these related to the case of alcohol. The published report of the expert committee which met in 1954 did not cover some crucial points made in the material used at the meetings: in a background paper (WHO/Ment/58) Jellinek had touched upon the vested interests in alcohol and the need for research to incorporate consideration of this factor, but this was omitted in the final version; also left out were arguments for taking on problems of alcohol rather than the problem of alcoholism. There were references to some points contained in a working paper by Harris Isbell in which he challenged prevailing tendencies to exaggerate the differences between alcohol and morphine addiction (WHO/Ment/83); it was acknowledged that physical dependence on alcohol existed and that withdrawal symptoms were far more severe for alcohol than for opiates. Nevertheless, in the printed report, alcohol was still seen as occupying an intermediate position between habit-forming and addiction-producing drugs.

If conflict arose, as seems likely, out of the incompatible positions maintained by the various people involved, it probably lost its edge with the departure from WHO of Hargreaves and Jellinek in 1955 and of Wolff at around the same time. These changes in personnel meant a virtual cessation of interest in the alcohol question, and nearly ten years elapsed before it was renewed. Under Hargreaves's successor, E. E. Krapf, a study group on the treatment and care of drug addicts was convened

(WHO/MH, 1957). But hardly any additional activity was undertaken. At about the same time, Hans Halbach was appointed as chief of the Drug Dependence Unit. Halbach and Krapf informally agreed that alcoholism was a matter of mental health (Halbach, interview). As alcoholism had low priority, there was little risk of its featuring in discussions of drug addiction and control and of confronting the international control system with the inconsistencies of the classification scheme on which it rests.

It was not until 1966, after Krapf had been replaced by P. A. H. Baan as chief of the Mental Health unit that another alcoholism expert committee was convened. This one was particularly concerned with the combined approach towards alcohol and other drugs, a subject discussed in a paper prepared by Joel Fort in 1965 (PA/100/65). Fort was a consultant first to the Division of Narcotic Drugs and later to WHO, but he was too critical of the international drug policy, especially as regards cannabis, to remain for long in the organization, and on at least one occasion after he left (at the International Alcohol Congress in Melbourne, 1970), he leveled direct criticisms at the work of the international bureaucracy (Fort, 1970). However, general acceptance of the combined approach was slow in gaining ground, and five years passed before the responsibility for alcohol problems and "drug dependence" was given to the same unit. This move does not, however, guarantee increased activity in the field of alcoholism, and the outlook is that the other drugs will continue to receive much more attention and attract more programs and resources.

To illustrate further the attitude of WHO towards alcohol control, we will digress a little and recount the events leading up to the International Council on Alcohol and Addictions (ICAA) being accorded the status of a "nongovernmental organization" (NGO) in official relationship to WHO. In early 1947, R. Hercod, the director of this organization, suggested to WHO that alcohol should be included in its program, considering the size of the problem, its international character, and the need for education and research in the field. An application was lodged for his organization to be accredited to WHO as an NGO. WHO had difficulties in deciding on the application and negotiations took place between its staff members and Hercod. In November 1948, WHO postponed a decision until, it informed Hercod, "it disposes of further information on the present tendency of your

Bureau's activity." It added that "only questions of a medical order should justify an official collaboration" and considered it "desirable that the moral and emotional aspects of the problem of alcoholism should therefore no longer play the preponderant part in your programme" (letter from Gautier, 1948). Additional correspondence followed, and when the Bureau's own executive committee came to review the situation in September 1949, it decided to appoint a medical committee and publish the medical papers presented at a recent meeting in Locarno as separate proceedings (Minutes of the Executive Committee, 13-14.9.1949). This excursion into medical territory attests to an intense desire to qualify for WHO acceptance. In October 1949 Hercod completed a lengthy questionnaire required by WHO, but in March 1950 he was informed that WHO had postponed its decision. In May Hercod provided yet more documentation and had a meeting with WHO's assistant director-general, Bertrand, from which he emerged declaring that "while recognizing the social aspects of the alcohol problem, this appears to us to be above all a medical problem" in an attempt evidently to accommodate to the WHO view. In June 1950 the WHO executive board recognized that "the evolution . . . into a more scientific body was taking place" but postponed its decision once again. This led to a spate of correspondence between Hercod and Wolff, who had become head of the drug addiction section. In the exchange of letters Wolff pointed to some members of the Bureau's medical committee as being not entirely to WHO's satisfaction. Although new information was transmitted yet again and adjustments were made to the composition of the medical committee (for instance, in a letter from Hercod to Wolff on 7 November 1950), no commitment on the part of WHO was forthcoming. The question was raised again in 1960 and this time the rejection was on the grounds that the organization was not sufficiently scientific. It was not until 1968, after a new application had been lodged, that a wish entertained from twenty years back was fulfilled, and the ICAA became a nongovernmental organization under WHO.

The foregoing history of frustration is to be compared with that of the International Federation of Pharmaceutical Manufacturers Associations (IFPMA), founded in 1968 and accorded NGO status in January 1971. There had been no change in WHO qualifications for admission; yet it is ironic that IFPMA, which is essentially a lobby for drug industry interests, should be so readily accepted into the system, while a procontrol candidate was barred. The standing committee on NGOs, at its meeting on 26 January 1971, had originally recommended that a decision on the IFPMA application be postponed because the organization was "still in a formative stage and should increase its international character" (WHO Off. Rec. 189 Annex 14). However, at a meeting of the WHO executive board the argument was advanced by some members that, in view of the executive board's recent decision to stimulate pharmaceutical industry in developing countries, relations with international pharmaceutical associations should be encouraged. Halter, the Belgian chairman of the committee referred to it as a "special case, for which the Standing Committee had assessed all possible factors and merely suggested postponing its admission." Afterwards, the board decided in favor of admitting IFPMA as an NGO (EB 47 SR 17: 275).

All that we have discussed so far does not, however, constitute the entire involvement of the UN system in alcohol control. An interesting form of drug control is embodied in the ILO Convention No. 95 on the Protection of Wages.* Article 4 of this convention stipulates that "the payment of wages in the form of liquor of high alcoholic content or of noxious drugs shall not be permitted in any circumstances"; article 13 states that "payment of wages in taverns or other similar establishments ... shall be prohibited except in the case of persons employed therein". The text of the convention as drafted by the ILO did not initially contain the provision relating to alcohol and noxious drugs, and the addition in the final text stemmed from an initiative of the workers' members who, despite opposition from the employers' members, secured this amendment to the original text (ILO Conference: 32nd, 1949, Report and Proceedings). Earlier ILO conferences had also dealt with this question: the Convention concerning Social Policy in Non-Metropolitan Territories (1947), for instance, contains a number of provisions for the protection of wages including one which reads as follows:

---

* Date of coming into force: 24 September 1952. According to Landy (1966), it had fifty-seven ratifications and twenty-nine declarations.

The substitution of alcohol or other spirituous beverages for all or any part of wages for services performed by the worker shall be prohibited;

Payment of wages shall not be made in taverns or stores, except in the case of workers employed therein (article 15, pars. 4&5).

SUMMARY

1. During the first four decades of the twentieth century, an international agreement for alcohol control existed for the African region. The effects of this control have not been systematically evaluated.
2. Trials to interest the League of Nations in international control of alcohol did not attract significant support. They were largely blocked by the resistance of wine-growing countries and the ideological conflict between the prohibitionists and the anti-prohibitionists. International cooperation was even lacking in controlling the illegal trafficking in alcohol: the United States worked on a bilateral basis and while an agreement was reached in the Baltic Sea area this was not extended with League support.
3. While action on alcohol problems was part of WHO's program from its inception, activity in this area, except for Jellinek's period, has been modest indeed.
4. The exclusion of alcohol from international control highlights the inconsistencies of drug classification by the WHO expert committee.
5. An example of drug control measures being combined with other instruments of social policy on an international level is afforded by the ILO Convention on the Protection of Wages.

13   Cannabis: International Diffusion of National Policy

> ... the drug (marihuana) is adhering to its old world tradition of murder, assault, rape, physical demoralization and mental breakdown. ... Bureau records prove that its use is associated with insanity and crime. Therefore, from the standpoint of police work, it is a more dangerous drug than heroin or cocaine.
>
> H. J. Anslinger, "Enforcement of the Narcotic Drug Laws in the USA" (paper communicated to the League of Nations Advisory Opium Committee, 14 May 1938)

Towards International Control

Cannabis (or Indian hemp, as it was generally referred to earlier) is probably the most widely discussed drug among those under control. Few other subjects have called forth so many contradictory viewpoints, all claiming to have been derived from scientific evidence. The purpose of this chapter is not to reiterate what is known about cannabis or to tell the truth about this drug; rather, it is to trace how cannabis came to be subjected to similar international controls as opium, heroin, and cocaine, to see what information was used as evidence of its fitness for control, and to throw light on the assumptions underlying the arguments which have been advanced to bring this about.

The first move to bring cannabis under international control was made by the Italian government, which raised the question during the preparations for the Hague Conference in 1911. Lowes (1966: 173) connects this with the fact that, after its war with Turkey, Italy became a colonial ruler in a part of Africa (Tripolitania and Cyrenaica) which had a problem with cannabis; Italian territory was used as a collection and storage center for smuggling into other territories (Taylor, 1969: 87-88).

At the Hague Conference, little interest was evoked by the cannabis question. Italy participated only at the first day's session (Musto, 1973: 51). Nevertheless, a cursory discussion of the subject resulted in the adoption of a resolution which reads as follows:

The Conference considers it desirable to study the question of Indian hemp from the statistical and scientific point of view, with the object of regulating its abuses, should the necessity thereof be felt, by international legislation or by an international agreement.

After the conference, efforts were concentrated on having the Hague Convention ratified and hardly any attention was paid to the cannabis question until the government of the Union of South Africa proposed to the Advisory Opium Committee in 1923 that "the whole or any portion of the plants cannabis indica or cannabis sativa" be included in the list of habit-forming drugs. In August 1924, the Advisory Committee decided on the suggestion of the British delegation to ask governments for information on the production, use, and traffic in cannabis. In November 1924, a circular letter was accordingly forwarded to all governments. However, before answers had been received and discussed, the topic was introduced at the Second Opium Conference of 1924–25 by Egypt, in spite of the fact that the question was not on the agenda. Previously prepared memoranda accompanied the stirring speeches made by the Egyptian delegation demanding the immediate inclusion of cannabis in the international drug control scheme. A description of hashish, the nature of "hashishism," and the effects of hashish formed the basis for this proposition; the illicit use of hashish was, moreover, said to be the principal cause of most of the cases of insanity in Egypt. The chief Egyptian delegate, El Guindy, was an able speaker and imparted much sense of urgency in his statements; he claimed that hashish was imported illegally from abroad and that Egypt itself had already prohibited cultivation in 1884; that, furthermore, this question concerned many countries due to the risk of hashish replacing other drugs. After two subcommittees had worked on the question, the conference agreed to include cannabis in the Geneva Convention of 1925 under the following regime:

1. ... the Contracting Parties undertake:

(a) To prohibit the export of the resin obtained from Indian hemp and the ordinary preparation of which the resin forms the base (such as hashish, esrar, chiras, djamba) to countries which have prohibited their use, and, in cases where export is permitted, to require the production of a special import certificate issued by the Government of the importing country, stating that the importation is approved for the purposes specified in the certificate and that the resin or preparation will not be re-exported;

(b) Before issuing an export authorization under Article 13 of the present Convention, in respect of Indian hemp, to require the production of a special import certificate issued by the Government of the importing country and stating that the importation is approved and is required exclusively for medical or scientific purposes.

2. The Contracting Parties shall exercise an effective control of such a nature as to prevent the illicit international traffic in Indian hemp and especially in the resin.

Although the control regime was not as strong as Egypt had wished, it nevertheless constituted a breach in the resistance of the opposition, represented primarily by Britain and India. The warnings of Malcolm Delevingne, the British delegate, were largely unheeded; he had expressed real concern over taking decisions, on a matter which was yet "in an unprepared state." It was indeed a remarkable instance of a decision being taken to place a drug under international legal control without there having been any documentation on the need of control, except from one country, Egypt, and without its being even on the agenda of the conference. But as Stephen Porter, the American delegate, put it: "Happily, as I understand it, no question of revenue is involved. That fact ought to make the decision easier."

In August 1925, when the Advisory Committee came to inspect the replies from governments concerning cannabis (OC 291), the committee was in effect discussing material which was already obsolete. Only twenty-four governments out of sixty replied. The majority had found no abuse of cannabis, but some considered cannabis a dangerous drug and remarked on its inclusion in their national legislation. Only a few countries expressed an opinion on the necessity for international control. It is probable that some governments, such as Egypt, did not answer in view of the planned intervention at the Geneva Conference.

Interest in the Advisory Committee

The inclusion of cannabis (or rather the resin of Indian hemp) in the Geneva Convention did not lead to immediate interest in research or in attempts to provide proper considerations for the framing of control policies. In fact, before 1933, little activity was undertaken, as far as can be discerned from the public records. Of course, details of the problem in Egypt were communicated to the Advisory Committee—for instance, in a letter of June 1929 in which the Egyptian government described its own activities in fighting hashish and in which it accused Syria of having super-seded Greece as the main source of illicit hashish in Egypt. The annual production of Syria was calculated at about 30,000 to 40,000 kg, about 90 percent of which was allegedly sent to Egypt and about 10 percent to the U.S. The French also provided information on activities to control hashish, giving statistics of large-scale crop destruction (O.C. 1503). However, these communications did not evoke much interest from the Advisory Committee.

Egypt tried other ways to capture interest in hashish. It brought to the attention of the Health Committee five preparations of Indian hemp to which the Geneva Convention was not applicable, but which, according to the Egyptian view, were liable to similar abuse as the variety of cannabis covered by the convention. At its twentieth session in 1933, the Health Committee avoided taking any clear stand but merely raised two problems: a medical one relating to the danger of the preparations and a legal one as to whether the convention could be made to cover preparations not intended to be included (CH 1127). The question was reexamined two years later, and on this occasion the Health Committee stated that preparations made from tinctures and extracts of Indian hemp might lead to similar abuses and might produce ill-effects similar to the variety of cannabis under the control of the 1925 convention (CH 1166). Meanwhile, the Advisory Committee was evincing more and more attention to cannabis; in its 1933 annual report the Committee observed that:

A smuggling trade in cigarettes containing Indian hemp ("marijuana" cigarettes) appears to have sprung up between the USA, where it grows as a wild plant freely, and Canada. It may well be that, as the control over the opium and coca derivatives makes it more and more difficult to obtain them, recourse will be increasingly had to Indian hemp for addiction purposes, and it is important that the trade in Indian hemp and its products should be closely watched.

Under apparent pressure from Egypt, but especially from the U.S. and Canada (Renborg, 1947: 216), the Advisory Committee began to pay increasing attention to cannabis. And in its eighteenth session in 1934 it made this explicit:

During its last few sessions, the Committee had already decided to devote particular attention to this question in view of the increase in addiction to Indian hemp in certain countries and the fear that, as the increasingly strict control of other narcotic drugs renders the acquisition of these products more difficult, addicts were resorting to an increasing extent to Indian hemp in order to gratify their vice: hence the necessity of keeping the trade in this plant and its products under close supervision.

In consequence, the secretariat was urged to report on cannabis to the next session. As to the content of this report, Carnoy, the Belgian delegate, indicated the kind of question he would like answered. He

wondered whether the committee ought to indicate the points to be studied, for instance:
(a) were the seeds innocuous?
(b) could substitutes be found for the use of cannabis indica in medical practice?
(c) was the use of cannabis indica, as permitted in Tunisia, to be regarded as a use of narcotic drugs or merely the use of a stimulant like coca-kola? (OAC Minutes, 1933: 47).

Nevertheless, the information to be given by the secretariat was not specified. However, another important decision was made at the same session: a new assessor—a Belgian pharmacologist, Dr. de Myttenaere—was proposed by Carnoy and elected.* His appointment represented a departure from the customary basis for choosing assessors, and this was acceptable because police expertise was already sufficiently represented on the Committee (by the Egyptian representative, Russell Pascha, and the Canadian, Colonel Sharman) (OAC Minutes, 1933: 76). Dr. de Myttenaere was to become a key researcher into the question of

---

* Assessors were experts with special technical knowledge appointed by the League Council to assist the Advisory Committee.

cannabis in the 1930s and a significant contributor to the knowledge which came to be acquired by the international organs on this subject.

At the following session of the Committee, the secretariat, as requested, presented the information it had compiled in a document entitled "Preliminary note on the chief aspects of the problem of Indian hemp and the laws regulating thereto in force in certain countries" (O.C. 1542, 23 May 1934).

As far as we know, this was the first systematic review of the subject to be prepared for consideration by the formulators of international drug control; this happened nine years after cannabis was placed under control in an international convention, twenty-two years after the Hague Conference resolved to study this question, and shortly before the Health Committee took the decision referred to earlier.

The document is, therefore, of considerable interest. The first part contained an outline of the general aspects of the question. The diversity of cannabis usage in different areas of the world was reviewed. The Geneva Convention was analyzed and attention was called to the fact that this convention actually covered only medicinal preparations of cannabis, not the raw materials. The latter part discussed cannabis in different countries and the various degrees of control to which it was subjected, such as prohibition of cultivation in Egypt and more or less unrestrained large-scale cultivation in Thailand and India.

However, discussions on the basis of this document were postponed in view of the obvious need for more information, and at the following session (the nineteenth, in 1934), the Advisory Committee was supplied with a large set of additional documents. These certainly provided a great deal of new information but there was, in contrast to the earlier document (O.C. 1542), a preponderance of poorly substantiated statements on the negative effects of cannabis, not only in the reports from France (on Syria and the Lebanon), the U.S., and Egypt, but also in the two documents prepared by the secretariat. One of the secretariat documents (O.C. 1542 of 4 July 1934), dated only one month after the closing of the last session, began with an informative discussion of all the different types of cannabis and concluded by saying, "Lastly it has been found, especially in Egypt, Siam and

USA that the effects of addiction to Indian hemp on the physical health and morale of the race may be even more disastrous than those of opium and other drugs (i.e., in inducing insanity and the development of criminal propensities)." The sources for the document were given: Dardanne (1924), Bouquet (1925), and Levin (1928). It will be seen that the evidence on which this conclusion rested was extremely slender. No attention was paid, for instance, to a source like the Indian Hemp Commission of 1894, and the tendency to overlook the findings of this important inquiry was apparent in later discussions as well.*

Among the other documents the most interesting was the one contributed by the U.S., because this contained the beginnings of a standpoint which was to crystallize later into the international position on cannabis. It attested to "the terrible effects of this form of drug addiction on criminality," on the basis, primarily, of a pamphlet entitled "The Marihuana Menace" by Dr. Forsier of New Orleans, a poor document from a scientific point of view, even when judged by the standards of the time. One other main reference was to a Dr. Yung of the U.S. who was said to have treated more than seven thousand addicts of various types and to have observed a shift in the pattern of addiction; while, earlier, addiction to opiates and cocaine predominated, barbiturates and marihuana had now come to assume, in order of importance, first and second place respectively. Yung's opinion was that marihuana should be controlled under the Harrison Act (the U.S. Federal law on narcotics). The report judged the number of people using cannabis in the world to be around 200 million, but how it arrived at this figure is unclear. Although Dr. Yung considered barbiturates a greater problem than cannabis, his paper was cited to support the contention that marihuana was the drug to be alarmed about and to bring under stringent control (O.C. 1542 [c] and addendum).

During the discussion of these documents by the committee, the Indian representative pointed out that the use of cannabis was associated with social and religious customs. The delegates of Poland and Switzerland said that there was "no thorough study

* A recent review sees the report of this commission as a "document unique in the history of cannabis" and commends it for the "thoroughness and rationality applied to the analysis of the data" (Kalant, 1972).

available of Indian hemp, particularly from the medical and scientific standpoint." A subcommittee was thus appointed

to study the whole problem of Indian hemp. The Sub-Committee might appeal in the course of its investigations for the co-operation of experts, doctors, and others who are duly qualified in the matter of Indian hemp and who have had local experience either in Africa or in Asia or in America. By way of preparation for the work on the Sub-Committee, the Committee requested the Secretariat on the proposal of the Swiss delegate to prepare a bibliography of all the literature relating to Indian hemp, and, in the probable event of no complete and authoritative work on the question being available, to consider the possibility of publishing, at some future date, a memorandum on the Indian hemp problem bringing up to date the existing information on the subject, particularly from the medical and scientific standpoint.

The subcommittee was composed of representatives from Canada, Egypt, France, Great Britain, India, Mexico, Netherlands, Poland, Spain, and the U.S., and also included the recently nominated assessor, de Myttenaere. Later Siam and Turkey became members of the subcommittee.

The Work of the Subcommittee

Working from 1935 to 1939, the subcommittee undertook research, produced reports, discussed practical problems of policy, and was to all intents and purposes a major factor in the evolution of the international policy on cannabis.

The subcommittee as such did not meet more than eleven times during this period; all these meetings were held during the session of the Advisory Committee. From 1935 to 1937 only four meetings were held. Fuller of the U.S. was elected chairman of the subcommittee and, on his resignation, was succeeded by Nind, the Indian delegate. Representatives of the other countries varied from year to year, and members of the Advisory Committee outside the subcommittee often participated in the discussions.

But it is clear that it was de Myttenaere and experts invited to collaborate with the subcommittee who in fact carried the bulk of the work load. The experts were appointed at the subcommittee's first meeting on 29 May 1935. They were:

Colonel A. G. Biggam, former professor of clinical medicine (Cairo), assistant professor of tropical medicine, London (proposed by Egypt);

Dr. Walter L. Treadway, assistant surgeon-general of the Public Health Service, U.S. (proposed by the U.S.);

Dr. J. Bouquet, chemist to Tunis hospitals and inspector of pharmacies; Colonel Martin, director of Syrian Health Service; and Dr. Charnot, head of Biological Chemistry and Toxicology, Rabat (proposed by France);

Professor J. Rodhain, director of the Prince Leopold Institute of Tropical Medicine, Antwerp (proposed by Dr. de Myttenaere).

Although all six were expected to collaborate with the secretariat and especially with de Myttenaere, it became evident by 1937 that Biggam, Martin, and Rodhain did not, in fact, participate in the work and that the experiments planned by Charnot were never actually carried out (O.C. 1542[u]). Thus, only Treadway and Bouquet were truly working, the former as a channel for the input from those working in the U.S. on the subject. Bouquet, on the other hand, made a sizeable contribution, not only by communicating a large number of papers to the subcommittee but also through his attendance of its meetings in 1938 and 1939. Although additional experts were brought in, their contributions were insignificant. It will be remembered that, in addition to Treadway and Bouquet, there was de Myttenaere, whose contribution to the subcommittee's work was probably as substantial. A proposal he made to have a meeting of experts was turned down by the chairman, Fuller, on the grounds that "serious practical difficulties" were involved: the experts were asked instead to exchange their views in writing (Minutes, Subcommittee, 7 June 1937).

The output of the subcommittee was substantial; altogether, fifty-four League of Nations documents on cannabis were produced (bibliography on cannabis, E/CN.7/479). A breakdown of these reports by their origin gives the following distribution:

by Bouquet	14
by de Myttenaere	9
by researchers in the U.S.	4
by other researchers	6
by the secretariat	10
on the cannabis situation in the U.S.	9
on cannabis in other countries	2
TOTAL	54*

* In some instances a report was merely an addendum to an earlier report. The

The tabulation shows that Bouquet and de Myttenaere contributed greatly to the data base which was being built up so that the
Advisory Committee could reach a decision on cannabis. The
proportion of data from or about the U.S. was comparatively large,
and while Bouquet provided some data on Africa, there was no
coverage of India or other parts of Asia. The American material,
expressing strong views on the subject, was largely communicated
by Harry Anslinger.

As to the contents of this work, they were to revolve around a
number of questions which the subcommittee had outlined to the
experts concerned, including:

—nomenclature
—adequacy of text in the 1925 Convention
—addiction, particularly in Africa
—the habit-forming capacity
—existence of withdrawal symptoms

The secretariat and de Myttenaere prepared a questionnaire to
be communicated to the experts (O.C 1542 [j], 16 January 1936).
The questions covered: the adequacy of the Beam reaction test in
determining the presence of cannabis resin; what was to be covered
by the concept of Indian hemp; whether there was only one or
several species of cannabis; causes of abuse; therapeutics and
treatment. To the director of the Opium Traffic Section, this
program represented a new field of activity for the Advisory
Committee "both in respect of chemical and medical research and
legislative provisions" (O.C. 1542 [k], 15 May 1936).

For the subcommittee's second meeting in 1936, de Myttenaere
tried to broach some broader questions in his note (O.C. 1542
[m]) by asking:

1. Should any person possessing Cannabis and its preparations be
punished, if the latter are not active?

2. As long as the effects of hemp and its preparations more or less
resemble those of alcohol, why should they be prohibited while
alcohol remains free, particularly in Mohammedan countries?

3. Is it possible that the stimulating and sedative action and the

---

Secretariat reports included some by the subcommittee and the so-called "Notes
by the Secretary General." There was much redundancy in this reporting. Some
documents of minor importance are not included here.

curious hallucinations in judging time and space are due to the same active principle, or that each of these disturbances is due to a different active principle?

One cannot tell from the minutes how these questions were handled, but it seems that the answers to them had to await further material.

Bouquet's answer to the questionnaire (O.C. 1542 [O and O Add.] of February and May 1937) was, together with de Myttenaere's work on the Beam reaction test, of prime importance. Bouquet contended that there was "only one species of hemp (C. sativa), of which there are several varieties," and based on this premise examined in great detail the relation which the different varieties of cannabis bore to the definition of Cannabis indica in the 1925 Convention.

His discussion of the situation in North Africa had also much of interest to offer and was considerably more comprehensive than earlier reports. He noted, for instance, the difference between urban and rural areas and said that the "countryside is far less affected by cannabis-addiction than towns and villages" (p.26). In the latter, "tea-addiction is the most widespread evil." In discussing causes of cannabis addiction, he pointed to three factors: "immemorial custom; the indolent character of Moslems; and the inconceivable family life" With regard to the effects of cannabis he described them as being experienced in the following stages:

(a) intense mental well-being accompanied by motor excitation
(b) mental confusion accompanied by illusions and hallucinations
(c) oneiric ecstacy
(d) depression and sleep.

Of hashish users, he had this to say:

Many hashish addicts never marry, but live as old bachelors between their pipe and their cooking-pot. Their tastes as a whole tend towards a feminine attitude in harmony with their inverted temperament (p. 25).

As far as control measures were concerned, the Tunisian monopoly system under which a cannabis product named Takrouri was sold (in 1934, sales amounted to 7,946 kg) was seen to be instrumental in reducing both the illegal traffic in, and the consumption of, hemp. However, the lower strata of the population had taken to habitual drinking of wine and other alcoholic beverages, and these persons were for the most part former "hemp-addicts." "White drugs" (heroin and cocaine) held a stronger attraction than hemp, Takrouri not being "sufficiently strong to satisfy heroin and cocaine addicts." In regard to the use of cannabis for medical purposes, Bouquet considered that "therapeutics would not lose much if it were removed from the list of medicines."

This report seemed to have captured the interest of the subcommittee because at its meeting in 1937 an invitation was extended to Bouquet to participate in the 1938 meeting. To the meeting of 1937, however, a large amount of material from the U.S. was communicated. This material pointed out that the definition of hemp in the 1925 Convention was not sufficiently inclusive, in contrast to the definition in the U.S. Marihuana Tax Act adopted by Congress in 1937, which appeared to be much broader. Anslinger reentered the picture, laying heavy stress once again upon the relationship between crime and marihuana—"there have been thirty cases of violent crime in the USA in 1936 which were directly traceable to the use of cannabis" (Minutes, subcommittee, 2 June 1937). The link between marihuana use and insanity was forged, and a paper by Wassenberg of the Health Section, which attested to this link, was communicated (Minutes, subcommittee, 7 June 1937):

the state of intoxication normally induced by Indian Hemp may, as the result of habitual abuse, particularly in the case of persons predisposed, develop into a genuine and clearly defined state of insanity of longer or shorter duration.

The period between 1937 and 1938 was marked by further data-gathering. Identifiable in some of the documents submitted at the time was the official standpoint of the U.S. government on cannabis. The adoption of the Marihuana Tax Act had reinforced its wish to influence international controls also, being now

in a better position to take a leading place in the international movement against cannabis, as it already has in the war against other dangerous drugs (O.C. 1733).

To marshal support for the U.S. policy, materials like Merrill's "Marihuana, the New Dangerous Drug"; Schicks's "Marihuana, Depraver of Youth"; and papers by Anslinger himself were communicated as evidence for the belief that marihuana is

the worst of all narcotics—far worse than morphine or cocaine; under its influence men become beasts (O.C. 1734).

The theme underlying all these documents was the alleged association between crime, insanity, and cannabis. On the basis of these documents and the Stringaris publication, *Hachice* of 1937, the theory that cannabis use might lead to heroin addiction was put forward—a theory which was going to play an important role in subsequent discussions.

In contrast to the views expressed in these papers, Bouquet insisted that the association between violence and cannabis did not occur in Africa, and it will be remembered that earlier he had attributed the use of heroin in Tunisia to the control of cannabis, a contrary hypothesis to that of the U.S. It was again Bouquet who prepared the most important paper of all, that entitled "Present State of Documentation Concerning Cannabis and the Problems to Which It Gives Rise" (O.C. Cannabis 3, 12 April 1939). The first part of the document, which contained 104 pages, was structured as follows: a historical study, a botanical study, tests for identification of cannabis, a summary of chemical investigations, and cases of cannabis intoxication. For our purposes, however, the latter sections are of more interest. For example, here Bouquet distinguished between different reasons for taking hashish:

   —as an exceptional supplement to food (comparable to tea, coffee . . .)
   —as a stimulant (similar to opium)
   —for politico-religious reasons (Vedas)
   —for perverse purposes (rape and murder, as reported in the U.S.).

Equally interesting are the views he expressed on control matters:

Dr. J. Bouquet is convinced that if measures of absolute prohibition had been taken twelve or fifteen years ago excellent results would have been achieved and the problem would no longer be so acute. He thinks, however, that at the present time total suppression (at least in countries where the consumption of hemp is an old-standing habit) would result in an increase in addiction to manufactured drugs, which are much more dangerous . . . (p. 93).

He went on to advocate "gradual repression" of use, imprisonment of native traffickers, and harshness towards those who were

simultaneously addicts and traffickers. He discussed how different control measures could have different effects depending on the
subgroup to which they were directed. He suggested a definition
of Indian hemp which he discussed in relation to that in the
relevant treaty text and which he attempted to align with the one
adopted by the U.S. Marihuana Tax Act (p. 101). The additional
control measures he suggested included restricted authorization,
progressive raising of retail prices, and the exclusive sale of drugs
with a resin content not exceeding a fixed percentage.

A shorter version of Bouquet's document was incorporated in a
secretariat paper submitted for discussion to the subcommittee
(O.C. Cannabis 7). This paper identified the problems for which
solutions had been found and those for which they had not.

The first problem was to ascertain which plants gave rise to
addiction. Only one species was thought to have addiction
potential, and the way to safeguard the rest was "to allow
cultivation with a view to obtaining seed for industrial purposes in
temperate districts only, where scarcely any resin is produced."

The second problem concerned the physical identification of
cannabis and here too a solution could be found: tests existed.

The determination of the resin content of hemp, which constituted a third problem item, had to await further research.
Similarly, the determination of the active principle of cannabis was
contingent upon the results of ongoing research.

The fifth problem was addiction. Here the subcommittee was to
undertake large-scale inquiries in order to establish the as yet
"uncertain causes of cannabis addiction." These were to be
supplemented with studies on "cannabism," insanity, and crime.
In this connection, alternative means of combating addiction, such
as prohibition versus supervision of use, for instance, were
discussed. Finally, there was a question of changing the existing
legislation governing cannabis, but no clear lines emerged from the
handling of this topic.

At its last meeting in May 1939, the subcommittee adopted a
report to the Advisory Committee which reiterated many of these
points. Perhaps the most interesting observation was that made on
the substitution of heroin for cannabis, a phenomenon reported
from North Africa, Egypt, and Turkey, and expressed as follows:

Heroin, and even opium, appear to have partly ousted hashish in the Mediterranean area, and this process seems to be continuing to an alarming extent. The Sub-Committee lacks precise information, however, as to whether the substitution is due to an inadequate supply of cannabis or whether heroin-addiction is gaining ground as a result of a ready supply of the drug and the intensive propaganda put out by traffickers, the two phenomena not being directly connected. Though there may be a danger of another and perhaps a worse drug being substituted for cannabis, the Sub-Committee does not consider that this constitutes any reason for relaxing the campaign against cannabis; rather, it con-stitutes a potent reason for combating all forms of drug addiction (O.C. 1763:8).

The meeting concluded that further studies should be undertaken. A new questionnaire, discussed by the meeting, was elaborated by Bouquet in a document produced after a further meeting (O.C./ Cannabis 10 [1]) in December 1939. This, together with another of Bouquet's papers (this time on the absence of intoxicating power in cannabis seeds) (O.C./Cannabis 14), marked the end of the work of the subcommittee on cannabis.

The Road to Prohibition

The process just described had led to the accumulation, by the end of the 1930s, of a rich store of information on cannabis. Yet more was necessary before this could be translated into an international control policy on cannabis, and quite clearly the opinions on this matter were by no means in full agreement.

While the Narcotics Commission did not, when it met for the first time in 1946, appoint a subcommittee on the cannabis question, it did in other respects follow the pattern which its predecessor had set in the handling of this subject. The debate on cannabis at this first meeting signaled future disagreement: on the one hand

some medical opinion in the United States and Mexico had been advanced that marihuana did not offer any real danger, and had little influence on criminal behaviour (CND:1st, 1946).

And the Mexican representative wondered if too many restrictions on the use of marihuana would not result in its replacement by alcohol, which might have worse results. The delegate from India thought that Indians were moderate in their use of ganja and bhang. On the other hand, the U.S. representative, Anslinger, did not share this view and quoted a number of concrete examples, proving the relationship between the use of marihuana and crime. He considered the recent report of certain United States physicians on the subject to have been extremely dangerous.

The report referred to, it seems, was the La Guardia report of 1944.

A secretariat paper (E/CN. 7/W 37) provided the background material to a resumption of the discussion in 1948. It was largely a summary of many of the studies done by the subcommittee in the thirties; noticeably missing from the sixteen U.S. references out of a total of twenty-six was any mention of the La Guardia report. The point was made, however, and with some force, that the United States Pharmacopoeia had dropped cannabis entirely. The Permanent Central Board, too, was of the opinion that (PCB, 1947):

the situation is one which requires drastic international action. The matter should be taken in hand at the earliest possible moment.

Work was soon underway to draw up the Single Convention, and the committee assigned this task found itself having to tackle the problem of cannabis. The fact of the industrial usefulness of hemp created difficulties for the prohibitory legislation which was being urged in the dominant quarters. Nevertheless, the complete prohibition of the cultivation of cannabis sativa for its resin was still thought feasible (E/CN.7/AC.3/1).

Support for the prohibitionist standpoint was elicited from WHO, whose Expert Committee on Drugs Liable to Produce Addiction declared that "cannabis preparations are practically obsolete. So far as it can see, there is no justification for the medical use of cannabis preparations" (WHO/EC DD, 1952:11). Evidence was not presented to substantiate this verdict. The expert committee's opinion coincided with that of its secretary, P. O. Wolff, who was the head of the section dealing with drug addiction in WHO and whose own publications on cannabis reveal the kind of views he entertained. The English edition of one of these contained a forward by Anslinger (Wolff, 1949) and typically abetted the earlier claims and arguments of the U.S. government during the Advisory Committee days, such as the estimate that there were 200 million cannabis addicts in the world, and the polemics leveled against the La Guardia committee. Marihuana "has been clearly associated since the most remote time with insanity, with crime, with violence and with brutality," Wolff wrote (p. 52). And as far as the expert committee's verdict is concerned, this too was echoed in Wolff's statement that "there is no medical indication whatsoever that will justify its use in the present day" (p. 2).

Reference was made to the WHO opinion in a secretariat paper addressed to the Commission meeting in 1953 (E/CN.7/256). The paper mentioned the fact that two alternative drafts of the Single Convention, each of which treated cannabis differently, were being considered. The problems which would be encountered in formulating cannabis control were enumerated: its alleged medical value, the social acceptance of cannabis use, the industrial use of hemp, the practical difficulties of controlling remote areas, and the risk of illicit traffic. In view of these difficulties a study program was proposed geared to describing the factual situation and to evaluating existing control regimes. The cooperation of FAO and WHO was also to be sought. The Commission approved of these studies. The importance of WHO's contribution was stressed, and a study on the physical and mental effects requested. Wolff, representing WHO, indicated that such a study could be carried out. He also referred to a study done in South Africa. In a letter to the chairman of the committee, Wolff made clear his feelings:

I am, of course, satisfied that in all the main questions your committee could confirm the view I have expressed. . . . I have just returned from New York, where I attended the session [of the Commission]. . . . At the request of the US delegate, I was pleased to refer at length to the main points of your report (Letter dated 23 April 1953 from Wolff to Schalkwijk).

The decision reached in 1953 may be interpreted as an acknowledgment of the difficulty of taking a stand without adequate knowledge. However, two years later the Commission was ready to make a provisional decision to include cannabis in schedule IV of the proposed Single Convention; in other words, to adopt a line of prohibition. While the formal decision was taken later, little material of substance was submitted after 1955 and, despite much talk, no one seriously challenged this position. We may therefore consider 1954 and 1955 as the crucial years for the ultimate decision and review in more detail the nature of the material submitted to the Commission.

To the Commision meeting in 1954 little new material was

communicated. Some data on the studies were reported and the cooperation with South Africa was stressed (E/CN.7/276). WHO's view on the obsolescence of the therapeutic use of cannabis was reiterated. At the Commission meeting in 1955, however, a great deal of material was offered. This material fell into the following categories:

—information from some countries forming part of the study program assigned to the secretariat

—an FAO report

—a report by Wolff

—proposals on the control regimes to be adopted.

As far as the reports on countries were concerned, only some countries in south Africa were covered (E/CN.7/286 and addenda 1–7). The contents of these studies supported the view that strict controls were needed. Whatever one might think of their quality, these studies covered only a small part of the world. Studies of other regions were reported to the Commission through the years 1955–60 (addenda 8–29 of the above document) but they had no perceptible influence on decisions. The secretariat did not undertake a comprehensive analysis of the information obtained from the various countries, and it seems unlikely that such information, uncollated as it was, formed the basis for the final decision on the type of control which was to be applied.

FAO contributed an exposition of "the possibility of replacing hemp fibre and hemp seed by other crops of similar industrial value or of developing narcotic-free strains of the cannabis plant" (E/CN. 7/297, 63 pp.) which set forth the arguments for and against the two ways of satisfying the need for control on the one hand, and the requirements of the hemp industry on the other. While both ways were considered possible, the second alternative was judged the easier of the two. Nevertheless, it would require considerable effort, and an element of uncertainty remained about the whole operation.

The report on "The Physical and Mental Effects of Cannabis" was prepared by Wolff (E/CN.7/L91, 35 pp.) and was dated 17 March 1955. It was transmitted to the Commission by the secretariat (that is, the Division) in a letter dated 6 April 1955 which stated that "WHO agreed to make the study." It appeared under the name of Wolff and, although it may be found in WHO's files (APD 56), it was not supposed to represent WHO's official standpoint. It certainly had not been endorsed by the relevant expert committee and was not mentioned in the latter's reports. In fact Wolff's successor, Halbach, referred to the report in a letter "as a working paper for the WHO Secretariat and made available for distribution by the WHO Secretariat" (Letter from Halbach, 27 October 1965 to Bureau of Narcotics). However, at the Commission meeting, this document was clearly regarded as embodying the WHO position. As to the contents, Wolff himself asserted that his earlier position was vindicated (Wolff, 1949). The literature cited was highly selective and the work of the League in the 1930s was barely acknowledged, although there was a reference to Bouquet's observation of the differences between the U.S. and Africa as far as correlation between crime and cannabis use was concerned. The conclusions were predictable:

It is important to realise that not only is marihuana smoking *per se* a danger but that its use eventually leads the smoker to turn to intravenous heroin injections . . .

. . . cannabis constitutes a dangerous drug from every point of view whether physical, mental, social or criminological.

The last document was concerned with the choice of the type of control. Two alternative regimes of cannabis control were provided in the first draft of the Single Convention prepared by Adolf Lande of the secretariat. The first alternative proceeded from the assumption that if cannabis was found to have no medical value, then prohibition was the consequent course of action. The second alternative provided for strict production control in the event that cannabis was found to be medically valuable (E/2768, 1955). Considering the buildup of pressure applied by the prohibitionist group and the position of power occupied by the U.S., the chief party in this group, it is hardly surprising that the first assumption came to be upheld. An ECOSOC resolution had, in fact, been passed urging countries to stop using cannabis in medicine (548 F/XVIII). The Commission thus agreed that "it should also be made clear in the new treaty that the use of cannabis would be prohibited for all purposes medical and non-medical alike, except that of scientific research" (CND: 10th, 1955).

It is clear that Lande's alternative formulations were so structured as to lead inevitably to a choice of prohibition. Curiously, no one questioned the assumption behind the alternatives. Why should medical utility be the crucial criterion? Why should prohibition hinge upon the verdict that medicine can do without cannabis? Earlier on, Bouquet had reached the same conclusion as to medical value but had not, nevertheless, advocated prohibition.

During the next few years, reports from twenty countries were presented to the Commission, but these had little, if any, bearing on decisions. The wide use of cannabis in indigenous Indian medicine was an obstacle circumvented by allowing reservations to relevant clauses in the Single Convention. Indian objections to cannabis prohibition made little headway against the massive anticannabis bloc.

The Defense of Obsolete Positions

The rest of the history of international cannabis control is a record of efforts to sustain the status quo, rendered immutable by the fact of too great an official and personal commitment to the concepts and decisions on which it is based. In 1955 the WHO expert committee had declared that it was "pleased to note" that cannabis was placed in schedule IV of the draft convention. In 1959 some Commission members observed that research in their countries offered prospects of using cannabis for the extraction of useful substances, particularly antibiotics; WHO was asked by the Commission to study this and to present its views before the planned plenipotentiary conference in 1961. WHO did this, but its report—"The Merits of Anti-Biotic Substances Obtainable from Cannabis Sativa" (E/CN.7/409)—did not see the light of day until the 1961 conference had opened in New York. In any event, the conclusions were carefully worded so as not to detract from the decision that was going to be made by the conference as to the fitness of cannabis for the most stringent international control.

That cannabis would be placed under the strictest control regime in the Single Convention was a foregone conclusion. At the 1961 plenipotentiary conference in New York, disagreement was voiced but did not amount to real opposition. Some modifications to the envisaged control regime were accepted. These included transitional provisions allowing countries such as India and Pakistan to continue to use cannabis nonmedically for twenty-five years after the convention came into force. It is clear that cannabis was subjected to the same controls as heroin on the grounds that its medical use was obsolete. In the case of heroin, the risk to public health was offered as an additional argument for prohibition, whereas in the case of cannabis its wide abuse was the argument used.

The irony is that the criterion of "medical utility" underlying the Convention has come to be an equivocal variable: until WHO pronounced cannabis use as medically unjustifiable in 1952, licit cannabis consumption was at a level of 1,000 kgs a year. In 1966, it was reduced to about 200 kg (PCB, 1966). In 1965, the WHO expert committee thought that cannabis might be found to have medical applications after all (WHO/EC DD, 1965:312) and the Commission was told of this possibility by the WHO representative at its twentieth session (CND: 20th, 1965).

Ironically enough, in the session of the Commission immediately following the 1961 conference, a debate sparked by some comments from professional persons in the Dutch press to the effect that "cannabis addiction was no worse than alcoholism" took place in which some members expressed views not wholly consonant with the international policy already embodied in the Single Convention. However, the INTERPOL representative mentioned that "cannabis consumption was known to produce aggressiveness in the intoxicated individual," and the WHO spokesman reminded the Commission of the opinion of the WHO expert committee. "which was still valid that cannabis abuse comes definitely under its definition of addiction." And there was the added danger of progression to more dangerous drugs; whereupon the Commission recalled that it had agreed that cannabis abuse was a form of drug addiction and emphasized that any publicity to the contrary was misleading and dangerous (CND: 16th, 1961: 18).

Since that time, several state commissions (for example, the Le Dain Commission in Canada and the U.S. National Commission on Marihuana and Drug Abuse) have been appointed to examine drug use and have recommended changes in the law on cannabis. Their reports have had no perceptible effect on the attitude of the international community, whose energies have continued to be directed towards the tenacious defense of the correctness of its own position. Officials in the UN who have strong views against the prevailing policy refrain from expressing them publicly, blocked by the general unwillingness to entertain changes which are likely to involve a departure from the basis of the current operations of the drug control system.*

Each year, the INCB's annual report contains injunctions against relaxation of cannabis control. The following statement in the Board's 1971 report provides an illustration:

In the opinion of the Board, the findings so far yielded by research afford no reason for relaxing that control. On the contrary, present indications are that cannabis represents a serious and growing danger to many countries, both in its inherent potential for harm and its association with other forms of drug abuse.

Some Commission members are also rigidly inaccessible to public and scientific opinion. Vaille, the French delegate, for example, is convinced that the Commission should not waver from its stand on cannabis, whatever new light scientific inquiries may throw on the subject. He pointed out to the 1973 session of the Commission that (E/CN.7/SR.727):

"The question of the relative harmfulness of different variants of cannabis, of taking the drug in small or large doses, etc., was doubtless of theoretical and clinical interest and WHO should certainly continue its investigations along those lines, *but such investigations should not be allowed to influence international control measures in any way whatsoever.*" (emphasis added).

SUMMARY
1. Cannabis came under a limited form of international control at the Geneva Conference in 1925, on the insistence of the Egyptian delegation. This was accepted despite the fact that the question was not even on the agenda.
2. Implementation of controls was urged by the U.S., which was troubled by the use of marihuana at home. This was particularly the case after the passing of the U.S. Marihuana Tax Act in 1937.

---

* R. E. Popham, rapporteur to the WHO Scientific Group on the Use of Cannabis (WHO/SG: 478, 1970) has spoken of his lack of success in trying to include in the published report of the group a statement to the effect that research into the possible therapeutic effects of cannabis has been inadequate and that this may have been due to the bias engendered by the control system in the choice of topics for investigations (Popham, interview).

3. During the period 1935–39, a cannabis subcommittee, appointed by the Advisory Committee, amassed a large collection of data. Although the Indian situation was overlooked in the research effort, the documents produced showed much awareness of cultural differences in cannabis use and an appreciation of the difficulties attendant upon control. The work of the subcommittee represents the most systematic effort made to date by the international drug control organs to arrive at control policy decisions based on research. There was little follow-up to this research, and later decisions relied on information and reports of a less relevant nature.

4. The definitive decision to adopt a prohibitionist line was taken by 1955. The U.S., the primary force, mobilized all the control organs concerned.

5. Despite increasing criticisms of the international stand on cannabis from both outside and inside the system, the official policy has continued to be a strict adherence to the provisions of the Single Convention. So as to reinforce this official policy, declarations regarding the undesirable effects of cannabis use have constantly emanated from the key agencies.

14   Crop Substitution:
Aid for Less Trade

> There is no industry in the country to absorb these
> workers in the event of suppression or serious curtail-
> ment of the opium trade, nor can the proprietors or
> peasants ... substitute other crops for opium without
> serious handicap and loss.
>
> Memorandum on Persian Opium (1927)

In 1968, a General Assembly resolution
recommended that governments seek assistance from international sources to "develop alternative economic programmes and
activities, such as the substitution of crops, as one of the most
constructive ways of ending the illegal or uncontrolled cultivation
of narcotic raw materials" (Resolution 2434 [XXIII]). In 1970,
when a special session of the Commission on Narcotic Drugs was
convened to consider the objectives and scope of an international
action program against "drug abuse," this resolution was cited as
containing an element of the basic approach which must underlie
all future United Nations action in this field (CND: 2d Special
Session, 1970).

Historical Background

The replacement of the opium poppy, coca bush, and cannabis
plant by alternative, non-drug-bearing crops in areas of uncontrolled cultivation is an idea which has been in existence for more
than fifty years. However, up till now, neither incentive nor
resources on the part of the countries concerned have quite risen
to the level which such an exercise would have demanded,
involving as it does the agricultural and social transformation of

extensive regions which are more often than not beyond the reach of governmental control. There have been a number of forays into the field, but no real inroads have been made.

Crop substitution is linked to the belief, to which hope has traditionally been pinned, that the answer to the drug problem lies in the limitation of drug production at the source, that is, at the level of cultivation. The notion was embodied in the so-called American Proposals to the Geneva Conferences of 1924–25 for the limitation of production to the amount required to meet medicinal and scientific needs. Several opium-producing countries pleaded economic and political difficulties in accepting these proposals. The delegates of the Serb-Croat-Slovene state and of Turkey, for example, indicated that they were not prepared to limit production without assurances that other resources for their peasants would be substituted. The U.S. delegation then proposed that a commission should visit Persia, Turkey, the Serb-Croat-Slovene state, Greece, and Egypt to study crop replacement possibilities. As Persia was prepared to entertain the American Proposals, given certain guarantees, a Commission of Inquiry* appointed by the League of Nations Council arrived in Persia in early 1926 to study:

(a) the existing situation with regard to the cultivation of the poppy;
(b) the replacement of a proportion of this cultivation by other crops (Report, Commission of Inquiry, 1926).

Two years prior to this event, Mrs. Hamilton Wright,† the American assessor on the Opium Advisory Committee, had proposed that a crop substitution program be devised for the opium-growing countries as a step towards achieving the direct limitation of opium production at which the impending Geneva Conference was aimed. The reaction to this proposal was negative: it was thought impractical by the British representative, and

* The composition of the commission was as follows: chairman: F. A. Delano (U.S.), a former member of the Federal Reserve Board; Members—Dr. F. Cavara (Italy), professor of botany at the University of Naples; V. Cayla (France), agricultural engineer; J. B. Knight (U.S.), agricultural expert.

† Wife of J. Hamilton Wright, U.S. delegate to the Shanghai Commission. She served on the U.S. delegation to the Second Geneva Conference in 1924-25, being thus the first American woman to receive plenipotentiary powers as a diplomat (Taylor, 1969: 304).

outside the Committee's competence by the French representative. The representative of India thought that Mrs. Wright was "under a misapprehension as regards the conditions under which the poppy was cultivated in oriental countries": substitution was something which the peasant would voluntarily undertake if it was to his advantage to do so, and it required no order from the government. In the end, Mrs. Wright withdrew her proposal (OAC Minutes: 5th, 1923).

The report of the Persian Commission of Inquiry is still the most thorough examination of the subject so far available. It was a sizeable document whose contents ranged from Persia's physical geography to an annotated list of the vested interests which would be affected and the possible crops and economic activities which might replace opium cultivation. It also offered an outline of the program for achieving the progressive curtailment of opium production, which may be summarized as follows:

> *Preparatory period of three years*
> Register and license poppy fields and traders
> Adopt identifying marks on opium
> Revise export and excise taxes on opium
> Carry out experiments in different parts of the country
>
> *At the end of the preparatory period*
> Continue the road program on the maximum possible scale
> Initiate development of a railway system
> Undertake an irrigation project
> Develop the farm demonstration work already embarked upon
> Adopt a system of tariffs which would promote home industries and reduce imports and thus help the balance of trade
>
> *Beginning in the fourth year*
> Reduce by 10 percent a year the area under poppy, starting with those areas where substitute crops and industries are most possible

The report, nevertheless, conveys a sense of the enormity of the difficulties entailed. And in a letter to the secretary-general of the League, the commission's chairman, Delano, summed up the situation as follows: "Persia should allow three years to put its house in order, by which was meant improving its internal economic condition, making a start on building its roads, adjusting its tariffs of import duties, improving its agricultural methods, building up its sources of revenue before it undertook a reduction in the production of opium and the substitution of crops and industries therefor" (Letter, 23 April 1927).

While the proposals for a program of reduction and the substitution of crops and industries were accepted in principle by the Persian government, it was nevertheless adamant that, to adopt the policy suggested, it would have to be granted—as the "absolutely necessary condition of success"—autonomy over the establishment of customs tariffs (Observations of the Persian Government on the Report by the Commission of Inquiry, 1927). It also asked if other governments might help by reducing their import duties on Persian goods. Persia's request for a measure of economic self-determination and for better access to the European market for its goods in exchange for its agreement to opium curtailment might have found sympathy in a forum like today's United Nations Conference on Trade and Development (UNCTAD) among the "trade not aid"-oriented countries of the Third World. At the time, however, ideas like "economic development," "technical assistance," and "international aid" had not surfaced, let alone the recognition that opium-growing is associated with conditions of economic underdevelopment or that international trade is an instrument of economic development. The request drew no response. When in 1955 Persia—now become Iran—decided to prohibit opium production, the situation was somewhat different; by that time, the UN technical assistance machinery for drug control was sufficiently evolved for some form of aid to be given on an international level.

UN Efforts

The international response to Iran's opium ban took the form of an exploratory mission in 1956 and a survey mission in 1957–58 to ascertain crop substitution and agricultural development needs in areas previously under opium cultivation, both undertaken by the FAO. One of their recommendations was that efforts should be focused less on finding a substitute crop for the opium poppy than on reducing the farmer's losses and enhancing his economic position (E/CN.7/327/Add.2, 1967). It would seem that little was accomplished, for, in a 1963 paper prepared for the Commission on Narcotic Drugs, it was stated that "so far as is known the most elaborate attempt up to the present to discover substitutes was the anti-opium mission to Iran, but for a number of reasons all that could be done then was to confirm already-existing ideas about the value of substitute crops. No field trials could be carried out; still less was there the opportunity to work out and demonstrate cultivation and production methods suitable for adoption by farmers" (E/CN.7/454, 1963:4).

It is clear that the UN's efforts in the crop substitution field have been modest. What was said of its role in the Lebanese sunflower operation in cannabis-growing areas might equally be said of its role in general, that it is of assistance "by expert advice, by liaison or co-ordination, but most important, by creating the international atmosphere in which other forms of assistance might begin to flow" (E/CN.7/508/Add.2, 1967:24). In concrete terms, the total UN response up to 1972 might be said to comprise the actions listed in Appendix F. The UN evidently lacked the means to do much beyond sending the occasional expert or survey team to assess the situation in a producing country and offer recommendations. In the aftermath of the Iranian ban on opium production in 1955, FAO was in the field to advise the government on substitute crops. However, cessation of opium production involved the country in so much financial loss and had so little impact on the incidence of drug addiction that in 1969 Iran decided to rescind its ban and resume opium cultivation. The availability of illicit opium from Turkey and Afghanistan, the capital loss suffered by Iran as a result of these imports, and the substitution of heroin for opium with a subsequent increase in drug-related problems all made it less than feasible for Iran to continue its prohibition (E/CN.7/r.18, 1971).

In 1971 the UN concluded an agreement with the Thai government to introduce new crops and economic activities in selected villages in northern Thailand as part of a Drug Abuse Control Project to be executed under the UN Fund for Drug Abuse Control (UNFDAC). Since then, pilot trials to replace opium growing in five "key" and twenty-five "satellite" villages by other types of activity have been undertaken.

Despite the claims made for the Lebanese sunflower operation (the "Green Plan") for replacing cannabis cultivation in the

Baalbek/Hermel district, skepticism prevails in the international forum, not least because there has been no apparent letup in the illicit consignments of cannabis that are found to have come from Lebanon. The UAR representative on the Commission contended that the amount doubled between 1967 and 1968 (E/4606, 1969), although sunflower planting began in 1966. In a paper prepared by the Division of Narcotic Drugs for the twenty-second session of the Commission in 1967, the lack of information on the fate of the sunflower crop was queried. The situation appeared unclear at the time, and the paper asked if it was "to be assumed that the experiment last year should be written off, or that it was only partially successful?" (E/CN.7/508/Add.2, 1967:27). At present, financial support by the Fund is under consideration, for without additional resources the Lebanese government is unable to carry through its program.*

With the coca leaf, it is even more difficult to obtain a basis for an assessment of results for, despite the ambiguous reference in the 1961 report of the Commission on Narcotic Drugs to "good results" being obtained "in the field of technical assistance from the Andean-Indian Project—a joint UN-ILO-WHO-UNESCO-FAO effort being administered by the ILO," suppression of coca-leaf-chewing has never been an objective of, or a serious consideration in the Andean-Indian Program. This is a program aimed at raising the living standards of the Indians of the Andean plateau and integrating them into the economic and social life of the countries concerned (Ghosh, 1968). Yet in *Everyman's United Nations*, published by the UN Office of Public Information, it is stated that "In 1949 there had been the Commission of Inquiry on the Coca Leaf to Peru and Bolivia,† while the Andean-Indian

---

* Lebanese officials have variously stated in private that they would not for political reasons induce any financial strains on peasants in the region (where there were battles a few years ago) and that if the U.S. or Egypt or the UN wishes to eliminate cannabis they can pay for it all; that is, by providing income guarantees to farmers or all the necessary capital investment in sunflower processing plants and transport. There are also former high officials residing in the region who own cannabis-growing estates, and one assumes they wish to protect their income (Blum, personal communication, 1973).

† This Commission, composed of H. B. Fonda (vice-president and director of the American Pharmaceutical Manufacturers' Association), J. P. Razet (inspector general of French Ministry of Agriculture), Dr. F. Verzat (professor of Physiology, Basle University) and M. Granier-Doyeux (professor of pharmacology, Central University of Venezuela), was sent to Peru and Bolivia to study, *inter alia*, "the

Program, involving co-operation by several United Nations agencies and dealing in particular with certain aspects and consequences of the coca leaf chewing habit, had also been initiated" (UN OPI, 1968:332). This is not borne out by other literature on the program (Sharp, 1961; Ghosh, 1968). Nor do ILO officers who have been administering the program in Geneva since 1967 think coca-leaf-chewing a direct concern of the program, whatever indirect results it may have on the habit (Migone, interview).

The stance of international bodies other than the Commission evinces somewhat more caution and realism. While it sees "seeds of genuine promise" in the "experimental economic measures being introduced in Thailand," the INCB lays stress on the immensity of the task involved, the deep-seated difficulties "imposed by the geographical remoteness and economic twilight of the regions principally concerned" (INCB, 1970). It sees supplies from other regions coming to fill the vacuum that will be created when Turkey stops production (INCB, 1971) and detects signs that "illicit traffickers in opium and opiates are turning their eyes to areas where there is little or no control over poppy cultivation" (INCB, 1970). The misgivings are probably well-founded when one considers that the amount of opium used by the U.S. market can be grown in an area of, at most, 2,849 to 5,957 hectares (based on Holahan's estimate), an area that can easily be absorbed in another producing region, even if opium were to be completely eradicated from the 31,000 hectares it covers in Turkey and Thailand (see table 14.1), which is a dubious proposition in itself.

The UN has become interested in another activity closely related to crop substitution that is worthy of note. In 1972 a research project was subcontracted by UNFDAC to the Commonwealth Institute of Biological Control (European Station in Delémont, Switzerland), aimed at discovering biological enemies (insect species or pathogens) of Cannabis sativa and Papaver somniferum which can be used to devastate the cannabis and

---

measures to be taken, should this habit prove to be harmful, in order to eradicate it from the population concerned". In its report, the Commission stated that the problem of "substituting other crops for the coca leaf cannot be resolved in a general and uniform way in all the coca leaf producing areas of Peru and Bolivia", but that, "generally speaking, substitution is possible and therefore to be recommended" (Report, Commission of Enquiry, 1950).

TABLE 14.1
Reported Acreage under Opium Poppy Cultivation

Country	Year	Hectares
India	1971	41,000[a]
Turkey	1971	13,000[a]
Iran	1927	28,000[b]
	1955	30,000[c]
	1972	20,000[a]
Thailand	1967	18,000[d]

SOURCES: [a]World Opium Survey, 1972, prepared under the
auspices of the Cabinet Committee on International
Narcotics Control.
[b]Neligan (1927).
[c]Report of FAO Exploratory Mission on Opium in
Iran, November 1956 (cf. E/CN.7/327/Add.2).
[d]Report of the UN Survey Team on the Economic
and Social Needs of the Opium-Producing Areas of
Thailand, 1967.

NOTE: India is included to give added comparison.

poppy fields in areas of uncontrolled production.* Concurrently,
the Division of Narcotic Drugs is encouraging research on the
botanic species, Papaver bracteatum, as a possible substitute for
Papaver somniferum. The former contains no morphine and its
high thebaine content can be directly converted to codeine. If the
research produces positive results, then the next step would
presumably be to reduce the world's legal production of opium
from Papaver somniferum by 80 percent, which is the amount
needed for the world's codeine supply. This recalls the earlier
study (see chapter 13) which FAO was asked to prepare on the
possibility of developing drug-free strains of the cannabis plant as
well as the replacement of the hemp fiber and seed by other crops

---

* It was reported by the *International Herald Tribune* (22 November 1973)
that this $150,000 project was proving unsuccessful. A number of insects and
diseases had been identified that attacked the cannabis plant and the opium
poppy, but none had been found which did sufficient damage to make its
employment worthwhile. Yet when the Commission met in 1974, and concern over
the project was expressed by some representatives, the Division responded that
"the project had been entrusted to an eminently qualified research institute and
that the action to be taken on the research findings would be left to the discretion
of Governments" (CND: 3d special session, 1974).

of similar industrial value (E/CN.7/324, 1957). FAO could not give a categorical opinion as to which of the two measures had more potential, but it did see possibilities in the crop substitution alternative, although only for countries where two conditions obtained simultaneously: one, where there was a serious problem with the drug, and, two, where hemp fiber and seed were not very important economically. It is ironic that these two factors—the existence of a perceived drug problem and the economic insignificance of the drug-bearing crop—are not juxtaposed in most of the countries where replacement programs are being encouraged.

Finally, there is the search for synthetic alternatives to opiates of natural origin for pain and cough relief (WHO/SG 4 and 5, 1972) which seems to be based on the assumption that, if this proves fruitful, then medical practice can dispense with opiates of natural origin, poppy need never be grown, and nonmedical use will disappear correspondingly. It is this last point which is open to question. So too is the implicit assumption that substitution of synthetics for medical use would not be associated with illicit synthetics (for example, methadone) for nonmedical use.

All these are not, strictly speaking, crop substitution projects, but they are expressions of more or less the same ideas, and like crop substitution they are tied to the belief that the solution to the problems related to drugs lies in eradicating opium at the source.

The U.S. and UNFDAC

Before the establishment of the Fund, there was a need to capitalize on other ongoing projects not specifically focused on cultivation control: thus the survey of the Riff region of Morocco approved in 1960 for execution by FAO, though geared primarily to the general agricultural development and reforestation of the region, was mentioned by the Commission in the crop replacement connection because within the pilot development area is a sizeable proportion of land formerly used for the cultivation of "kif," or cannabis. Encompassing anti-coca-leaf efforts within existing projects in the Andean-Indian Program has also been urged (CND: 20th, 1965). When geographical coincidence does not occur, however, this possibility is ruled out. Afghanistan, for instance, has made it clear that its development priority lay in the western part of the country, which yielded quicker returns on investment than the opium-growing areas of Badakhshan, and UN assistance in opium cultivation control was acceptable only insofar as it did not prejudice the assistance Afghanistan might receive under the United Nations Development Program (UNDP), and insofar as it was not expected to make counterpart contributions (E/CN.7/r.18, 1971:19).

The Fund has brought the hitherto virtually dormant crop substitution program into greater activity and prominence. Crop replacement of opium in Afghanistan and Burma is now a projected program under the Fund. The possibility of executing either remains uncertain. It is doubtful, for example, if the Burmese government's agreement to consider a UN plan for opium crop replacement means a great deal in reality since the production and distribution areas are beyond the government's control.*

The Fund is not the only active force in this area. Preceding the UN missions were visits by high U.S. officials to Burma to discuss means of interdicting the illicit opium flow from Burma. However, due to Burma's go-it-alone ideology, American help was refused (Gross, 1972). Also independently of the UN and through bilateral diplomatic and economic pressure, the U.S. induced the Turkish government to decree the abolition of opium production with the harvest of 1972. To give effect to this decree, a general program of agricultural and economic reform, including the substitution of the opium crop in the area designated "Development Region to Replace Poppy Income" has been drawn up. An initial $3 million made available to the Turkish government by the U.S. Agency for International Development (AID)—of which half was to assist in developing alternative crops—was supplemented by a later pledge of $35 million divided into two parts: $20 million to be spent on crop substitution and $15 million to compensate Turkey for losses in foreign exchange (Murphy and

---

* The recent trouble (1973) in Burma's eastern frontier region underscores the lack of realism of the projected replacement program. The trouble is said to be fomented by a newly arrived Kuomintang (KMT) intelligence band, an organ of the Taiwan government which has got itself established in the Golden Triangle region (see chapter 15). It has taken under its command the leftover KMT forces stranded since the 1950s. The organ's activities are said to be espionage and subversion against Peking. It has tried to lure into its fold with offers of arms and money local Burmese defense units, most of which have turned into gangs of opium and arms smugglers (*Far Eastern Economic Review*, 1973, *81*, 27: 19).

Steel, 1971; Cabinet Committee, 1972). With bilateralism, it is
easy to arouse the feeling, as happened in Turkey (where it was
abetted by opposition among a number of politicians to the ban),
that controls are being imposed for the benefit of another country
in what is seen as a capitulation to American pressure (Spong,
1972).* While the U.S. government places considerable emphasis
on foreign crop eradication (Goldberg and DeLong, 1972), other
governments do not. Thus some UN Commission members see
the American contribution of $2 million to the UN fund as a
means whereby the U.S. can pursue its crop eradication objectives
in Thailand in a project which bears the semblance of a multilat-
erally aided operation. The latter has the advantage of being
relatively free from the kind of resentment which bilateral aid has
created in Turkey. It is clear (see table 14.2) that all of the $2
million contribution by the U.S. is going to the Thai project.
Independently of the UN, the U.S. State Department has signed a
U.S.-Thailand memorandum of understanding that will make
U.S. aid available to Thailand for drug control in that country.
Thus the contrast between Turkey and Thailand in the level of
funding assured by 1972 is probably smaller than the table
indicates.

The U.S. has also given Mexico, through AID, considerable
grants, light planes, helicopters, remote sensing equipment, and
chemicals to eradicate marihuana. Similar grants made in 1961
and 1965 have apparently been without effect. This is not surprising considering that the marihuana trade may be worth an
additional $100 million in foreign exchange to Mexico, whose
total legitimate exports are about $1.1 billion (Goldberg and
DeLong, 1972).

Obstacles
In the report of the second special session of the Commission on
Narcotic Drugs to which reference has already been made, it was
noted that "the importance of crop substitution in the areas of
illicit or uncontrolled production of narcotic raw material was by
now well established as an essential part of the world effort to
fight drug abuse and illicit trafficking" (CND: 2d special session,

---

* Turkey has decided to restart opium cultivation. A government resolution
authorizing this will go into effect before July 1974 (*International Herald Tribune*,
27 June 1974).

TABLE 14.2
Financial Aspects of Crop Substitution Programs

Country	Year	Amounts available or earmarked	Sources
Persia	1925	2 million tomans[a]	Persia's original proposal for an international loan was replaced in 1926 by a request for tariff autonomy
Turkey	1968 1972	$1.6 million $35 million	US AID loan[b] pledged by the U.S. government, divided into two parts: $20 million for crop substitution and $15 million to compensate for Turkey's losses in foreign exchange
Thailand	1972	$2,084,400[c] +$5 million (in cash and kind)	UNFDAC
Afghanistan (projected)	1973 1974 Future	$800,000 $1 million $3.2 million	UNFDAC
Burma (projected)	1973 1974 Future	$500,000 $800,000 $2.7 million	UNFDAC

[a]This sum represents an estimate of the cost. One toman was approximately equal to U.S. $1.00 (League of Nations Document A.8.1927.xi).
[b]E/CN.7/r.18
[c]These are starting funds. In 1973 a further $5,580,000 was committed to the project.

1970:12). This statement belies the fact that up until then (and now) none of the attempts at replacement can be said to have reached a stage where results can be discerned, let alone assessed.

The Iranian experience illustrates the inherent and oft-recounted difficulties which any effective program of crop replacement must first overcome. The areas involved are often those which are least capable of supporting alternative economic activities, or are most impervious to governmental controls, or both. They may also be yielding illicit revenues for local or central government officials who, if crop substitution were successful, would lose their income and—unlike the farmers—not be reimbursed.

The enormous scale on which any effort must be predicated will already be apparent from the outline of the reduction program offered by the Persian Commission of 1926. A look at what is entailed in the projects being initiated elsewhere makes this even clearer. Some idea of what is entailed in terms of the acreage which has to be brought under control and the number of cultivators whose livelihood will be jeopardized is given in tables 14.1 and 14.3. The Thai data in the tables are based on estimates made by a UN survey team of the economic and social needs of the opium-producing areas of Thailand carried out in 1967, but

TABLE 14.3
Estimated Number of Poppy Farmers Affected by Crop Substitution Programs

Country	Year	Number	Population of country (in thousands)
Persia	1927	Unknown, but poppy was cultivated in 18 out of 26 provinces[a]	12,000
	1955	300,000[b]	18,325
Turkey	1972	80,000[c]	35,230 (1970)
Thailand	1972	55,000–300,000[d]	35,810

SOURCES: [a]Memorandum of the Persian Government to the Second Opium Conference, Document O.D.C.24.
[b]Report of FAO Exploratory Mission on Opium in Iran, 1956, Rome.
[c]World Opium Survey 1972, Cabinet Committee on International Narcotics Control.
[d]United Nations Report of the South East Asia Consultative Group on Narcotics Control 1960, TAO/AFE/11. A survey carried out by the Thai government in 1965–66 gave a total hill-tribe population of 275,249 persons (Report of UN Survey Team on the Economic and Social Needs of the Opium Producing Areas in Thailand, 1967).

are presumably relevant to the current endeavor as well, even though this is limited to pilot trials in a number of selected villages.

Of the many difficulties, the agricultural factor is not the least. Conditions of climate, soil, water, and labor that are conducive to the raising of drug-bearing crops can militate against alternative crops that have potential for success on other counts. FAO wrote in 1967, for instance, that "it would appear that the attempts at growing sunflower as a substitute for cannabis in the non-irrigated land has been a complete failure" (E/CN.7/518/Add.2, 1967: 9), and this despite the fact that "agronomically the sunflower might be the most suitable crop to grow as a substitute." The attendant problems cited for opium substitutes are an echo of those noted by the Persian Inquiry of 1926: the fact that, as noted in the report of that inquiry, opium is largely an autumn-sown crop harvested in the spring means that it can be followed by other crops in what amounts to a rotation scheme; this advantage is shared by few other high-yielding crops. In terms of return per unit of land, no crop comes anywhere near opium. In Iran, for instance, it was found that, although the best alternative use of erstwhile opium-poppy land was to grow alfalfa on it for livestock feeding, the exercise could not, without supplementary activity, make up for the loss of income accruing from the cessation of opium production (E/CN.7/454, 1963). FAO reckoned that poppy cultivation in the Hamadan area in Iran was four to five times more profitable than wheat-growing and that this relationship was true for other areas (E/CN.7/327/Add.2, 1957). Similarly, attempts to substitute Mexican wheat for opium failed in Pakistan because the unit return of the wheat was roughly half that of opium, assuming opium to be sold at official prices (Holahan, 1972). An added difficulty in replacing opium is its easy marketability and high profitability, a point made by the Persian Commission and recapitulated in more recent discussions; FAO, for example, has alluded to the "institutional and marketing problems, and possibly, questions of international trade" which must first be settled (E/CN.7/454, 1963: 5). That many substitute crops have been proposed for opium, cannabis, and coca leaf (see table 14.4) is not because they are easily replaceable, but because no single alternative suffices.

Giving subsidies for producing other goods or making direct

payments to the farmers can compensate for some of the income loss. As adjuncts to crop substitution measures, they can go some way towards alleviating the latter's unpopularity. But unless the subsidies are sufficiently high, or increase sufficiently quickly to keep abreast of the rise in price which will inevitably result from a drop in production level—due not only to the nature of demand but also to the wide margin between the producer price and the consumer price, which allows an appreciable raising of the former without greatly narrowing the margin—they are unlikely to be effective. It was noted in 1967 that the subsidy paid to cannabis farmers in Lebanon was working to make cannabis less profitable than sunflower. But as the price of illicit hashish rose with the reduction of supply by sunflower replacement, there was a risk—if the Lebanese government were to keep on increasing the

TABLE 14.4
Proposed Substitutes for Opium, Cannabis, and Coca Leaf

Country	Crop	Substitutes
Persia (1926)	Opium	Silk, dried fruits, cotton, wool, nuts, pharmaceutical raw materials, flower extracts, dried fruits, hemp[a]
(1957)	Opium	Wheat, sugar beet, vegetables, cotton, maize, sorghum, millet, tobacco, oil seeds (sesame, sunflower, cotton seed), specialized crops (e.g., saffron), livestock[b]
Peru and Bolivia (1950)	Coca leaf	Coffee, tea, fruits (orange, lime, grapefruit, apple, peach, grapes), rice, sugar cane, yucca[c]
Lebanon (1966)	Hashish	Oil-bearing crops, especially sunflower seeds, fruits and vegetables, safflower, sunflower, alfalfa, vetch, wheat[d]
Thailand (1967)	Opium	Peas, vegetable seed, pyrethrum, tobacco, tea, coffee, livestock, silk, forestry[e]

SOURCES: [a]Report of the Commission of Inquiry to Persia, 1926.
[b]Report of Exploratory Mission on Opium in Iran, E/CN.7/327/Add.2, 1957.
[c]Report of the Commission of Inquiry on the Coca Leaf, 1950.
[d]UN document E/CN.7/508/Add.2, 1967.
[e]Report of the UN Survey Team, 1967.

sunflower subsidies—of entering into a "race with the traffickers" (E/CN.7/508/Add.2,1967:19). This would involve Lebanon in staggering costs, even if there was the remotest chance of its winning the race.

FAO has, in recognition of the fact that the less one does about compensating for income loss the more difficulty one will have in suppressing cultivation, pointed to the possibility of relieving the farmer of the need to grow or buy food through the distribution of foodstuffs under its World Food Program as a means of offsetting some of the loss suffered in being made to abandon a remunerative crop (CND 2d special session, 1970:13; E/CN.7/454, 1963). The program was likewise invoked by the Commission on Narcotic Drugs in connection with supplementing the diet of the coca-leaf-chewing Indian in the Andes (CND: 20th, 1965). But, as admitted by FAO itself, this is at best an interim measure.

Successes

A widely accepted view is that the high profitability of opium production will diminish as the producing areas become more developed economically and opportunities for wage employment increase, so that, given a particular stage of economic and technological development, opium cultivation will be abandoned in favor of other types of activity. Although this view has some of the optimism of the Indian representative's rebuttal of Mrs. Hamilton Wright's arguments in 1923 for devising a crop substitution scheme, and neglects changes in the demand for opium (Holahan, 1972), what has happened in Yugoslavia would appear to support it. There, opium growing has apparently given way to other less labor-intensive activities. Opium production has fallen from eighty tons a year before World War II to a mere four tons in response to the general economic progress of Macedonia, the producing area (GE.70–13174). One of the conditions for successful crop replacement would seem to be the integration of the program into an overall development plan. This was done by Algeria with respect to the reduction of its wine-growing areas in favor of other forms of agriculture (Thörnander, 1971).

The People's Republic of China offers another example of successful opium crop replacement. Opium-growing, once a major activity in the south-western provinces, has been wiped out through agricultural transformation in all but a few remote pockets. In these remote pockets, which are found in the mountainous frontier regions between China and Burma, opium growing has persisted among the indigenous national minorities (that is, non-Han Chinese) to satisfy local needs. Such concessions to local peculiarities are in line with the overall gradualist approach followed by the Chinese Communist party towards national minorities. But even here changes have occurred. How social reforms succeeded in bringing about the substitution of opium by other crops in one such area was documented by a British journalist in his account of the breakup of a slave society in northwest Yunnan, where the Norsu, a minority people, have lived for centuries in isolation (Winnington, 1959).

There has not been any evaluation of the functioning or the results of crop substitution programs; nor can there be until at least one such program becomes fully operative. It will, therefore, be a long time before it is possible to judge its effectiveness as a means of reducing drug availability, although it is already apparent that the expectations and hopes which have hitherto been attached to crop substitution are out of step with the supply realities. Apart from the examples mentioned, there has been no demonstrable success in this field over the last fifty years.

SUMMARY
1. Crop substitution is considered by the UN to be a central strategy in its action against "drug abuse."
2. The concept of crop substitution is linked to the notion of controlling opium at the source, propounded by the U.S. at the second Geneva Conference in 1924–25.
3. The first country to contemplate crop substitution was Persia. A Commission of Inquiry visited it in 1926 and drew up a plan. Nothing happened until 1955, when Iran prohibited opium production. Even then little was achieved by way of developing alternative economic activities.
4. Until recently, the UN did little beyond sending an occasional expert or survey team to assess the situation and offer recommendations; it also encouraged the inclusion of drug reduction considerations in general development programs, for example, in the Andean-Indian program.
5. Lebanon has embarked (it seems unsuccessfully) on a project to substitute sunflowers for cannabis, and Thailand on a trial to replace opium-growing in its hill-tribe areas.

6. UNFDAC has provided an impetus to crop replacement programs, which take up the largest proportion of the available funds. Independently of the UN, the U.S. has financed crop replacement programs in Turkey.

7. A related exercise—one based on equally questionable premises—is the search for synthetic alternatives to opiates and research on Papaver bracteatum.

8. The difficulties which replacement programs have to overcome are enormous. The areas concerned are often beyond governmental control. Before a program can be instituted, fundamental economic reorganization is necessary. Other activities are less lucrative. Many vested interests are involved. Although no program of substitution has ever "got off the ground," the tone in which such programs are discussed by the Commission is unrealistically optimistic.

9. However, in Yugoslavia reduction of opium production has come about not through deliberate drug-control programming but naturally, as a result of economic progress. China offers the only example of successful, deliberate control of opium availability through crop replacement.

10. On present evidence, expectations of what can be achieved are excessively high.

15 The Illicit Traffic

> ... it is fair to say that if there were no opium in Turkey, there would be no heroin in New York. But it is also fair to say that if there were no addicts in New York, there would be no smugglers in Istanbul.
>
> Jean Nepote, "The International Police Fight Against Drugs"

If there is one aspect of the problems associated with drugs to which the international community pays more attention than others, it is the illicit traffic. We will not attempt in this chapter to analyze the enormously complex international drug trafficking business, but will confine ourselves to tracing the way in which the policies of the drug control organs towards trafficking have evolved, the forces in the world's marketing structure to which these policies have responded, and the conceptions or misconceptions on which they are based.

The Prewar Period

The context within which international policies developed has undergone several changes, some of which were effected by the control system itself. Drug trafficking has always existed, but restructuring has taken place, depending on what has been defined as legal or illegal. Opium was prohibited in China before the war of 1856–58, but under the Tientsin treaties which ended the war Britain and France (the victors) secured not only the legalization of opium but also of Christianity (Lowes, 1966:50). With legalization, "smuggling" naturally ceased, and opium entered China through authorized channels.

Although the illicit traffic is sometimes described as though it were a business separate from other activities, it is, in fact, intimately bound up with other types of commerce, both legal and illegal. In the 1920's, drug trafficking was a business which was mostly carried on by supposedly law-abiding European pharmaceutical firms. The Opium Advisory Committee saw it as a question of overproduction and the diversion of "surplus" drugs into illegal channels. As was pointed out by the Chinese member of the Committee, Germany, Great Britain, Japan, Switzerland, and the United States were all turning out "morphia by the ton, which was purchased by smugglers by the ton." It was as if, he observed, the manufacturing countries were "competing with each other owing to the fact that the business was a very profitable one, although the profits went only to smugglers and a few manufacturers.... He could not understand why civilized countries should allow such a scandalous state of affairs to continue unchecked" (OAC: 5th, 1923:73). The large influx of European morphine and heroin into China during the 1920s had been in response to the elimination of the Indian opium trade and the suppression campaign within the country. Small quantities of both drugs were imported for medical use from Europe—for a time they were believed to be a cure for opium addiction—but the distinction between "medical" and "nonmedical," as that between legal and illegal, became progressively blurred, and a great deal of smuggling occurred (Adams, 1972).

The illicit traffic in manufactured products from Western pharmaceutical houses became a major problem in the Far East in the 1920s, "constituting a more serious menace to Orientals than the use of prepared opium" (Taylor, 1969: 231). Attempts to control diversion from drug manufacturers often came up against the problem that those manufacturers knowingly supplied drugs to smugglers (OAC: 10th, 1927) and that the authorities of some countries were negligent about checking such diversion. Switzerland, for instance, was a particularly safe place from this point of view, not only for irresponsible drug firms but also for money transactions associated with drug deals. What came to be known as the "Canton Road Smuggling Case," handled by the Mixed Court of Shanghai in 1925, offers an illustration of this. The case involved 180 chests of opium shipped from Constantinople and sold in China, and 26 boxes containing mostly heroin imported from Basle, Switzerland, by a Chinese dealer, Gwanho. Documents produced at the trial revealed that a considerable trade had been plying between Gwanho and the Swiss drug firms Hoffmann-La Roche and MacDonald and Co. The latter had been "notoriously engaged in the illicit traffic" and had operated for a time from Germany, where it transacted a considerable trade in drugs and arms to the Far East.* German inquiries into the dealings of this company had driven it to seek a "more convenient centre," which it subsequently found in Switzerland. A Stuttgart firm was involved too, and a telegram was found showing that Gwanho had remitted £2,000 sterling to it through the Schweizerische Kreditanstalt of Zurich (OAC: 7th, 1925, Annex). But pressure applied to Switzerland by other members of the Advisory Committee was steadily resisted. When another case of illicit traffic involving Hoffmann-La Roche was discussed and protests were voiced by the British delegate that this threw "a lurid light on the character of the firm," protests supported by the chairman, Sir John Campbell, who personally "had no doubt whatever that Hoffmann-La Roche and Company was not a firm to which a licence to deal with drugs should be given," the Swiss representative persisted in his attitude that the Swiss government was neither responsible nor could it justifiably intervene (OAC: 10th, 1927: 67–69).

The records of the Opium Advisory Committee abound with cases of illicit transactions implicating European pharamceutical firms. One of the most widely publicized cases involved Naarden, a Dutch firm, which, between 1927 and 1928, had amassed about 850 kilograms of morphine, 3,000 kilograms of heroin and 90 kilograms of cocaine, most of which was smuggled into China. In general terms, the supplies came mainly from three firms in Germany, Switzerland, and France (A.86.1929.XI).

Gradually, however, international pressure succeeded in persuading drug manufacturing countries to apply adequate controls over their drug industries, and overproduction was by and large brought under control. But the implementation of the 1925 and

* Drugs and arms have continued their close association. See a League of Nations memorandum, "Analogies between the Problem of the Traffic in Narcotic Drugs and that of the Trade in and Manufacture of Arms," which was presented to the Conference for the Reduction and Limitation of Armaments in Geneva, 1933. See also page 241.

1931 conventions had a double-edged effect: while authorized manufacture was regulated, underground factories started to appear, often close to areas of uncontrolled production of raw materials. Turkey was a case in point. Drug trafficking persisted, but the sources of supply had shifted. It has remained that way to this day.

International Response: The prewar period

International legislation enacted from 1925 on, established a system of control over the distribution of opium, cocaine, and cannabis so as to confine the movement of these drugs within regular, legal trade channels. Under the Hague Convention of 1912, obligations were placed on the "treaty powers" to take measures to prevent the smuggling of opium, morphine, cocaine, and their respective salts into Chinese territory and into the Far Eastern colonies of these powers and the leased territories which they occupied in China. The focus in those days had been on China, which was then the chief consumer.

Paralleling the controls instituted over supplies was the introduction of penalty provisions in the international legislation. The Hague Convention enjoined its signatories to "examine the possibility of enacting laws or regulations making it a penal offence to be in illegal possession of raw opium, prepared opium, morphine, cocaine, and their respective salts," whereas under the 1925 Convention, the parties agreed to punish "by adequate penalties" breaches of the laws giving effect to the provisions of the convention (Art. 28).

The development within the international framework of a purely penal approach towards trafficking came to a head in 1936 with the conclusion of the Convention for the Suppression of Illicit Traffic in Dangerous Drugs. The last treaty to be concluded under the auspices of the League of Nations, the Convention was drawn up by the International Police Commission (IPC)—the predecessor of the International Criminal Police Organization (INTERPOL)—established in Vienna in 1923. It was based on the 1929 Convention for the Suppression of Counterfeit Currency, in whose formulation the IPC also had a hand. The Convention called for the severe punishment of offenders "particularly by imprisonment or other penalties of deprivation of liberty"; the application of the principle of universality of jurisdiction in national criminal law, that is, punishing violators irrespective of their nationality or the place where they had committed their offence; and for the extradition of offenders. In effect, therefore, illicit drug trafficking became under this Convention a crime of international character. It is perhaps a sign of the times that in 1972, when states came to reconsider the extradition provisions of the Single Convention, it was not a treaty on counterfeit currency but one on aircraft hijacking which was used as a model for drug legislation (E/CONF.63/C2/SR 11, 1972).

Thus, the mode of action against the illicit traffic established by the prewar treaties was based on controlling availability (through administrative regulation) on the one hand, and on the pursuit of a criminal policy on the other. In terms of practical measures, a number of schemes had been proposed. It was suggested, for instance, that a blacklist of drug firms and traffickers be established on the basis of information sent to the Committee by governments. This would establish a moral boycott of drug firms which had allowed their products to go into the illicit market. The German, Swiss, Japanese, and Portuguese representatives voiced strong oppposition to this proposal, and the idea of a blacklist of firms was dropped, although that of individual dealers was retained (OAC: 3d, 1923). Nationalization of the drug industry was another proposal (OAC: 10th, 1927), a unified system of police action yet another (OAC: 13th, 1930). The IPC came into the picture with its draft convention on the suppression of the illicit traffic which, among other provisions, called for the centralized organization of police offices.

Under a system of reporting established by the conventions, seizure information was submitted by governments on an annual basis to the Permanent Central Opium Board. Cases of illicit traffic were reported to the Advisory Opium Committee, and summaries of these were distributed to individual countries and enforcement agencies.

The Postwar Period

We have seen in earlier chapters that action by international organizations has to be based on information officially supplied by governments. The characteristics of this information-base thus determine to a large extent the picture which the international community has of drug trafficking and its perception of the nature of the problem. The documents forming the basis of the

discussion in the Commission of the illicit traffic consisted of:
  —review of the illicit traffic in narcotic drugs (during the
  preceding year), prepared by the secretariat, based on in
  mation submitted to the UN by governments;
  —chapter 11 of annual reports (for the preceding year);
  —summaries of reports on illicit transactions and seizures.
In 1949 ECOSOC granted consultative status to INTERPOL,
which was thereby entitled to receive the Commission's agenda
and to be represented by an observer at its meetings. Soon
INTERPOL was contributing a memorandum on the illicit
traffic, and this became a regular addition to the documents
listed above. In 1960 the Division of Narcotic Drugs and the
secretariat of INTERPOL decided to simplify the system of
reporting seizures to international bodies, and the review of the
illicit traffic became a joint document amalgamating the information supplied by governments to the UN and to INTERPOL
separately. Another addition to the set of documents regularly
presented to the Commission was the report of the Ad Hoc
Committee on Seizures.

A significant input into the Commission's meetings on the
illicit traffic were the written statements, notes, or memoranda by
the U.S. delegation. These were often added to the list of
documents given above: in a few instances the U.S. submission
was published as an annex to the Commission's report (for
example, in 1950 and 1966). The earlier reports of the Commission reveal a significant reliance upon U.S. sources of data: the
review of the traffic throughout the world during the war years,
for example, was based on three documents, two of which were
presented by the U.S. delegation.*

The data contained in official government reports on seizures
were not always complete, nor were they consistently communicated, but they were considered an important source of information. The criteria for the selection of cases to be communicated
to international and national bodies were laid down in article 23
of the 1931 Convention: cases should be reported which might be
of importance "either because of the quantities involved or

---

* "Review of the Illicit Traffic in Narcotic Drugs Throughout the World
During the Years 1940 to 1945 and the first half of 1946," presented by Mr. J. W.
Bulkely of the US Treasury Department (E/CN. 7/10); "Review of Illicit Traffic
in the US in 1945," presented by the representative of the U.S. (E/CN. 7/10).

because of the light thrown on the source from which drugs are obtained for the illicit traffic or the methods employed by illicit traffickers." Annual world totals of drugs seized, as reported by national governments and INTERPOL between the years 1931 and 1969, are given for roughly five-year intervals in table 15.1. It will be seen that opium seizures have declined, while those of morphine and heroin have been climbing since 1946, although they still have not reached the levels attained in the 1930s. Clearly, seizures are connected with legislation, as is indicated by the appearance of stimulants, depressants, and LSD in the contraband traffic. The fluctuations in the size of cannabis seizures are suggestive of the turns which international interest and enforcement efforts took for this drug over the years; it may be possible for instance to relate the steep increase between 1950 and 1955 to the fact that 1954 and 1955 were crucial years in the process leading to the international decision to control cannabis.

The distribution of seizures among countries for one year, 1971, may be seen from table 15.2, in which we have listed the three leading countries in decreasing rank-order for each of the following measures: total weight seized, number of seizures, number of arrests, and number of nationals implicated. Iran led on all four counts for opium, and the U.S. for cannabis. Sweden reported the largest seizures of stimulants and made the largest number of arrests of dealers in stimulants. While the largest number of heroin seizures and arrests were made in France, the largest amounts were seized in the U.S. (45 percent of the total). Seizures of cocaine in the U.S. accounted for over half of the world's total in terms of quantity, number of cases, and arrests.

Despite the merger of its report with that of the UN, INTERPOL has continued to make its own studies. One such study was referred to during the 1969 session of the Commission: statistics collected during the first ten months of 1968 on illicit traffic involving tourists and migrant workers in Europe showed that, of the 675 seizures examined, 40 percent related to "tourists" and 5 percent to migrant workers. The largest number of seizures were of cannabis (255, constituting 51 percent of the total), followed by opium (24, representing 28 percent of the total), then amphetamines (16), LSD (9), morphine (4) and heroin (1). The drugs had been bought in 21 countries, and of the 986 offenders arrested, 442 were "tourists" of 42 nationalities and 60 were foreign workers.

TABLE 15.1
Total Quantities of Drugs Seized (All totals expressed in kilograms unless otherwise indicated)

	Raw opium	Prepared opium	Morphine	Heroin	Cocaine	Cannabis	Synthetic drugs under international control	Stimulants	Depressants	LSD
1931	48,392	7,179	1,354	943	70	20,888				
1936	124,497	18,063	393	867	97	16,283				
1946	22,413	5,191	40	27	24	24,411				
1950	54,614	4,345	42	80	12	133,536				
1955	59,312	3,232	209	137	11	1,331,371	1			
1960	35,970	672	332	390	10	875,849	4			
1965	37,612	585	413	320	180	157,124	1			
1969	40,709		847	463	152	1,828,480 (+29,362 resin)		319 434,001 tablets	249 250 tablets	43,143 doses
1971	37,841		1,600	1,446	562	4,625,173 (+50,022 resin)		684 854,635 tablets	243 14,363 tablets	272,961
1972a	39,413		1,751	1,928	775	2,926,787 (+61,834 resin)		94 9,546,171 tablets	142 748,449 tablets	206,096 doses

SOURCES: Reports to and by the Commission on Narcotic Drugs.
NOTE: Miscellaneous ampoules, tablets, etc. have been omitted, except where significant quantities are involved.

aFigures for this year are provisional.

TABLE 15.2
Distribution of Seizures by Country for 1971

	Quantity	No. of seizures	No. of arrests	Trafficker nationality
Opium	Iran (63%)	Iran (22%)	Iran (18%)	Iranian (15%)
	Hong Kong	France	France	Turkish
	Singapore	India	Turkey	{ French
		Turkey		{ "Chinese"
Morphine	France (54%)	Iran (20%)	Turkey (25%)	Turkish (27%)
	Turkey	Turkey	France	French
	Hong Kong	{Hong Kong	Hong Kong	{ Iranian,
		{ France		{ "Chinese"
Heroin	U.S. (45%)	France (39%)	France (43%)	French (40%)
	Spain	Iran	Iran	Iranish
	France	U.S.	U.S.	U.S.
Cocaine	U.S. (65%)	U.S. (57%)	U.S. (51%)	Chilean (20%)
	Mexico	Mexico	Mexico	U.S.
	Italy	Italy	Italy	{ Colombian
				{ French
Cannabis	U.S. (67%)	U.S. (28%)	U.S. (27%)	U.S. (21%)
	India	France	France	French
	Lebanon	Spain	Spain	German
Stimulants	Sweden	Sweden	Sweden	
	Denmark	Denmark	Denmark	?
	U.K.	{ U.K.	France	
		{ France		
LSD	Denmark	Sweden	Sweden	
	Italy	France	France	?
	Sweden	Netherlands	Spain	

SOURCE: Report submitted by the General Secretariat of INTERPOL to the forty-first General Assembly Session, Frankfurt, September 1972.

NOTE: Within each cell countries are listed in decreasing order of magnitude for the category indicated. Brackets indicate equal magnitudes for the countries bracketed. "Chinese" refers to ethnic origin, not nationality.

The information collected, stored, and disseminated by INTERPOL relates chiefly to criminals: in 1966, its representative to the Commission claimed that they had information on three hundred thousand criminals, and that many of these were drug traffickers.* Its sources are generally police forces in member countries, of which it had only nineteen in 1946 and ninety-eight in 1966 (CND: 21st, 1966). The number of communications received from countries by its secretariat in 1971 totalled 12,259, the number sent out 1,208.

The Committee on Illicit Traffic used to meet in closed sessions that were attended by a large number of observers, including the Permanent Anti-Narcotics Bureau of the League of Arab States. Here, accusing fingers could be pointed at drug-supplying countries and imputations made with less restraint than in the open sessions.

Although the Commission admits that assessing the dimensions of the illicit traffic hinges on a number of factors, such as the adequacy of national data and the effectiveness of law enforcement services, and that therefore the apparent trends revealed by seizure figures might be merely illusory (CND: 24th, 1971), the seizure information nevertheless forms the basis of its discussions. Assessments are, in fact, also made, albeit on different criteria, by another body, the INCB. This latter organ has repeatedly pronounced on the volume of raw materials supplying the illicit drug traffic; in its 1965 report, for instance, it stated that while opium produced licitly for the world's medical and scientific use amounted to 800 tons a year, the amount available annually from illicit sources was around 1,200 tons; the corresponding quantities for coca leaf and cannabis were vast. Again, it reported in 1971 that the quantity of illicitly produced opium was substantially larger than the quantity absorbed in manufacture for legitimate use and that illicit traffickers were increasingly drawing upon this large source of supply. How the INCB arrives at these estimates is not known.

According to the INCB, "ebbs and flows in the illicit traffic, occasioned by variations in demand, on the one hand, and by problems of procurement, on the other, have not materially altered the central position which opium has occupied since international control was first imposed" (INCB, 1971). The Commission's reports often note that opium and the opiates, cocaine and cannabis continue to be the main drugs in the illicit

---

* Doubt has been cast on this claim by a member of the UN Narcotics Division (interview).

traffic (which is hardly surprising since they are by definition the focus of international concern and control). The procurement aspect, however, has changed in the postwar period, and looking back over the years the INCB noted that (INCB, 1969):

> during the formative stages of the control measures introduced by the treaties the illicit traffic supplied itself more or less freely by recourse to unprotected sectors of the licit trade. As the controls began gradually to take effect this became progressively more difficult and traffickers have been obliged to look more and more to sources which are still beyond control. . . . Unfortunately these sources are both extensive and prolific and they constitute an enormous reserve. Some of these sources are remote and even now are difficult of access.

Many of these sources are located in Southeast Asia. The share of the illicit opium market by the various regions is difficult to assess, as is the level of illicit production in the different uncontrolled producing areas. Estimates of the latter made by the U.S. BNDD in 1970 and by the Cabinet Committee on International Narcotics Control in 1971 are given in table 15.3. The highest concentration of illicit production is in the Golden Triangle region—northern Burma, northern Thailand, and

TABLE 15.3
Estimated Illicit Opium Output (in Metric Tons)

Producing country	Amount[a] produced	Amount[b] produced
India	175–200	100
Turkey	100	35–80
Pakistan	175–200	20–160
Afghanistan	100–125	100
Burma	400 ⎫	
Thailand	200 ⎬	700
Laos	100–150 ⎭	
Mexico	5–10	10–20
Other	5–10[c]	20–50[d]

[a]BNDD estimate, 1970, as quoted by Holahan in *Dealing with Drug Abuse* (1972).

[b]Estimate by the Cabinet Committee on International Narcotics Control, in *World Opium Survey, 1972.*

[c]Mainly North Africa and the Near East.

[d]Mainly Eastern Europe. Additional amounts are probably produced in Latin America, North Africa and the Far East.

northern Laos (Holahan, 1972; McCoy, 1972), accounting for about 70 percent of the world's illicit supply. Turkey, although the major source for the American market in the last decade, accounts for only 7 percent of the total illicit supply (McCoy, 1972).

The traffic in cocaine subsided in the 1950s but a resurgence is apparent in current statistics (see table 15.1). The decrease in cocaine traffic in the earlier period is thought to be due less to the effect of international legislation than to fluctuations in demand; the renewed interest has been attributed to users switching from amphetamines.

The illicit-traffic chapter of the 1959 report of the Commission stated that "geographically, cannabis is the most widespread drug of addiction," but that a large proportion of the traffic is based on indigenous production and consumption in the Far East, Africa, Central and South Africa. Annually, reference was made to the "traditional traffic" in hashish in the Near and Middle East, and to Lebanon and the Syrian areas of the UAR as principal sources. More recently, the discussions in international circles of the traffic in cannabis have taken an alarmist turn. The INCB spoke in 1970 of the "widespread, almost epidemic, resort to indulgence in cannabis in recent years" and INTERPOL of the "tremendous upsurge" in cannabis trafficking. Sources were said to be expanding, Nepal and Afghanistan being the most frequently identified.

The Commission's sessions are occasions for some countries to identify others as sources of supply for the drugs found in the illicit traffic. Countries from which seized drugs were alleged to have originated had defended themselves either on the grounds that they lacked the means of control or that the charges were unfounded. There were, in any event, frequent charges and countercharges. The importance attached by the Commission to the need to settle the question of origin led to the collection of "authenticated samples" and to the establishment of the UN Laboratory, whose sole raison d'être seemed to be the scientific determination of the geographical origin of opium seized in the illicit traffic. What is referred to in UN documents as "scientific research on opium" (a regular item in the agenda for the Commission's sessions) is often not much more than that. As earlier stated, testing for opium origin is an obsolete exercise, but, previously, considerable belief was invested in the method.

Although these tests purported to afford countries protection against ill-founded charges (CND:10th, 1955), they have, in fact, been used for quite opposite purposes. Anslinger's determination to misrepresent the People's Republic of China as the source of most of the heroin entering the western United States and as a sponsor of an illicit trade aimed at earning foreign exchange and at "undermining the morale and health of the population of other countries" is well known. Despite the protests of the members of the socialist countries on behalf of the Chinese government, which was not even present in the Commission, Anslinger persuaded a number of countries that "the continuation and expansion of a twenty-year-old plan to finance political activities and spread addiction among other peoples through the sale of opium and heroin, and the extension of these operations to areas which had come under the jurisdiction of the Chinese mainland had mutilated and destroyed whole sections of population which, during the past 40 years, had been freed of the danger of addiction through the efforts of the enforcement authorities of the free countries" (CND:9th, 1954). At one session the representative of Poland raised a query regarding the identification of samples of opium, and the reply of the representative of the Laboratory was as follows:

in the determination of the origin of a sample of seized opium, the analytical data for the seizure were compared with the data obtained for all the authenticated samples in the UN laboratory. The basis for the determination of origin was, therefore, the range and number of authenticated samples available. . . . The firmness of a conclusion as to the origin of a seizure was thus dependent upon the number of authenticated samples available from the particular region in question. In the case of the mainland of China, there were only four authenticated samples, which were received in 1951 from the National Government of China (CND: 18th, 1963).

It is obvious that the charges against the Chinese People's Republic were based on opium samples sent to the UN by the Nationalist government in Taiwan. Both Anslinger and the UN apparently thought this to be in order, since they considered the Nationalist government to be the only recognized government of China, but the situation was anomalous, to say the least, for the UN Laboratory was accepting as authenticated samples those sent to it by a government which neither ruled nor had any access to the country in question (CND: 18th, 1963). Lately, the USSR has been making allegations in the press (*Pravda*) that China earned "at least $12,000 to $15,000 million a year" through opium trafficking, while the U.S. government has admitted that there has been "no evidence of any trafficking from China into any other area" (*Far Eastern Economic Review*, 1973, *79*, 2: 5). It seems that there never has been any concrete evidence of such trafficking, but, while this fact has remained constant, the foreign policies of countries towards China have been reversed. In spite of allegations by the Taiwan government that the People's Republic was smuggling opium out of China, a UN mission accompanied by U.S observers in northeast Thailand could find no evidence of Chinese involvement in drug trafficking (*Report on World Affairs*, 1972, *53*, 3: 167).

While INTERPOL publishes monthly lists of traffickers, and the Commission's reports sometimes record the names of those arrested, a long-held belief among the international control bodies is that drug trafficking is operated by criminal underworld syndicates and that it is "to some extent the prerogative of a hierarchically organized criminal elite headed by 'sleeping partners' who often displayed a respectable facade and were difficult to unmask" (CND: 20th, 1965). The Mafia was mentioned in connection with heroin smuggling in the United States (CND: 14th, 1959); and the image of the traffickers was one of those who, "prompted by predatory greed, were amassing fortunes by exploiting the morbid craving of drug-dependent persons" (Steinig, 1971). In the 1940s, merchant seamen were identified as the chief trafficking group, and there were proposals to persuade governments to revoke their licenses or certificates and to bar them from unions. Of late, the international bodies must have felt their beliefs challenged, for, in its 1971 report, the Commission noted that:

A new category of traffickers appeared to be emerging between the highly organized gangs working on a large scale and the individuals smuggling one or two kilogrammes for the use of themselves and their friends. Among the latter there was a growing awareness of commercial possibilities, and small groups were now dealing in quantities of 10–25 kg. of cannabis or opium.

The following quotation from the INCB's report for 1969 likewise illustrates this:

The flow of illicit traffic has been aided and expanded by the swelling stream of young people travelling from one country to another, frequently as students, sometimes in the guise of students or as wandering musicians who, both by their number and by their often innocent appearance, aggravate the problems of the preventive staffs. On the not infrequent occasions when young people from several countries assemble in mass gatherings the scope for trafficking is greatly facilitated as well as enlarged and the problems of narcotic enforcement staffs are intensified.

The two stereotypes—"the victims" of the traffic, that is, the drug addicts, and "its organizers, the professional criminals"—also exist (CND: 20th, 1965). How simplistic these beliefs are compared to reality is shown in recent studies of drug traffickers and users (Blum, 1972). Many dealers engage in drug trafficking in order to finance their own consumption.

A category of traffickers which has not been discussed in the international forum is, on the other hand, the diplomat who travels under special immunities (McCoy, 1972); between 1960 and 1969 the BNDD arrested and convicted two ambassadors and one ambassador-designate with a total of 168 kg of heroin in their luggage (Gaffney, 1969). Also missing from international discussions today (cf. Advisory Opium Committee discussions) is the illicit side of legitimate drug supplying. It is estimated in the U.S. that 20 percent of all amphetamines are diverted from licit channels; this suggests some collusion on the part of those in charge of the channels involved. Such collusion also exists in the alcohol trade. It has further been shown that, in the U.S., pharmacists not only violate regulations but also sell drugs illegally (Blum et al., 1974).

While the question of illicit traffic comprises the bulk of the work of the Commission, it is illicit traffic in a rather narrow sense which actually occupies it. Perception is typically focused on the opioids, cocaine, and cannabis. The Single Convention itself defines illicit traffic as cultivation or trafficking in drugs contrary to its provisions and, in spelling out measures to combat it, does not venture beyond the usual reliance on prohibition of cultivation (article 22), coordination of repressive action (article 35), and the punishment of drug production, acquisition, possession, and distribution (article 36).* In the 1972 amended version of the

* The wording of this provision is as follows: "Subject to its constitutional limitations, each Party shall adopt such measures as will ensure that the cultivation production, manufacture, extraction, preparation, possession, offering for

Convention, the harshness of the last provision has been toned down by the introduction of the possibility for parties to provide, "either as an alternative to conviction or punishment or in addition to conviction or punishment" for the "treatment, education, after-care, rehabilitation and social reintegration" of offenders.

Nevertheless, the tendency is increasingly towards perceiving the problem of drugs as one of illegal trafficking, and towards a narrowing of intervention options to that which is directly geared to controlling that particular aspect. One of the aims of amending the Single Convention was to enhance the involvement of the INCB in the control of the *illegal* production of opium as well as the legal production. As originally proposed, the new terms would allow the Board to obtain information on the production of raw materials from which the illicit traffic draws its supply, to use information from all sources, official or private, to make on-the-spot checks of suspect drug activities within a country, to modify estimates to limit a country's production to the amount of illicit diversion or illicit production or both that has occurred in that country, and finally, to impose an embargo when it decides that a country is becoming a center of illicit traffic: in short, to increase the INCB's enforcement powers. In the actual protocol adopted, the Board's functions have been defined in such terms as to include an explicit reference to the prevention of "illicit cultivation, production and manufacture of, and illicit trafficking in and use of, drugs" (article 2). Moreover, countries are encouraged to supply the INCB, as well as the Commission, with data on illicit drug activity within their borders; the Board, on the other hand, is empowered to offer its advice on the party's endeavors to reduce the illicit activity.

A further illustration of the increased emphasis on the illicit traffic aspect is afforded by the drastic emasculation of an amendment introduced by Costa Rica, providing for education, for control of "advertising which explicitly, subtly or by omission

---

sale, distribution, purchase, sale, delivery on any terms whatsoever, brokerage, dispatch, dispatch in transit, transport, importation and exportation of drugs contrary to the provisions of this Convention, and any other action which in the opinion of such Party may be contrary to the provisions of this Convention, shall be punishable offences when committed intentionally, and that serious offences shall be liable to adequate punishment particularly by imprisonment or other penalties of deprivation of liberty."

incites to the consumption of drugs," for the promotion of national centers to deal with rehabilitation and prevention in relation to drug consumption, and for regional centers for investigation, education, coordination, and control (E/CONF. 63/C.1/L.20, 1972). This was redrafted by the conference to read as follows:

If a Party considers it desirable as part of its action against the illicit traffic in drugs ... it shall promote the establishment, in consultation with other interested parties in the region, of agreements which contemplate the development of education centres for scientific research and education *to combat the problems resulting from the illicit use and traffic in drugs* (article 38 bis) (emphasis added).

The accepted text bears little resemblance to the original, and the problem itself has been redefined as one resulting from the illicit use and traffic.

A constant theme in the Commission's discussions of illicit drug activity has been the imposition of penalties of greater severity than are found in a number of countries. The 1968 report records that "the Commission recalled its long-held conviction that severe penalties for drug trafficking were an effective deterrent, and its appeals to governments to ensure that long periods of imprisonment should be imposed on drug traffickers, since fines alone were insufficient punishment." A resolution adopted in 1961 called for the imposition of "adequate sentences"—the word "adequate" to be interpreted, according to the representatives of Canada, France, Turkey, and the UAR, as meaning "severe."

The diversity of penal sanctions applied in different countries for what appear to be similar offenses is considered undesirable, and the harmonization of legislation is often urged. Domestic laws do differ widely; a study of selected countries by a staff member of the Division of Narcotics noted that there was an "obvious lack of a common international point of view on the subject" (Memorandum on Penal Sanctions for Narcotics Offences, 1972: MNAR/3/72). To take a few examples: the Afghani criminal code of 1924 expressly forbade the local use of alcohol, cannabis and cannabis resin, and opium, and punished such offenses with imprisonment or fine; however, the exportation of "Afghani production" of narcotics was expressly authorized.

Under new legislation (1956) an across-the-board penalty comprising confiscation of the drug and imprisonment and/or fine was introduced for all drug offences. In contrast, Iranian legislation bases penalties upon the quantity of drug involved; in cases involving more than 2 kg of opium or 10 kg of morphine, heroin, cocaine, and cannabis, capital punishment by firing squad can be ordered. The study noted that since 1969 over 110 executions have taken place, and eight life sentences were imposed in 1970. While Japan places as heavy an emphasis on penalizing possession as trafficking, most European countries punish import/sale/manufacture more severely than possession. Some countries do not distinguish between classes of drugs: the United Arab Republic of Egypt is an example. It is noteworthy that a feature shared by many of the legal systems surveyed is the severe penalization of the user; this is seen by the study as a sign of society's frustration at not being able to strike more effectively at the suppliers.

The study points to the vastly different concepts that different countries have of what constitutes fit punishment for a particular offense but sees these as being linked to local conditions which may possibly justify them. Yet in the Commission, countries are urged to harmonize their drug legislation. If the Commission is in favor of stiffer penalties, then what is being urged is uniformity towards greater severity. In withholding any criticisms it may have of the death penalty, is the Commission tacitly advocating that other legal systems, too, should adopt the Iranian firing squad?

As an adjunct to heavier sentencing policies, effective law enforcement and better intelligence services are thought necessary. More than once, the Commission had recorded its recognition of the "bravery of officials killed or wounded" in reported battles between enforcement officers and traffickers (for example, CND: 22d, 1968). What has not been admitted is the high incidence of corruption in some narcotics police forces (see Blum et al., 1974). Training programs for law enforcement officers designed to impart or improve investigative and other techniques have been instituted by the UN on a regular basis. INTERPOL also organizes international training seminars for police officers, and the U.S. Bureau of Narcotics Training School has likewise trained officers from other countries. Along with INTERPOL, BNDD—now DEA—is a frequent participant in

UN technical assistance missions and seminars on narcotics control (in the study tour of Latin America in 1965; seminar for narcotics law-enforcement officers in East Africa, 1967; inter-regional seminar on narcotics control, Beirut, in 1968, and so on). The UN itself awards fellowships to enforcement officers both under its technical assistance program and under the aegis of the UN Fund (UNFDAC). The importance attached to enforcement is reflected in the infusion of funds into the Central Training Unit, which conducts courses designed for law enforcement officials specializing in countering illicit traffic (UN Information Letters, 1972: 9; 1973: 3). Financial support for this unit represented the second largest allocation (the first being the Thai project) from the resources available to the Fund in 1972.

A great deal of the discussion of penalties for trafficking is, in fact, vitiated by the failure to take account of the political context within which the drug trade is embedded. McCoy's study (McCoy, 1972) alleges, for instance, that the drug business in Southeast Asia is intimately linked to the cold war crusade of the United States. He reports that in Laos, for example, the U.S. working through the CIA to build up the Meo guerillas to counter Communist wars of national liberation, indirectly provides support by way of money, guns, aircraft, and the like to the very individuals who are engaged in the opium trade; while in Burma, the opium shipment business is for the most part in the hands of the remnants of the Kuomintang (KMT) army of the deposed Nationalist government of Chiang Kai-shek, again CIA-financed. The involvement of the KMT troops had been pointed out to the Commission as early as 1960 (CND: 15th, 1960). A Southeast Asia Consultative Group on Narcotics Control organized by the UN had reported that "the presence of military irregulars (KMT) in Upper Burma ... added to the difficulties of control. These irregulars had facilitated the opium traffic and were notorious as the 'opium army' " (TAO/AFE/11). The intricacies of the situation are further illustrated by an incident reported in the *Far Eastern Economic Review* (1973, 79, 7: 13). A Thai police helicopter carrying Thai police and three Americans, one of whom was an official in the U.S. embassy in Bangkok, was shot down in eastern Burma. The explanation of the Thai officials was that they had come to persuade Thai farmers to stop growing opium poppy, but had strayed into Burmese territory by mistake. The area over which this occurred was where the

Burmese troops had been engaged in skirmishes with the opium-growing Lahu hill-tribe insurgents. When the government began to set up administrative bodies in the villages, the Lahus had felt threatened and had sent an emissary to Thailand to acquire arms in exchange for opium.

UN discussions, however, eschew the total set of conditions of which the drug trade is only a part. A realistic appraisal of the situation is avoided. Perhaps attention is concentrated on the well-organized professional criminal for the reason that the other elements involved are both complicated and raise awkward questions. UN officials justify their inaction by saying that they are unable to originate anything which does not stem from official information supplied to the UN by the government concerned.

SUMMARY

1. Illicit drug traffic is bound up with other types of commerce, both legal and illegal. Its contents and sources have been affected by legislation and law enforcement.
2. International action against the illicit traffic has been based on controlling availability on the one hand, and the use of the criminal sanction on the other.
3. International control over drug availability has had a double-edged effect: it regulated authorized production but gave rise to unauthorized production, especially in areas beyond local government control, for example in the Golden Triangle region of Southeast Asia.
4. Under international legislation, drug trafficking became a crime of international character.
5. A system of governmental reporting of drug seizures and transactions to international bodies has been established. The information reviewed by international bodies is sometimes uncertain. International organs also entertain some misconceptions of drug dealers and drug trafficking.
6. In its discussions of the illicit traffic, the Commission has constantly emphasized the need to impose stiffer penalties on traffickers. These discussions are also characterized by imputations of illicit consignments to various countries.
7. A wide diversity of penal sanctions exists in national laws despite injunctions to harmonization; a common feature, however, is the penalization of the user.
8. There is a tendency among international bodies to perceive the "drug problem" as a problem of illegal trafficking.

9. A large proportion of the resources and efforts of UN drug organs have been committed to increasing the effectiveness of police officers.
10. The political context in which the drug trade is embedded tends to be overlooked.

16   The Vienna Convention

> Times had indeed changed since Governments had been
> prepared to go to war to protect the commercial interests
> of [their] factories, which used to flood the markets of
> distant countries with heroin.... Amphetamines and
> the barbiturates ... [are] at present being exported by
> the ton to those same distant countries, and that trade
> [is] legitimate. It [is] essential to give those distant lands
> the right to protect their peoples.
>
> > J. Mabileau, delegate of France, in a statement to
> > the Vienna Conference, 1971

         The Vienna Convention on Psychotropic Sub-
stances was adopted on 21 February 1971 by a plenipotentiary
conference in Vienna. Under it, amphetamines, barbiturates,
tranquilizers, and hallucinogens will be brought under international control. How did these controls come about?

Behind the events leading up to Vienna was the underlying fact
that problems related to the use of these "psychotropic" substances occurred. Japan, for instance, had serious problems after
World War II with widespread intravenous use of amphetamines.
The WHO Expert Committee had taken note of this problem
several times since 1949, though it had not, on those occasions,
considered international action warranted. The Commission too
had discussed amphetamines as well as barbiturates and hallucinogens a number of times. At the 1961 conference which adopted
the Single Convention, some participant states had agreed that
amphetamines, barbiturates, and tranquilizers constituted a
public health hazard. However, a resolution calling for strict
national control and for looking into the necessity and possibility of
international control had failed to attain a two-thirds majority.

Moves towards International Control

At a session of the Commission later in 1961, the question of the
national and international control of barbiturates was re-intro-

243

duced by Turkey, the United Arab Republic, and Yugoslavia
(CND: 16th, 1961). The proposal was reconsidered the following
year, when it was rejected. Instead, the Commission agreed on a
recommendation for national control of production, distribution,
and use. Themes which were to recur were already developing. One
was the concern of the Commission with drugs outside the scope of
existing treaties. Another was the tendency of the developing
countries to use this as an opportunity for turning the tables on
Western industrialized countries and have the weight of control
(hitherto felt most by them) spread equally over production of raw
materials and synthetic manufacture. Yet another was the insistence by some of the protagonists that national, not international,
control was the preferred and sufficient response.

In 1963 and 1964 the Commission considered LSD, a drug for
whose control the U.S. was the chief proponent. In 1965 Sweden
came on the scene, advocating international controls over some
stimulants. Sweden had been grappling with problems related to
stimulants since the 1940s, when in response to a high rate of oral
consumption it had exerted national control through making most
of the existing narcotics regulations applicable to these drugs.
With the occurrence of intravenous stimulant use, Sweden had
formally classified stimulants as narcotics and had sought to affect
availability through law enforcement and a close watch over
prescriptions. An illicit market developed with the reduction of
licit supply, and the fact that other European countries did not
control stimulants made for a great deal of smuggling. Sweden saw
that international cooperation between police and customs authorities was difficult to achieve unless other countries felt it incumbent
upon them to accept treaty-bound obligations and enforce compatible drug controls. At the World Health Assembly in May 1965,
Sweden was one of the sponsors of a resolution on sedatives and
stimulants (WHA 18:47) containing recommendations for prescription control, health education, and research. The WHO
secretariat was asked to study the "advisability and feasibility of
international measures of control."

The WHO Expert Committee made a significant move when it
recommended the following measures of control over stimulants
and sedatives (WHO/EC DD, 1965):

    1. Availability on medical prescription only
    2. Full accounting for all transactions from production to
    retail distribution

3. Licensing of all producers
4. Limitation of trade to authorized persons
5. Prohibition of unauthorized possession
6. Establishment of an import-export authorization system
However, of these actions, only the last is international in character.

When the Commission met in 1965 a special committee was established to consider controls over such substances outside the drug conventions then in force as barbiturates, tranquilizers, and amphetamines. Before the time the committee met—this was eight months later in August 1966—the situation "was to change radically." LSD was singled out by it in a special resolution condemning all usage other than for medical and scientific purposes (E/CN.7/498, 1966). To amphetamines, barbiturates, and tranquilizers, the committee gave second place. Among the views of the committee regarding these drugs were those of some observers that the market for these drugs was "being overexploited"; that "superfluous production and stocks" continued to increase the risk of diversion; and that "professionally and commercially the risks involved had been viewed too lightly." They also referred to "irresponsible prescribing and dispensing by doctors, improper self-medication by individuals," and "illicit introduction of these drugs into countries for abuse" (E/CN.7/498, 1966). At its session in 1966 the Commission accepted the committee's report and asked the Division to undertake, in consultation with WHO and the Board, a study on the legal, administrative, and other questions involved in initiating international action (CND: 21st, 1966). In May 1967 ECOSOC adopted a strong resolution for *national* controls over LSD (E/RES/1197 [XLII]). This was followed by a World Health Assembly resolution of a week later, similarly focused on LSD, in which a study on the feasibility of *international* control was urged (WHA/20.42). The Assembly also adopted a resolution on sedatives and stimulants, asking for those *national* controls that were enumerated by the WHO Expert Committee in 1964, to which reference has already been made. In the Commissions's 1967 session a working group was appointed to study the implications of control.

The Positions Taken

Linked to the events just recapitulated are the views, reactions, and preferences promoted by nations, groups, and individuals with varying degrees of access to and influence on decision-making. What these were on the part of the Board and the Division are expounded in a document prepared by the Division in response to the Commission's request for a study on the administrative and legal aspects of control mentioned earlier.* On the assumption that a consensus existed on the necessity for international control, the document proceeded to spell out the choices which were available to the international community in the selection of control measures.

When the Commission asked for the study, it had directed that special priority be given to "the problem of LSD and similar substances." However, the Division's paper pointed out that the common denominator of the various positions held by WHO and the Commission was the necessity for mandatory national controls through an international treaty, new or adapted, and that this was fully consonant with the position held by these bodies in relation to amphetamines, barbiturates, and tranquilizers. A treaty "covering the whole field of psychotropic substances" would, however, have to reflect the "greater gravity" attributed to LSD.

The Board's views were expressed in a memorandum appended to the Division's paper. It considered several possibilities. One was the restriction of "undesirable commercial advertising of dangerous drugs" through articles 21 and 22 of the WHO constitution, authorizing the adoption by the World Health Assembly of, among other regulations, those concerning "advertising and labelling of biological, pharmaceutical and similar products moving in international commerce." The Division's paper considered such restriction only "an ancillary measure of control" and advised against it. The Board had also considered the amendment of the Single Convention, and the conclusion of a special treaty. The Board argued against amending the treaty, and the Division concurred, with the comment that such an amended treaty would be a jigsaw puzzle. The Division's paper also ruled out the application of article 3 and proposed a new treaty. Although the Division emphasized considerations of practicality in the selection of control measures and the Board was mainly concerned with legal arrangements, the two bodies arrived at essentially the same conclusions.

* "The Control of Psychotropic Substances Not under International Control— Legal, Administrative and Other Questions." Note by the Secretary-General (E/CN. 7/509, 1967).

The Board's paper also tackled the question of the application of article 3 of the Single Convention providing for the inclusion of drugs liable to *similar* abuse and productive of similar ill effects as drugs already included or readily *convertible* into drugs showing such a similarity. It was up to WHO, the Board thought, to interpret the term "similar," but some similarity in ill effects appeared to the Board to exist between morphine and barbiturates or some tranquilizers, between cocaine and amphetamines, and between cannabis and some hallucinogens. Nevertheless, the Board agreed with the WHO representative (Halbach) when he spoke to the Commission about the legal difficulties of applying article 3: "the drafter of the Single Convention had not intended to include dependence-producing drugs other than those listed in the schedules." The crux of the matter was what degree of similarity WHO considered a drug should display before it could be placed under existing international control. The Board's opinion was that a narrow definition of "similar" had in fact been intended. According to the Board it had been the understanding of the Commission when drafting the Single Convention and of the delegates who adopted it at the conference in 1961 that ampehtamines, barbiturates, and tranquilizers could not be included on grounds of similarity. The draft resolution moved by some delegates on international control of these drugs would have been unnecessary if article 3 of the Single Convention were applicable to the drugs in question. The Board also thought it interesting that no government in favor of international control over psychotropic substances had initiated a procedure under article 3.

The Division's commentary provided the counterpoise to the Board's arguments. It stated that "in very general terms" depressants of the central nervous system "might be assimilated" to the group of drugs of the morphine type, the stimulants assimilated to cocaine and the hallucinogens assimilated to cannabis or cocaine or both. It further noted that the contents of the control schedules of the Single Convention had not been determined on the basis of a finding of similarity between the drugs controlled, and some national governments had not balked at including amphetamines and hallucinogens in narcotics legislation. Theoretically, "given the heterogeneous character of the substances in the first two Schedules of the Single Convention, other heterogeneous stimulants and depressants of the central nervous system might be assimilated to it." The paper concluded that "if for empirical or pragmatical reasons, control measures of a selected degree are to be applied to these substances, this is not absolutely precluded by the terms of article 3 of the Single Convention." Although it was unambiguously and unanimously affirmed by the 1961 conference which adopted the Single Convention that the Convention was not intended to cover, for example, tranquilizers and barbiturates "but only substances of a definitely narcotic kind" (Official Records II, 1964: 86), there were those at the conference who were in favor of the principle of international control over these substances, but their views failed by one vote to obtain a two-thirds majority. The basis for the rejection was thus merely procedural. It could therefore be argued, the Division contended, that the drafters of the Single Convention had not intended to "keep out the other psychotropic substances at all costs for all time." The Division believed that "It is not legality which can stop the international community from using the instrument at hand, it is whether it would be practical and effective to do so."

The Board had also pointed to the practical difficulties of applying the Single Convention. On this point the Division agreed. Such application would entail amending the Convention and adding schedules, and this would result in the creation of a very complicated treaty causing "intractable administrative problems."

Further Moves

In late 1968 Sweden did what the Board had previously thought interesting that no one had yet done. It sent the UN secretary-general a notification asking that six stimulants (amphetamine, dexamphetamine, methamphetamine, methylphenidate, phenmetrazine, and pipradol) be placed under control in terms of article 3 of the Single Convention. Behind this move may have been a sense of frustration at the slow progress toward control, a pressing national problem, the continued lack of cooperation from other countries in stemming illicit drug supplies, and a reaction to the attention claimed by LSD at the expense of the other drugs.

Sweden's assumption of a more active role in international drug control was preceded by several preparatory steps. Its representatives attending as observers at the 1968 meeting of the Commission had pleaded for controls over stimulants (CND:22d). At the World Health Assembly in 1968 the Scandinavian countries and Yugoslavia had moved that the Assembly should recommend the inclusion of stimulants in Schedule I of the Single Convention, although the resolution eventually adopted (WHA 21:42) was one which merely took account of the fact that the Commission was working to develop a new international instrument. Also in 1968 the Swedish National Board of Health and Welfare organized an international conference on the abuse of stimulants to secure an information base on which to plan further action. On 1 January 1969 Sweden became a member of the Commission.

After the 1968 Commission session, the Division circulated a questionnaire to national governments on possible control measures. The answers were analyzed in a special document for the Commission (E/CN.7/518 and Corr.1). The Division also distributed a document entitled "Protocol on Psychotropic Substances Outside the Scope of the Single Convention on Narcotic Drugs" (E/CN.7/519). This draft consisted of two versions: A and B. Version A spelt out control measures which had to be applied in sets, whereas in B these measures could be applied separately. Version B also allowed each party not to apply the controls decided upon.

Sweden followed up on its initiative with a further proposal that stimulants be placed under provisional control pending the definitive decision. In contrast to the position held earlier, the Division's response to this move was to invoke the arguments which had been offered by the Board against the applicability of the Single Convention to these drugs. In support of this new position, reference was made by the Division to the UN Office of Legal Affairs which had "consistently held that there were legal doubts" about the applicability of the Convention. Reference was also made to the Commission's opposition to the international control of amphetamines in 1955 and of barbiturates and tranquilizers in 1957 and 1959 to 1962 (CND: 23d, 1969).

The various postures adopted in response to the Swedish initiative confronted each other at the twenty-third session of the Commission. The following extract from the report of the meeting is a record of some of the views that were articulated (CND: 23d, 1969).

Some representatives, including those of India and Yugoslavia, argued that ... it was for the Parties themselves ... to decide whether [the 1961 Convention] could or could not be applied to any substance or substances. These representatives reiterated their view that the 1961 Convention was applicable to the psychotropic substances. Accordingly they held that the most dangerous of the psychotropic substances could immediately be put under control by action in terms of article 3 of the Convention, by including them, for example, in Schedule I or Schedules I and IV. They argued that the criteria for applying the Convention consisted of similarity as regards the liability to abuse, and similarity as regards ill effects; there was ample medical evidence to indicate that the more dangerous psychotropic substances disqualify, in terms of these criteria, for control under the 1961 Convention. Nor were the arguments about the understanding at the time of the drafting of the 1961 Convention decisive; today, there was much greater evidence of abuse liability and ill effects as concerns these substances, and had this evidence been available in 1961 the doctrine as to the scope of the 1961 Convention might well have been conceived differently. As regards the administrative and practical difficulties, these difficulties had been unduly exaggerated and were far from insuperable. The representatives of Sweden and Yugoslavia felt that it was entirely appropriate to bring the six notified amphetamine-like substances under the control of the 1961 Convention, but that other psychotropic drugs should be reserved for a new international instrument. (E/CN.7/523 Rev. 1:67).

Even if Sweden thought it could secure majority support for its proposal for *provisional* control over stimulants, it nevertheless withdrew this proposal in favor of a unanimous resolution calling for immediate voluntary national action on stimulants. The major Western countries had been in opposition, and some had threatened to withdraw from or withhold ratification of the Single Convention. It had seemed to Sweden that a better dividend would be had from a general agreement to take rapid action at the national level and to bring stimulants into the new treaty than from a mere majority of votes to which those cast by the manufacturing countries did not contribute.

The contents of the resolution ranged from observations on the abuse of stimulants and the Commission's inability to reach agreement on the applicability of the Single Convention, to recommendations that governments should apply national controls corresponding as closely as possible to those provided by the

Single Convention and that they should cooperate with each other and seek assistance from international bodies. The formal communication from Sweden regarding *permanent* control was not withdrawn, and the Commission noted that it was being transferred to the parties and to WHO, which would consider it.

The Draft Protocol

The Commission decided to accept version A as a basis for its work on the draft protocol despite the initial opposition of, among others, the U.S. representative, who argued for flexibility and the right of a party to reject a control decision. The proponents of version A—particularly Yugoslavia—held that national rejection of controls should not be allowed and that it would be inconsistent to prepare a weak instrument of control when there was agreement that the dangers arising out of the abuse of the psychotropic substances were grave. The Indian representative noted that the opium-producing countries had accepted strict controls in the interest of all mankind, and he expressed the hope that the developed countries manufacturing psychotropic substances would now cooperate in ensuring truly effective measures for control of their products.

The Commission decided to have four schedules of drugs, instead of the six which draft A had provided. Hallucinogens were to be placed under the most severe control regime, under schedule I. Following a discussion as to whether some stimulants should be controlled in the same way, agreement was reached that highly dangerous substances which were generally acknowledged to have medical utility should be listed in schedule II and be subject to controls "nearly analogous in most respects" to those of schedule I of the Single Convention. Schedules III and IV were to contain controls in decreasing order of stringency.

On the criteria for applying control, the Commission decided that potential for dependence should not be specified since the emphasis should be on the public health and social problems created by a drug's liability to abuse. The criteria should also encompass the capacity of a drug to produce stimulation, depression, hallucinations, or disturbances in perception or thinking.

On the placement of drugs under control, both drafts A and B left it to WHO to initiate the procedure. The Commission proposed that each party should also have this right. The USSR, supported by India and Switzerland, further proposed that the possibility of applying provisional control be incorporated. The Commission's work resulted in a new draft protocol, with a number of provisions left open or accompanied by alternatives.

Work on the draft protocol continued at a special session of the Commission at Geneva in January 1970. In addition to the draft protocol the Commission had to consider the seventeenth report of the WHO Expert Committee (WHO/EC DD, 1970), which recommended that the psychotropic substances proposed for control be divided into four groups. The basic criteria for control should be on the one hand the degree of risk that the substance was liable to abuse, and on the other its medical usefulness. As far as stimulants were concerned, the Committee proposed that:

to meet the immediate emergency, urgent attention be given to the elaboration of a special temporary instrument that will provide for speedy international control (p. 23).

In response to the Swedish notification of stimulants, the WHO director-general, in a *note-verbale* dated 7 October 1969 to the UN secretary-general, merely called attention to the "special temporary instrument" recommended by the expert committee without a commitment on his own part. He further stated that amphetamine, dexamphetamine, methamphetamine, methylphenidate, and phenmetrazine, but not pipradol, were pharmacologically similar among themselves and sufficiently similar to cocaine in their pattern of abuse and ill effects to be assimilable to Schedule I of the Single Convention. He believed that "on purely technical grounds therefore . . . he would be obligated to make a recommendation" that the five substances be added to Schedule I of the Single Convention. He added, however, that this might not be appropriate, as the plenipotentiary conference which adopted the Single Convention had rejected control of stimulants, and a new treaty was being considered.

The lists proposed by the expert committee were accepted by the Commission as the basis for the negotiations of the coming plenipotentiary conference. Sweden thereby secured the inclusion of stimulants in the second schedule, against the initial resistance of, among other countries, the U.S. and Canada.

On the procedure for bringing drugs under control, the manufacturing countries secured a relative weakening of WHO's role and a corresponding strengthening of the role of the Commission.

A clause provided that the Commision should take into account the findings and recommendations of WHO and, "bearing in mind economic, social, legal, administrative and other factors that it may consider relevant" decide whether a substance should be added to any of the schedules. A minority composed of Ghana, India, Iran, Jamaica, Sweden, Turkey, and the United Arab Republic proposed that the Commission's role be limited to accepting or rejecting the proposal of WHO. The representative of WHO declared that while they preferred the standpoint of the minority, they were willing to accept that of the majority, since it had been agreed that the decisions of the Commission would be based on grounds other than those considered by WHO.

Also noteworthy is the statement of the chairman, made on the demand of several delegations, that alcohol and tobacco were not to be included under the scope of the new international treaty. This may have been motivated by a wish to preempt future moves to bring these drugs under control. The 1961 conference, too, had been "expressly instructed" by the secretary-general's representative (Official Records, II, 1964:94) and by the chairman that alcohol was outside the conference's terms of reference. No member had objected.

Finally, Sweden introduced a draft resolution calling for interim application of national and international control over psychotropic substances. Although weaker than the Single Convention, the controls embodied in the draft protocol were considerably stronger than those advocated by the critics of the protocol. These critics were making themselves heard in 1970.

Countermoves

Ranged against the interests of those nations pressing for control were the countervailing tendencies of other nations and groups. The statement of the Swiss delegate at the 1966 session of the Commission, that amphetamines should not be placed under international control regimes because "the effects of amphetamines on the individual and society were far from being as harmful as those of cocaine, cannabis and synthetic drugs," is a reflection of the resistance by which the control-minded countries were constantly being checked (E/CN.7/SR 552).

A case against the protocol was being built up by the pharmaceutical industry when the instrument was still in preparation. At a meeting in Stockholm in June 1968 the Pharmaceutical

Industries Association (PIA) adopted a resolution expressing its views on an international instrument for the overall control of "certain dependence-producing drugs." In essence, what the resolution said was that legislation should be on a national level only, and that free international drug trade should not be unnecessarily hampered by complicated import/export rules. Reference was made by PIA to WHO's recommendations on national controls. The view was expressed that controls should be preceded by investigations of actual risks and based on statistical evidence of "social harm caused through use of drugs obtained from legitimate sources."

The keynote of the principles enunciated by the International Federation of Pharmaceutical Manufacturers Associations (IFPMA) in its resolution adopted in Rome in May 1969 was likewise the sufficiency of national controls. On the other hand it thought "the exchange of information and introduction of effective national legislation might usefully be co-ordinated by the establishment of a special international treaty." Concern was expressed about the draft international agreement under consideration by the Narcotics Commission. It envisaged, in the opinion of IFPMA, an overextensive system of control, which gave international organizations the exclusive right to determine which substances to control and the degree of control. IFPMA instead pledged its support to a draft convention which the organization itself had worked out, based on the principles it averred.

Further criticisms of the proposed treaty were voiced at the Twenty-ninth International Congress on Alcoholism and Drug Dependence organized by the International Council on Alcohol and Addictions (ICAA), which took place in Australia in February 1970. In a paper delivered by Walter von Wartburg, legal adviser to Hoffmann-La Roche, the proposed controls were critically examined (von Wartburg, 1970). His thesis was that decisions on the final draft of the treaty should be based on consideration of "administrative practicability" and "medical availability." The psychotropic substances were different, according to von Wartburg, from narcotic drugs in a number of respects. The number of substances in the former category was considerably greater; they belonged to different groups pharmacologically, whereas narcotic drugs presented similar "ill effects to the individual and to society"; and many of the drugs being considered for control were in "extensive medical use and admin-

istered daily to an untold number of patients all over the world."
Thus one could not generalize from the apparent value of
narcotics controls to the value of control of the psychotropic
substances.

Other points made by von Wartburg may be summarized as
follows. The heavy burden imposed by the new controls would
lead to an increase in personnel and expenditures. The burden of
rigid controls would outweigh advantages. The dissipation of
resources might weaken existing international control, and organized smuggling might profit. The effect of the American alcohol
prohibition had been an increase in alcoholism and a growing
disrespect for the law in general. Only an optimal level of control
could bring about a minimum level of abuse; and while complicated controls might be acceptable or even desirable for a relatively
small, homogeneous number of substances of no, or limited, use,
they would be "unbearable in respect to the many untold
substances" eventually to be covered by the new treaty.

As far as the problem of medical availability is concerned, von
Wartburg thought that therapeutic use of psychotropic drugs did
not, as a rule, induce physical dependence. Their abuse constituted a problem only in a few countries. The control regime of
narcotics might "sometimes even discourage the use of narcotic
drugs for medical purposes." Von Wartburg stated further:

It is well known that administrative controls do not as such
prevent the abuse of drugs by dependence-prone individuals.
Control measures may be very useful in general, but in the case of
psychologically defective persons they are directed at the
repression of the symptoms rather than at the treatment of the
underlying psychological difficulties. The cause of addiction is
not drugs but human weakness, as has once been observed by Dr.
Isbell from Lexington.

Von Wartburg's over-all conclusion was a plea for voluntary
enactment of adequate *national* controls. On the specifics of the
draft protocol, he argued that the coverage of the international
instrument should be by definition limited to substances whose
abuse posed an *international* problem, that emphasis should be
placed on existing problems rather than potential ones, and that
prime attention should be given to dependence-related abuse
rather than to misuse contrary to medical practice.

To indicate the variety of ideas which were being expressed
about the Vienna protocol and to see what their origins may have

been we will sample another round of discussions, this time at the International Institute of the Prevention and Treatment of Drug Dependence, an international conference organized again by ICAA in June 1970 in Lausanne. Criticisms came this time from members of the pharmaceutical industry as well as from prominent medical scientists from the U.S., whose dissatisfaction was with the use of the criminal sanction in drug legislation and the encroachment of controls on scientific research and the freedom of medical practice. At the end of the conference, a panel, consisting of some of the speakers, presented a paper entitled "Principles of Effective Drug Abuse Control" for general discussion. The views contained in the paper included the following: drug laws should focus on the evil-minded rather than on the weak; they should enable concentration rather than dissipation of control effort; society should not impede the search for therapeutic relief; an international treaty would not by itself abolish undesirable conduct; national action was preferable; the extension of narcotics control concepts to nonnarcotic drugs of great therapeutic value would "constitute an irresponsible interference with established medical practice on an international scale." The criteria for control proposed by the paper were similar to those advocated by von Wartburg. The increased consumption of psychotropic drugs for "medical, scientific and other legitimate purposes" which a "rapidly changing environment" was bringing about should not, the paper held, be arbitrarily prevented.

The paper was subjected to severe criticism by the representatives of the international drug organs and other members of the audience. The director of the UN Division of Narcotic Drugs (Vladimir Kušević) stated that narcotic control had not restricted legitimate availability. WHO's representative (Dale Cameron) said that it was not intended to subject unauthorized drug possession to heavy penalties. Adolf Lande, ex-secretary of the INCB, advised the meeting against drawing the conclusion that innovative scientific inquiry would be hampered by control. After a vigorous debate, the subject was dropped.

One of the papers delivered at the conference is worthy of special note. This was Adolf Lande's "Principles of Effective Drug Control." Lande was one of the authors of the draft protocol and had played an influential role in the stimulants controversy. In an internal UN memorandum he had argued against the inclusion of stimulants under existing drug treaties on the same grounds as those on which the Division's views, expressed at the Commission's meeting in 1969, were based. In the paper delivered at Lausanne, Lande conveyed his views on drug control in general:

I think most governments would not be inclined to deprive numerous people of their sleep by imposing the narcotics regime on barbiturates.... In deciding whether controls should be imposed and what measures should be applied, both the extent of medical use and the size of abuse must be taken into account.... The possibilities of international drug treaties to deal with the problems of personality and environment are even more limited than those of national laws. In fact they deal nearly exclusively with the agents, i.e., with the drugs.... The Legal Office of the United Nations ruled that the Single Convention on Narcotic Drugs could not be applied to barbiturates, amphetamines and tranquilizers, without an amendment. It did not exclude LSD and similar hallucinogenic drugs which in my view could be brought under international control by the operation of the Single Convention on Narcotic Drugs. In rejecting the application of the Single Convention to the psychotropic drugs with whose control it dealt, the Commission was not exclusively guided by legal considerations, but also by the opinion that the narcotics regime was not suitable for the drugs under consideration, that it was for some of them too strict and for others not strict enough.... The more broadly defined authority under the Single Convention on Narcotic Drugs was radically narrowed down by the understanding of the plenipotentiary conference which adopted this treaty that barbiturates, amphetamines and tranquilizers are excluded from the scope of the convention.... A satisfactory solution of the problem of the right of countries to reject control decisions of the Commission is in my view necessary to ensure the general acceptance of the protocol.... It is also essential that the control efforts of the international and national authorities are not dissipated, but concentrated on the real problems of abuse.... In particular, the international regime should not be burdened by the control of drugs which constitute only a national and not an international problem.... *If I am correctly informed, none of the drugs listed in Schedule IV of the Protocol constitute at present such a problem* [emphasis added].... In order to carry out this system of quantitative limitation [the estimate system], each country must allocate quotas to its manufacturers and/or import-ers. This restrictive system has proven its value in preventing the diversion of narcotic drugs from licit into illicit channels, particularly in the earlier years of its application. The

Commission on Narcotic Drugs has, however, rejected the
proposal of some of its members to introduce this system into the
Draft Protocol on Psychotropic Drugs and—as I think—rightly
so.... I think that an elimination of the import certificate and
expert authorization system from the draft would make the
Protocol more generally acceptable.... It appears also that the
requirement of an advance approval of research projects involving
use of drugs in Schedule I on human beings would be inconsistent
with sound principles of free research.... The punishment
meted out should be effective, i.e., sufficiently severe to be
deterrent. (Lande, 1970).

It is interesting to note how close these views were to those of von
Wartburg and the pharmaceutical industry. Lande in fact
appeared at the Vienna Conference on behalf of the American
Pharmaceutical Manufacturers Association.

In July 1970 IFPMA issued a commentary on the revised draft
protocol. The commentary acknowledged the usefulness of an
international protocol for the exchange of information on abuse
and countermeasures and for a framework for the coordination of
national activities. Its other comments were as follows: the treaty
should be flexible; the revised draft protocol still bore too much
resemblance to the Single Convention, whereas the two treaties
should be unrelated in view of the basic difference in coverage. An
extension of international narcotic control to valuable drugs of
daily medical use would be an error. Among such unsuitable
provisions was the necessity to furnish world-wide statistical
figures and the penal provisions. Further, the coverage was too
heterogeneous. There was consensus within "the international
community" only about the need for international control on
dangerous hallucinogens and some stimulants. "To achieve a
reasonably quick international control solution of the drug-abuse-
related public health problems of today, a concentration of
international control efforts primarily on the existing abuse would
appear to be the preferable course of action." The proposal of the
WHO Expert Committee for a limited temporary instrument was
noted. The treaty should deal exclusively with dependence-
producing psychotropic substances and base control on actual
proof of substantial abuse. Precursors should not fall under the
control, unless a problem existed. It "would be in the best interest
of public health if manufacturers were to remain free in their
ways and means to guarantee that industrially used substances"

did not give rise to an abuse problem. A differentiation in degree of control had, "contrary to the wisdom of WHO," been made most prominently between schedules II and III although these substances were declared to be of equal risk. No differentiation, however, existed between schedules III and IV, "whereas it is exactly between those two Schedules that WHO has found a significant dissimilarity of risks." The Commission should only have the power to accept or reject recommendations by WHO. A consultation prodecure should be mandatory for WHO. "This would ensure that no substance is eventually placed under international control without anybody being aware of the reasons and merits for such a decision." Any party should have an absolute right of rejecting control decisions (except in regard to substances under schedule I and in regard to request for mutual legal assistance in combating drug abuse). "Finally, a provision should be inserted to the effect that at least a reasonable number of important manufacturing countries must have ratified the new protocol before its entering into force."

Vienna

The diverse opinions confronted each other at the plenipotentiary conference in Vienna in early 1971.

We will examine article 2 as a test case. It deals with the scope of control of the various drugs and is of interest for two reasons. First, it represents an important departure from the Single Convention in the mechanism it spells out for putting drugs under control; and, second, the negotiations over it provide a good illustration of the generalizations we made earlier about the interests and conflicts of the various parties involved. It was one of the articles which had met with the most opposition in the committee which debated it, and the establishment of its text had taken four weeks (Official Records II, 1973: 66).

The mechanism differs from that of the Single Convention in its criteria for including drugs under control. In the new treaty these criteria are broader and more evidence is needed for a decision to control a drug. In the draft version, the requirement had been limited to a finding by WHO that the drug in question had the capacity to produce certain effects, but in the version which was actually adopted *sufficient* evidence that the substance in question *was being or was likely to be abused* was required before a control decision could be taken. The U.K. delegation pushed more than any of the others at Vienna for the necessity to have a strong basis of evidence for drug evaluation.

There were divergent opinions on the scheme of control. The West German representative, for example, repeatedly argued against controls over drugs listed in schedule IV: "Since it was not sufficiently clear," he declared, "that they did give rise to dependence and since no appreciable risk of abuse was involved, there was no need for any special regulations" (Official Records II, 1973: 7). In this he was supported by Belgium, Switzerland, the Netherlands, and Denmark. France thought it patently clear that these delegations "had set their minds" on weakening the protocol (Official Records II, 1973: 57). The developing countries, notably India and Togo, wanted fairly strict controls over all four drug schedules. The U.S. was also in favor of having four schedules but rather more relaxed associated controls than those sought by India.

The second departure from the Single Convention concerns the role of WHO, which had been reduced in the draft to that of assessing the medical and scientific factors relevant to control while the decision as to whether a drug should be controlled would be taken by the Commission based on social, legal, and administrative factors. At Vienna, Sweden and others proposed and secured a relative strengthening of WHO's role through the provision that WHO's evaluation should be determinative as to medical and scientific matters.

Another distinctive feature of the Vienna Convention is that it requires a two-thirds majority of the Commission to decide on an alteration to or change of schedule. At Vienna, the U.S. delegation abandoned its earlier compromise on this issue and proposed, unsuccessfully, a voting procedure requiring a three-fourths majority. Other delegations (USSR, Sweden, India, Yugoslavia) protested at this proposal, and the voting ratio of a two-thirds majority was retained (Official Records II, 1973: 183-4).

To gain support for the protocol from developing countries, Sweden emphasized that the Single Convention affected these countries' agricultural production adversely, whereas the Vienna protocol sought to regulate synthetic substances manufactured by industrialized nations (Official Records II, 1973:6). Others considered that, on the contrary, the difference in the nature of the drugs covered by the two treaties justified less stringent controls over "psychotropics." The Belgian delegate, for example, thought that the administrative burdens imposed by the protocol were unwarranted, that it would be simpler to check the quantities of *raw materials* imported and exported and to "control consumption without entering into the detail of preparations" (Official Records II, 1973: 8). The financial burden that implementing the protocol would entail was a plea used against extensive controls, ironically enough, by the wealthier nations (for example, Switzerland—see official Records II, 1973: 21). The assignment of control functions to the Board encountered much opposition from the very countries which argued in favor of this with respect to the Single Convention. Switzerland stated at Vienna that "The Board should not have the power to take action which might ruin the economy of any country" (Official Records II, 1973: 77). Export and import restrictions accepted as necessary by the adherents to the Single Convention were considered "impossible to carry out" and therefore unacceptable (to West Germany) in regard to "psychotropics." Control measures should befall (according to Austria) importing and not exporting countries; statistics of manufacture and trade were of doubtful value (in the Danish delegate's opinion), and international trade in schedule IV would be hindered by the export declaration system that was being contemplated (Official Records II, 1973: 50-51).

Differences from the Single Convention apart, other features of the Vienna Convention bear noting. Against the opposition of the U.S., two drugs, diazepam (Valium) and chlordiazepoxide (Librium), which had been proposed for control under schedule IV, were deleted by the Conference. This created a curious situation where one of the American competitor drugs in the tranquilizer range, meprobamate (Miltown), came under control while the Swiss tranquilizers did not. The American position was dictated by the fact that, within the U.S., control of Valium and Librium had been advocated (President's Advisory Commission on Narcotics and Drug Abuse, 1963).

The view has been expressed in Hoffmann-La Roche (the manufacturer of the two products) that the U.S. move in the international context was dictated in part by the internal failure, now overcome, to bring these drugs under control in the U.S. following a suit brought against it by Hoffmann-La Roche.* Through international control over Librium and Valium, national control of these drugs could be facilitated. La Roche's defense against this move was based on an analysis of 6,625 scientific papers on benzodiazepines (which include Librium and Valium) in which there were only forty-seven reported cases of abuse. The total number of cases reported by these papers was 254. Control was successfully evaded when the conference finally decided, on the proposal of the Technical Committee, that Librium and Valium be excluded from the control schedules.†

A number of delegations expressed surprise at the decision of the Technical Committee to drop these two products from the schedules. The Australian delegate, for one, observed that:

The deletion . . . seemed to have been due to a change of attitude on the part of some delegations between the first and second consideration of Schedule IV by the Technical Committee. *Yet no new pharmacological data or information on social factors had come to hand in the interval to justify such a change* [emphasis added]. The reasons for it therefore seemed to be of a pharmaco-political or pharmaco-sociological nature (Official Records II, 1973: 113).

The chairman of the Technical Committee indicated to us later that the deletion was one of the necessary concessions for securing agreement on having a treaty at all (Bror Rexed, interview). This is an instance of the horse-trading which took place throughout the conference.

An omission with possibly more far-reaching consequences was that of the salts of the substances considered by the conference. The salts were not expressly included; yet it is in the form of salts that the substances are usually marketed. In the Single Convention such inclusion was secured by the use of special footnotes associated with the schedules. At one of the last plenary sessions,

* United States Court of Appeals for Third Circuit, No. 71-1299. Hoffmann-La Roche, Inc. v. Richard G. Kleindienst, Attorney General of the United States and John E. Ingersoll, Director, Bureau of Narcotics and Dangerous Drugs, United States Department of Justice.

† The votes of the Technical Committee were as follows: for and against retention of chlordiazepoxide—6 and 14 respectively, with 3 abstentions; for and against retention of diazepam—6 and 12 respectively, with 4 abstentions. Cf. corresponding votes on meprobamate—17, 3, and 2.

the chairman of the Technical Committee raised the question of providing for such inclusion in the schedules of the new treaty. Another member of the Technical Committee supported him, explaining that the committee's only reason for not including these salts was that it "had been hurried in its final report" (E/CONF. 58/SR.27). Both the USSR and the U.S. held that it was not possible to generalize about the salts of all the substances involved.

In the course of the conference the U.S. delegation bargained for the right of rejection of controls on the part of a state which does not notify its acceptance of a control decision within a specified period. After hard bargaining between the contending parties, the model from the draft was retained, which allowed a state the right of partial acceptance under exceptional circumstances provided that it notified its decision. Agreement was reached that this right would be extended to all four schedules.

A Retrospective View

We will begin our review by asking who acted, for what interests, and through what means.

It will be clear from the foregoing section that the U.S. and Sweden were the initiators. In the chain of events leading up to the treaty, the Commission and Division had provided inputs of one kind or another. But the crucial role played by countries such as India, Yugoslavia, and the USSR must not be overlooked, even if their influence on events derived less from taking initiatives than from the support they rallied or the objections they raised to certain issues. A number of countervailing powers were obviously at work, chiefly among the industrialized countries (the Netherlands and West Germany, for example), offsetting the zealous endeavors of those pressing for controls. However, disentangling the various forces that worked on the decisions is complicated by the fact that the line between the procontrol and countervailing forces was seldom sharp. No one was against all controls, and those who were for controls had different ideas about how far to go.

To what extent did the UN organs fulfill their duty of responding to new drug problems? WHO advocated controls at a fairly early stage but considered national ones sufficient to meet the problem. The Swedish notification of stimulants for control under the Single Convention elicited an uncertain response from WHO, and it appears that the basis of this response was largely political.

The WHO director-general had admitted that on "purely technical grounds" he would be obligated to make a recommendation for control under the Single Convention. Since it is precisely on technical grounds that WHO is required by its treaty obligations to make recommendations, there was no justification for its not doing so. By not making a recommendation, WHO froze the initiative to include stimulants in the Single Convention. Although the expert committee's recommendation of an interim instrument to cover stimulants was a positive step towards control (WHO/EC DD, 1970), in retrospect it appears ill-advised, since the realization of the proposal for an interim instrument would have further deferred the conclusion of the full Vienna Convention, or even have lessened the chances of its being concluded at all. The Swedish initiative to bring stimulants under the control of the Single Convention is open to the same criticism, although it may have served tactical purposes, if the final effect was to prompt other countries to agree to stringent controls over stimulants in the new treaty.

The Commission was a step or two behind WHO in proposing new controls. On the whole none of the international organs can be said to have played an active part in bringing about the new convention. Their usefulness lay in the mechanism they provided for the bargaining that went on between the main protagonists.

What interests were at work? The Vienna Conference was as much a battle of interests as any other UN conference. Some nations contended that public-health interests would be better served if others would agree to cooperative action. Others were particularly concerned with warding off any limitation upon the exercise of their national sovereignty; this was exemplified by the socialist group's insistence on the right of reservations and the demand by the U.S. for the right of rejection of controls. Commercial interests were there, the most significant expression of them being not so much the presence of pharmaceutical industry representatives on the delegations of the U.S. and Switzerland as the coincidence of national and commercial interests. A dividing line was perceptible in the manner of voting and argument between countries which manufacture psycho-tropic substances and countries without such industry. France was astride both camps, arguing, as it has nearly always done, for the necessity of controls, in contrast to the other Common Market countries.

A pressure group which made itself heard during the events leading up to the Vienna conference was the scientific community. Acting as advisers to national delegations, medical and social scientists were instrumental in influencing governmental readiness to consider more varied social controls, alternatives to punishment, and new provisions for treatment and rehabilitation of drug addicts. Scientific opposition to drug controls modeled on those of the international treaties manifested itself before as well as after the Vienna Conference. It will be recalled that at the ICAA meeting in Lausanne in 1970, a case was presented against the proposed treaty. Later, in the U.S. Senate hearings on the ratification of the psychotropics convention, the scientific community was again among the opponents to the treaty, arguing against the new imposition of controls which had merely been sanctified by usage and had proved ineffective against the illicit traffic. One of their spokesmen, Neil Chayet, made a statement at the Vienna Conference itself expressing dissatisfaction with the use of the criminal sanction and concern for the challenge which drug controls represented to the independence of scientific research (Official Records II, 1973: 18-19).

What means were used? To gain their ends the various interests employed such means as influencing opinion by argument and entreaty, and enlisting support in voting. The arguments used in Vienna revolved around a number of themes: at one end, the primacy of public-health interests and the need to protect developing countries from being injured by the products of developed ones; at the other, considerations of practicality and the need to ensure wide acceptability (as an argument against specificity and stringency of controls). Because of the disinclination of many countries to accept international obligations, a large number of arguments were directed at minimizing the degree to which the provisions were binding. Necessarily, the consensus on the final document could only be obtained at the cost of much weakening of its contents and much lowering of the level of control desired by the control-minded countries. One of the most decisive arguments for a lowered level of control was that this was a necessary price for having an international agreement. The force of this argument lay in the fact that there were moments during the conference when the countries desiring controls were not even certain that they would obtain a treaty which bore any resemblance at all to the original draft, so assailed were they by opposition. Their readiness to make concessions (as in the Valium and Librium case) was thus dictated to a large extent by their own estimation of how far they could go without jeopardizing their chances of securing a reasonable level of control.

Earlier we discussed the case presented by the pharmaceutical industry against international controls. A basic argument of the industry which was never explicitly challenged was the contention that the more widely a drug was used, the less it should be controlled, other things being equal, since the practical problems of enforcing controls, given the extent of the demand, would outweigh the vestigial benefit of control. However, even granted that in the case of marihuana, this is a cogent argument for relaxing controls, it is possible to interpose a contrary argument, that the more used a drug is, the more it should be controlled. Another tenet of the pharmaceutical industry's position is that a drug should not be controlled until found guilty of harmful effects. A differing view is that embodied in the 1931 Convention, in which whole classes of drugs were placed under provisional control with provisions for individual drugs to be freed from control when shown not to be dangerous. This is the view underlying the Norwegian system of drug control, for example. Norway has limited its range of permissible pharmaceuticals to about three thousand only, and a new drug cannot be registered unless it demonstrates valuable propensities not possessed by those already registered. This makes for a cheap and effective form of drug control, easily supervised. It is not control for control's sake; rather it rests on the basic assumption that because of its profit motive, the drug-producing industry cannot be relied upon to market only those drugs that are strictly necessary, or to be the first to alert the public against using certain drugs. Current discussions on international drug control have not gone as far as envisaging such alternatives as public ownership of the drug industry, but it is worth mentioning that the 1931 Limitation Conference passed a resolution to that effect, with only one country, Germany, voting agianst it.

Neither are the arguments advanced by the Division of Narcotic Drugs in its brief to the Commission immune to criticism. As noted earlier, a perceptible change of position occurred between 1967 and 1969; however, both positions were poorly argued. To say, as it did in 1967, that it was not a critical factor whether the drugs proposed for control satisfied the "similarity" condition for inclusion under control, is to pursue a dangerous line of argument, since this is in contradiction to the treaty criteria. The switch in 1969 to the legalistically based position that the 1961 conference had excluded central stimulants and other psychoactive drugs from the Single Convention (and that they could not therefore be assimilated to the drugs controlled by it) is equally weak, for the very reasons which the Division spelt out in 1967 in its brief when it argued against the judgments of the PCB. Only WHO did not evade the crucial question, when, in its *note verbale* in 1969, it said that some stimulants were similar to cocaine in the meaning of the Single Convention.

The point of all this is not one of legal interpretation; it is the importance of the role which differing legal interpretations can play in the political process.

Apart from arguments, other means were used by the various interests involved, in a way which is not immediately obvious to the outside observer. One such means was the use of technical literature to buttress a case. The pharmaceutical industry, the U.S., and Sweden all used it extensively. Representation was another; Sweden secured a hearing only when it obtained a place on the Commission.

The outcome was that the conference concluded a treaty which was broader but considerably weaker than the Single Convention. The conference's purpose, after all, was (as the Danish delegate observed) to adopt a protocol that "would provide protection for all countries and *could be accepted in practice by the producing countries*" (Official Records II, 1973:59) (emphasis added). The necessity to facilitate ratification and adherence, it has been argued, justifies the lack of rigor of the control provisions. However, in the three years since it has been adopted, the Convention has acquired only sixteen ratifications.

SUMMARY
1. The development of the Vienna Convention is a paradigm of the treaty-making process which had led to the earlier drug conventions.
2. The chief movers for control were Sweden, the U.S., and African and Asian developing countries, led by India. Resis-

tance came mostly from West Germany, Belgium, the U.K., the Netherlands, and Switzerland.

3. Various positions were taken vis-à-vis the draft protocol. Its critics, who included members of the drug industry, argued for national as opposed to international controls.
4. The international organs were less movers for control than tools for maneuver by the contending interests.
5. The breadth and strength of the new controls were decided on the basis of their acceptability to countries opposed to control.

IV   A Choice of Futures

17 Conclusions and Recommendations

> "Opium smoking among our people is as widespread as
> whisky drinking among you, and has no more effect on
> us than whisky drinking on you." Evidently, he (our
> witness) meant that the Kachin people should have as
> much right to enjoyment as us Whites.
>> Eric Ekstrand, head of the Opium Traffic Section
>> and chairman of the League Inquiry into the
>> control of Opium Smoking in the Far East (1929),
>> in his memoirs (translated from the Swedish).

Here we will review the implications of the
conclusions of earlier chapters in order to identify fundamental
issues and to make recommendations. What has emerged from
the study makes a fairly straightforward case for some of the
propositions we are about to make, but others will not derive
directly or entirely from our findings. However, we will have due
regard for these findings in making our recommendations, and
will, where necessary, make known the line of thought on which
they rest.

In this study we have described the operations of the control
system and the influences affecting its development. A modest
enterprise, it has deliberately avoided some of the broader issues
on which the subject impinges. Our study differs from other
investigations in its inclusion of alcohol and in its attempt to go
behind the formal procedures to actual operations. In doing so we
have referred to occurrences in the system's history, finding that
despite changes in vocabulary and in the world at large, the
system has been so stable, its arguments and underlying views so
unchanged, that, without a consideration of the past, one's
understanding of it would be incomplete.

Success or Failure?

Until now the system has not been subjected to a comprehensive evaluation, nor have we ourselves been capable of performing that task adequately. Ours is a beginning. An overall and final evaluation is not possible in an absolute sense; it is necessarily tied to particular criteria and levels of aspiration, and, depending on these, the conclusions drawn will differ. Nevertheless, comparing the manifest outcomes with the professed goals of the international drug control system, it is possible to conclude as to where it has succeeded or where it has failed. One can ask, given a set of goals, if the strategies adopted in their pursuit were reasonable and the outcomes satisfactory. We shall, however, momentarily suspend judgments of the correctness of the goals pursued and criteria selected by the international control system.

To begin with achievements: first, the international cooperation begun at Shanghai and The Hague does constitute the first positive step towards the regulation of international transactions in drugs. The acceptance by countries of the necessity for such regulation was itself no mean achievement. The adoption later of the principle that a country could export narcotics to other countries only with their permission has helped to prevent the recurrence of the kind of situation exemplified by the Anglo-Indian opium trade. Whatever other factors might have been involved, the pressure of international opinion did contribute to an alleviation of the Chinese problem.

Second, the establishment of the statistical reporting system managed by the Board was a worthy achievement. Although the international organs see this more as a potential means of control, we would accord it a higher value: it is a feature of the information base which must underlie any control machinery.

Third, during the Jellinek era in the 1950s great strides were made in the development of alcohol programs in Europe and Latin America. These included new views on alcoholism, its nature and treatment. This was not accomplished through the creation of a large administration but came about as a result of the combination of Jellinek's talents with WHO's prestige. Even more needed than new resources were new concepts, and these certainly developed in an important way during the period in question.

Fourth, the widespread diversion of narcotic drugs from pharmaceutical houses to illicit markets in the 1920s and early 1930s was reduced to a negligible amount. To what extent this was due to the influence of the international system rather than national self-restraint is difficult to determine. It is evident, however, that there was little sign of voluntary control within the drug industry itself, and that, had it not been for the pressure exerted by some members of the Advisory Committee and the Board, national controls would have been even more tardy. Thus at least one of the goals underlying the provisions in the Geneva Convention governing international trade was fulfilled.

Fifth, there is the limitation, to a small number of countries, of *legal* opium production for export. Even though ambiguity has often surrounded the question of limitation of production and the means to achieve it, there can be no doubt that the scheme has been brought about by the international control system and that the designation of producing countries has been an obstacle to new countries starting opium production legally for export.

Sixth, the relative stabilization of the number of synthetic drugs of the morphine type on the market is a situation which the international system has been instrumental in sustaining. Without international control, there might have been a proliferation of such drugs on the market, most or all of which would probably not have added to the therapeutic benefit of those already being used but which could have constituted an increased risk to public health. The WHO expert committees were mainly responsible for this restraint.

Seventh, the significant decrease in the use of heroin and cannabis preparations for medical purposes can be attributed unequivocally to the effects of international drug control. The groundwork was laid in the League period but its success must be acknowledged to have been due to the joint efforts of WHO, the Board, and the Commission, the first being probably the most influential. The resistance of some countries to this development diminished with time, as revealed by the consumption statistics, and although the idea was propagated by the U.S. government, the international system played a significant part in bringing this situation about.

We turn now to the failures. The first failure is simply that the goal of eliminating the "evil," be it cannabis use, coca-leaf-chewing, or the opium habit, has not been achieved. It may of course be said that the expression of such a goal is mere rhetoric and idealism, and serves only as a spur to action—that such expressions are no more than political maneuvers. Yet there are those within the establishment in whom an acceptance of tactical necessity is combined with at least a partial commitment to this rhetorical goal, and who are thereby led to subscribe to utterly unrealistic expectations and operations.

Second, the international control system has failed to become truly international. Its dominant values tend to favor the interests of one or two countries over those of others in the international community. Of course no one is surprised that there is so little similarity between the ideals of an international organization and what the organization actually does, but the extent to which the drug control system is dominated by U.S. interests and constrained by "superpower" politics makes it a travesty of internationalism.

Third, the system has been unable to adjust to the changing world situation: the rapid development and increased use of "psychotropics" and the awareness of the problem of alcohol, both by itself and in association with that of other drugs, have not been accompanied by corresponding modifications in the international response. The system has thus lost its social relevance, moral strength, and scientific thrust. Even though there were reasons for neglecting alcohol, this cannot be said of the "psychotropics": in contrast to the vigor of efforts to bring new synthetic opiates under control, the process of enacting controls over the "psychotropic" drugs has been marked by hesitation and legalistic quibbling.

Fourth, the international administration has failed to meet the demands of its task. The fault lies partly with the international civil servants, who form the core of the permanent administrative machinery. The aimlessness of the whole system may be attributed in part to their inability to confront the actual situation and to make real efforts to explore alternative ways of operating. The Secretariat has not been what the onetime UN secretary-general Dag Hammarskjöld had said it could be: "a living thing ... it can introduce new ideas. It can in proper forms take initiatives. It can put before Member governments new findings which will influence their actions" (Foote, 1963). It is often admitted by international civil servants in private that the system is not what it pretends to be, but in their official behavior they continue to subscribe to the evasion of reality through defensiveness and the employment of false arguments. However, in extenuation of the apparent inertia of the staff members, it must be said that their work is bound to be affected by the masters they serve, and there have undoubtedly been occasions when constructive efforts and suggestions on the part of the personnel have been rebuffed by the dominant powers in the Commission.

Fifth, the attempts at crop substitution have failed. The failure has occurred on two levels. On one level, substitution programs have simply failed to get off the ground, to either materialize or survive. Technical mistakes, the inadequacy of auxiliary structures (such as marketing arrangements, outlets for substitute products and agricultural training, and so on), the consequences of heavy-handed pressures from outside, and the lack of respect shown for social traditions that were likely to be affected: all these factors operated to render crop replacement unsuccessful. On another level, crop substitution has clearly failed to reduce drug supplies. Although it is possible that reducing drug availability through crop substitution might be an element in an all-round drug policy, it is unlikely to be the all-important one. Treating it as the central policy, as the international system is apt to do, or as representing the fundamental approach underlying all future UN action against "drug abuse," is tantamount to an evasion of the realities of the drug-using world.

The sixth failure is that international control has contributed to the replacement of opium by heroin use in a number of countries. Iran offers an example of the wastefulness and harmful consequences of sudden, isolated repressive action; yet the lesson it affords is unlearned and unheeded. The international system continues to press for cessation of opium supplies and to attach opprobrium to countries unable to enforce prohibition.

The seventh failure is the inability of the present system to curb the illicit traffic. No control system is without its costs, and it is obvious that international control has itself contributed to the development of a black market, although even without the existence of international controls the mere fact that countries differ in terms of drug production, availability, and controls is in itself a sufficient condition for smuggling to occur. Several factors militate against effective law enforcement: the fact that illegal sale is not spontaneously reported by the "aggrieved" party but has to be detected through enforcement efforts, the practice of corruption in the narcotics police forces, and the existence of national sanctuaries for production, storage, investment of illicitly gained funds, for the refuge of wanted offenders, and for certain protected roles (diplomats, political leaders).* The international control system has furthermore abetted a situation where some countries severely punish individual drug offenders when at the same time they tolerate the ready facilities for illicit trafficking afforded by their illegal domestic drug production (for example, cannabis in Lebanon and stimulants in Italy).

The catalogue of seven cases each of success and failure is of course by no means exhaustive. And it will be remembered that they have been judged in terms of the outcomes sought by the system itself.

General Comments

The instances of success have a common denominator: none of them is directly aimed at affecting the individual drug-taker at the behavioral level. Two of the seven cases concern international trade; two seek to influence production; and two have a bearing on medical practices. In four examples commercial interests were affected. The discontinuation of the medical use of cannabis and heroin in most countries stemmed from the pursuit of a policy of prohibition; but, as was the case with alcoholism, the change involved was one of medical custom and perception of norms. In six cases of success, it has been the conduct of professions and private enterprise which has been influenced; and indeed, they appear to be more susceptible to regulation and control than individual behavior.

With regard to the failures it seems possible to distinguish between those due to inherent defects in the system and those associated with unintended or unforeseen consequences of its action, although the difference is by no means clear-cut. The weaknesses of the system include the goal of eliminating all

* The sanctuary problem is basic to many forms of international crime. As Blum, Kaplan, Lind, and Tinklenberg (1974) have recommended, it requires a more integrated international approach. They have suggested that international law enforcement in the drug area constitutes an opportunity and a test case for general coordination in the international administration of justice.

proscribed individual drug use—or supplies catering to that demand; the slowness of the control strategies to adjust to changes in the external drug situation (such as the appearance of problems connected with the use of new psychoactive drugs); and the lack of recognition of cultural diversity. These have their foundation in a more general inability to develop alternative policies of control and to shed the pretence, perpetuated by words and argumentative techniques, that all is well with the control system. The other failures also signify a lack of appreciation of the range of possible action and consequences. They also involve an intrusion into what are considered "problem countries" (which tend to be only the poor and uninfluential), through the exertion of pressure to engage in activities unacceptable to local customs and without sufficient regard for the cultural setting. Drug-taking is approached as though it were an isolated phenomenon. An illustration of the failure to conceptualize the drug problem adequately or broadly enough is the extent to which the skills which are engaged in the work are confined to a narrow range of disciplines and occupations.

The failures are more pronounced in the years after the Second World War, whereas some of the basic achievements occurred earlier. The late 1920s and early 1930s constituted the peak era of international drug control. This is reflected in the fact that very little written in recent years approaches the quality of the report of the Persian Commission of Inquiry or Bouquet's paper on cannabis. The Board, too, was more forthright in its dealings with governments and the pharmaceutical industry, and less reluctant in those days to take an independent stand. Also, underlying the work of the earlier years was a better understanding of cultural heterogeneity, perhaps because many of the active figures had worked in foreign cultures.

In making our recommendations we will be careful not to repudiate the laborious efforts which have gone into the making and acceptance of the present control system. On the other hand, it must be admitted that the defects of the system stem in part from an inability to adjust to new problems as they emerge. To find a balance between continuity and innovation is indeed a difficult matter. It is necessary to make our recommendations on two levels: that of an immediate and more practical order and that which entails changes of a more fundamental and long-range character.

Short-range Recommendations

These recommendations relate to the structure and functioning of the control machinery and are made on the supposition that the goals which are now being pursued will remain unchanged. Although we term these "short-range" recommendations, we are fully aware that their adoption would entail time-consuming reforms of a basic character not only to the bureaucracy but also to the legal framework.

First, we consider that a reorganization of the system is necessary, and we will take each key structure in turn to pinpoint where this should occur.

A reorganized system would still consist of a policy-making body, similar to the present Narcotics Commission, and a secretariat service, such as is being provided today by the Division. It is with the Commission and the Division that the information-gathering and goal-setting processes largely begin, and it is in these processes, as they are actually being carried out, that many of the system's weaknesses lie. The Commission's discussions on goals and programs lack inspiration, direction, frankness, awareness of alternatives, and information both sound and relevant to policy-making. It seems to us that expert advisory bodies should be periodically appointed to assist the Commission in its policy-making functions. Such bodies could prepare repertories of goals and alternatives from which the Commission could then make its choice; they could make predictions of costs and evaluate the consequences of adopting various courses of action. Very little work of this kind has hitherto been undertaken by the Commission. At present, the materials for decision-making are prepared by the Division, but analysis and evaluation of data in relation to decisions prior to their employment by the Commission can usefully be carried out by bodies with more specialized knowledge and greater diversity of viewpoints.

One of the weaknesses of the Division lies in the recruitment and composition of its personnel. As the Jackson and Bertrand studies tell us, the exclusion of youth, independence of thinking, and vigor from the ranks of the professional staff is a general characteristic of the UN administration. The persistence of the status quo in the Narcotics Division may owe much to the practice of retaining past or retired officials as "consultants" to programs. Thus the ideas and atmosphere of yesterday continue to inform the policies of today. Avoidance of misguided and obsolete action calls for a change in the selection criteria of personnel so as to ensure a bureaucracy receptive to new ideas and modes of operation. There ought also to be a greater readiness to contract work out to, or at least cooperate with, universities and national research institutions. Indeed it was Dag Hammarskjöld's policy, when he was secretary-general, that this should be so, at least insofar as research undertakings were concerned (Symonds and Carder, 1973: 73, 81).

When we look closely at who sets the tone of operations in WHO, we see that the balance of emphasis has always tipped strongly towards pharmacologists and the medical profession. WHO is performing a necessary function with respect to the pharmacological evaluation of drugs and the promotion of preventive programs, but because its role in recommending the level of control of drugs necessarily involves it in the shaping of drug policies, it should diversify the professional composition of its Drug Dependence Expert Committees to include other than pharmacologists and physicians. Hitherto there has been a tendency for the same people to make pronouncements on drug effects, on treatment, and on control measures, without sufficient recognition of the necessarily limited perspectives they bring to bear on these subjects. There has also been a tendency of late for the expert committees to involve themselves in matters having little to do with their drug-classifying obligations under the international treaties. So that these widened horizons will not overtax the expert committees—characterized as they have been by a fairly narrow professional base—we suggest that they differentiate between the technical task of evaluating drugs for control on the one hand, and the consideration of broader matters of policy, research, and social concerns on the other, with a concomitant division of work between differently composed committees.

So much for the professional basis of policy-making. In looking at organizational structure and performance, we see that the chief problem is one of obsolescence. The continued existence of a laboratory within the Division is not justifiable. It conveys the erroneous impression that the scientific basis of international action is narrowly chemical and botanical. It also lends an unwarranted aura of broad scientific expertise to the Division.

Since its role is that of coordinating, rather than actively engaging, in research, many of its functions can be absorbed by the Division proper and by WHO. Its collection of drug literature can be incorporated into the drug section of the general UN Library, and developed into an information resource available (more freely than it is now), to all research workers and to the public. Consideration should be given to the possibility of developing a research program by the Division which will yield information helpful to the Commission in its policy-setting task.

With regard to the Board, its creation, given the circumstances in the 1920s, was not without justification, and its earlier performance appears also to have been effective. But we have seen that its "independence" is more and more of a myth, and the "still, small voice" it purports to be has become louder and louder with regard to matters beyond its ken. Interest in its own survival has made the Board timorous where it should be bold, bold where it is ill-informed. Its members are increasingly political, rather than independent technical appointees. Unless these trends are reversed, it seems to us that there is increasingly less justification for having the Board at all. It would anyhow be preferable to strip the body down to its statistical functions and incorporate the secretariat, which would then be concerned only with statistical matters, within the structure of the Division. The Board itself should cease to be a separate institution, and we suggest that the parties to the treaties consider suitable amendments to bring about its termination. The Board's members could, however, serve as independent experts in the Commission which, though at present composed entirely of government representatives, could in fact be transformed by ECOSOC into a mixed organ of government representatives and experts (UN Commentary, 1973:7).

This raises the question of the future of the estimates system, which has hitherto been operated by the Board. We have already discussed the limitations of the system, but would point out that its effectiveness and relevance have not been adequately studied by an impartial outsider. It has been the international control system's answer to the question of how to maintain drug supplies at a level comparable with the desirable level of consumption, and it is conceivable that if it were inserted into the Vienna Convention, it could be of value in the initial stages of the treaty's application as a means of affecting the volume of "psychotropic" drugs prescribed. But its continued worth with respect to the Single Convention should be critically assessed; rigorous study of the system is called for.

The setting up of the UN Fund has so far had more negative than positive consequences. It has provided wide opportunity for the pursuit of narrow national and organizational self-interest. Coordination of activities between "rival" agencies, already difficult, is now even more of a problem. Instead of facilitating action on a broader base than that on which UN intervention has hitherto rested, the Fund has stiffened, through selective financial infusions, the mold in which UN drug programming has traditionally been cast. A large proportion of the money allocated to the Fund's various programs is in fact spent on supporting an ever-expanding bureaucracy to administer these programs. Indeed many of the Programs appear to serve no purpose other than to provide occupation for the enlarged secretariats. If this is the case, then one is prompted to suggest that, in order to avoid wastage, such programs should be relinquished. We view with skepticism the Thailand program and the Papaver bracteatum project. Our earlier suspicions of the unfeasibility of the project to discover means of waging biological warfare on drug-bearing crops have been confirmed, as it has now been abandoned as being unworkable. Behind such questions as how to obtain larger contributions to the Fund, or how to persuade Burma to join in the fight against the illicit traffic, there lie the larger ones. How can priorities for international action be set? What are the effects of international aid for drug programs on the recipient country? With regard to the latter, little thought has been given to the manner in which aid can distort—through upsetting national priorities and the choice of allocation of national investment between sectors and regions—the economic and social development of a country. Crop replacement programs have been justified by their advocates on the grounds that they have the instrumental and independent value of bringing about economic progress and raising living standards, but is it not equally possible that opium-growing by a poor country may contribute more to general economic development by increasing foreign exchange earnings? If so, the problem is to see the proper distribution of those earnings beyond the privileged class of criminals and their police and political supporters.

We suggest the transfer of the Fund to the United Nations Development Program (UNDP). Under UNDP proper consideration can be given to a country's real aid and development requirements. The Commission's role under this arrangement might be that of initiating proposals and making recommendations regarding the choice of projects to be embarked upon. The expert advisory groups earlier suggested might also be involved in helping to identify needs, formulating programs, and evaluating the long-term effects of implementing them.

While all this pruning of the international control organs is taking place, the question of the illicit traffic is obviously lurking just offstage. Present efforts to combat this traffic have tended to concentrate on making seizures and apprehending dealers. But an alternative course may lie in employing international relations to effect changes in previously overlooked or underplayed facets of the illegal trade, such as the acquiescence of governments, on political or economic grounds or both, to facilities on their soil for illegal production and distribution, and for the holding of profits (for example, in Swiss banks). A key aspect of the illicit traffic is the existence of the profitable market for drugs in the U.S. The demand which exists in the U.S. makes it a problem country of the first magnitude. We believe that no appreciable impact can be made on the illicit traffic until the international community tackles the problem of how to ease the American drug situation with a view to alleviating the world situation. A first step in this direction might be the initiation of an independent, "outside" study of the American drug problem: an analogy which comes immediately to mind is Gunnar Myrdal's classic study (1944) of race relations in the U.S. One might even envisage a latter-day Commission of Inquiry such as the one that was sent to Persia by the League of Nations. In fact, the Commission should direct the energies it has hitherto applied to studying problems in developing countries to Western industrialized ones; and the U.S., being the most problematic, should be the first to be studied. The need for this is all the more urgent because the world is more affected by the domestic policy of the U.S. than by that of any other country, and so far none of the nations which have accepted the American definition of the problem and its solution has had a chance of judging how compatible the policy of the U.S. is with its own situation.

Finally, we question the appropriateness of inserting mandatory penal provisions relating to drug possession and use in the text of international treaties. It provides fuel for national punitive action bordering on infringement of the code of human rights. Penal legislation and enforcement have been put to work in situations patently calling for other kinds of intervention: provision of better housing, welfare, work, and so on. These factors have worked to reduce confidence among many groups in drug control in general; the inclusion of the criminal sanction in the Vienna Convention, for instance, had the effect of dissipating support for it. And there is evidence that, in some countries, criminal policies have been a costly failure.

The recommendations contained in the foregoing pages may be summarized as follows.

1. We propose that the Commission reorganize its use of information and expertise to (a) allow external research institutions to be drawn into the process of data collection and analysis and (b) have ad hoc advisory groups to help formulate and evaluate policies.
2. There should be a clearer differentiation between the WHO Drug Dependence Expert Committees' drug evaluation responsibilities and their work on broader questions; the professional composition of their membership should correspondingly be diversified.
3. We recommend that the UN Laboratory be dismantled and its functions distributed among the existing units. International research efforts should in any event be deflected to areas of higher priority and relevance.
4. The structure of the INCB might, by suitably amending the Conventions, be changed as follows: the members might be absorbed by the Commission as independent experts, and the secretariat should be incorporated in such a way as to form a statistical-technical branch of the Division.
5. We propose that a thorough study of the estimates system be carried out by impartial outsiders to judge its continued usefulness in regard to Single Convention drugs on the one hand, and its applicability to drugs yet to be controlled on the other.
6. The Fund should be integrated into UNDP; the Commission's function vis-à-vis the Fund should be that of originating and evaluating project proposals prior to their acceptance, while the final decisions on the allocation of money should rest with

UNDP. The Fund's programs should anyhow be critically appraised and some of its current endeavors relinquished.

7. We urge a shift of emphasis in the international organizations' conceptions of "problem countries" from developing nations to industrialized ones, and we suggest that this change of emphasis should first alight upon the U.S. The Commission should seriously consider the problem of demand in America and promote the undertaking, by an impartial external group, of an inquiry into its international ramifications.

8. Penal provisions should not be detailed in international drug treaties in a way that would lead to their adoption by countries where their application is unsuitable.

Basic Issues

These proposals for adjustments to the system have been arrived at on the basis of an assumption that events will run their course without a major departure from the original, officially endorsed goals. But should these goals be perpetrated, considering what has emerged from our study? Is there no alternative choice of future controls? We believe that there is, if one takes a longer view in formulating one's recommendations. However, before such recommendations can be made, a number of issues and matters of principle must first be resolved. These issues do not appear here for the first time, but so far they have only been touched upon obliquely, and no stand has explicitly been taken on them. These issues, which we will now briefly discuss, are the following: national versus international control; the inclusion of alcohol under international control; the goals of the control system; and, finally, the relation between drug dependence control and the broader concerns of agricultural policy and drug consumer-protection in general.

There exist contrasting views on the necessity for international, as opposed to purely national, controls. In our introductory chapter we offered reasons for having controls as such, but took no stand as to whether these should be at the domestic level only, or set up internationally. One frequently encounters assertions that alcohol control is a national matter, but that cannabis is of international concern. And in the earlier discussions on amphetamines in WHO, the expert committees advocated national, rather than international, measures of control. Yet we know of no published work dealing at any length with this fundamental issue.

The controversy between those who consider international controls necessary and those who think otherwise cannot be resolved without resort to historical evidence. When seen in a historical context, it does not appear likely that whatever has been achieved in the way of regulated trade could have come about through the enforcement of national controls alone. It is also difficult to argue that the need for international controls is decreasing; increased trade in alcohol and other drugs between countries points in the opposite direction, and, in a world of economic integration and multinational corporations, national control is encountering more and more hindrances to effective enforcement. We think that some form of international control is indispensable (later we will discuss in what respects such control should differ from that which is currently being exercised), but we also accept the argument, often advanced in the Commission, that national controls are a necessary complement to international ones.

The next issue is: how does one perceive alcohol control in relation to the control of other drugs? We have seen that the international organs have paid little attention to alcohol and that only in one key organization, WHO, has there been formal recognition of the usefulness of a unitary view of alcohol and other drugs. The other organs, being more constrained by the treaties than WHO in what they can do, are less able, all of a sudden, to consider alcohol in the same light or within the same legal framework. The situation today is understandable from a historical point of view but is otherwise scarcely defensible. After all, the consensus of opinion today holds that alcohol has considerable harmful effects and that its use gives rise to serious public-health problems. The need to control alcohol is widely recognized, as is evidenced by the efforts of many countries; the need to do so on the basis of international cooperation is, on the other hand, less readily admitted. Nonetheless, in the report of a WHO Expert Committee on Mental Health, we find this statement (1967:41):

While recognizing that there are important differences between types of drug dependence, the Committee recommends that problems of dependence on alcohol and dependence on other drugs should be considered together, because of similarities of causation, interchangeability of agent in respect of maintenance of dependence and hence similarities in measures required for prevention and treatment.

If an international body has gone as far as recommending the above, the question that one is led to ask is: why not proceed even further and bring alcohol under international control? The case for placing alcohol under international control could be argued on the following grounds:

—it satisfies the criterion of "dependence liability" and, contrary to earlier notions, does not constitute a "special case" separate from the other drugs;

—the dependence-producing drugs under international control are a motley group and adding alcohol would not undermine their homogeneity;

—alcohol gives rise to more problems than any of the other drugs;

—the phenomenon of multidrug use and of the substitution of one drug for another makes it imperative to consider all the drugs involved as a totality;

—alcohol is an item of international trade the increase of which has not been accompanied by an internationalization of the measure designed to control it; it is also a commodity which figures prominently in internationnal life, as witness tourism and diplomatic activity.

—alcohol smuggling across national borders occurs.

There are, on the other hand, strong counterarguments, such as its near universal use and the integration of its use into the customs of many cultures. But the objections to international control of alcohol arise mainly from a particular way of looking at international controls. In proposing that alcohol be internationally controlled we are not thinking in terms of adding it unreservedly to the existing control schedules, or of an extension of the present control regimes to cover it. The mechanisms we do envisage will become apparent as we tackle the next issue.

The stands we have taken on the foregoing two issues are predicated on the presumption of a redefinition of the goals of international control. The present system aims at fighting "abuse" and "dependence" and at the suppression of all use other than for medical and scientific purposes. As "abuse" has in any case been identified with nonmedical and nonscientific use, there is no practical distinction between these two concepts. The terms "abuse," "dependence," and "nonmedical use" carry with them connotations of the approaches which have strongly influenced the development of international controls, namely the moralistic, the pharmacological, and the medical. The present formulation of goals does not relate drug control to broader social policy and leaves little room for the expression of cultural differences. Policies spawned by these goals are apt to focus narrowly on one or two drugs and to be careless of the all too likely drug substitution effect, which, as we have seen, has manifested itself as one of the by-products of international control. In pursuit of the absolute goals set by the system, countries are under a certain constraint to entertain unrealistic aspirations and to lay claim to achievements where in fact none obtains. A case in point is the rule under the Single Convention that nonmedical use of cannabis must be prohibited by the end of 1989; the onus is on India to say on that date that it has abided by its international obligations and has prohibited cannabis use, regardless of what this means in practice. The absoluteness of the present goals is such that, to uphold them in the face of diminishing credibility, all manner of distortion and falsehood is countenanced by the system, whether in the information it receives on the workings of the system in individual countries, or in the information it gives out to the unsuspecting public.

The ultimate purpose of any social policy is presumably to reduce human misery; a drug control policy inspired by this end might therefore be primarily directed at minimizing the harmful effects of drug use. In preferring to address the harmful effects of drug use, we are underlining the need to specify, with some concreteness, what these effects might be. Similarly, our preference for the term "drug use" over "drug abuse" and "drug dependence" stems from our wish to avoid using obscure concepts in formulating the objectives of control. Moreover, we reject the view that what is to be controlled is a uniform phenomenon. Drug use is something quite variable after all; it may, for example, serve medical needs or, alternatively, it may be compulsive or recreational. By the phrase "minimizing harmful effects" is implied the necessity of giving due consideration to the negative effects of control itself. Although we do not think that such effects are amenable to a strict cost-benefit estimation, we must nevertheless acknowledge the persuasiveness of the scientific school which has drawn attention to these effects (Becker, 1964; Lindesmith, 1965). A goal conceived under such a perspective and formulated in terms of the minimization of harmful effects can thus be translated into a broad strategy which takes account of the possible and unintended consequences of its implementation which, though not always predictable, can at least be anticipated sufficiently early in many cases for irrevocable mistakes to be avoided.

Use of drugs can be viewed as risk-taking behavior. Individual reactions to drugs, affected as they are by personality, mood, social setting, and experience, can be difficult to predict. It would be futile to direct control efforts at individual reactions; they must work on a more general level. A starting point might lie in a way of thinking to which many research workers in the alcohol field subscribe today, and this is the notion that the rate of alcoholism in a given population is related to the general level of consumption in that population, so that measures aimed at lowering the general consumption will also diminish the harmful effects. Although this view is not without opposition there is accumulating evidence which lends it credence (de Lint and Schmidt, 1971; Mäkelä, 1972; WHO/FFAS, 1974).

If harmful consequences of drug use are related to overall use—and the empirical evidence yielded by alcohol research is strongly suggestive of such a relationship—then one of the things which a drug control policy might seek to do is to decrease overall consumption. Although there is much to be learned still about the relationship between rate of use and degree of risk, we nevertheless consider that at the present stage of knowledge this proposition provides a useful and pragmatic starting point for the further elaboration of an international drug control policy.

It would be wrong to exaggerate the difference between the goal which we have been criticizing and the goal which we are now trying to insinuate in its place. There is indeed little conflict between these two goals, and most of the successes and failures of international control earlier enumerated can be judged as such independently of which goal is being used as a yardstick. Nevertheless, because the goal we propose is more clearly defined and lends itself more readily to an operational definition on the practical plane, it will be easier to evaluate the outcome of policies directed at achieving it, and thereby to detect mistaken strategies, not perpetuate them. Furthermore, our goal is compatible with the system's past successes in that it focuses on institutional rather than individual actions.

The last issue is the relationship of psychoactive drug control to such broader concerns as agricultural economic planning and drug consumer-protection in general. Should we not see opium and alcohol production as a matter falling within the province of agricultural development policy, and control for drug dependence and for drug "misuse" as part of the larger area of ensuring drug safety and efficacy? We have seen that reduction of opium and alcohol production can, without any element of conscious drug control strategy, follow naturally from changes in general agricultural policy. An expanded and inclusive view of control encompassing drug safety, efficacy, dependence, and other matters might also be possible on the common basis of acknowledging the desirability of increased responsibility on the part of drug manufacturers. And indeed, there has been a perceptible move among some members of the international community to extend international controls to the elaboration of consumer protection procedures aimed in the long run at making the pharmaceutical industry adopt more cautious and responsible attitudes to drug production, marketing, and use. The protection of public health does call for the international supervision of standards for drug purity, safety, efficacy, labelling, advertising, and so on, particularly in importing countries which rely for their supply of drugs on the pharmaceutical industries of other countries. It would be advisable, in the case of some drugs, for these controls to be coordinated with the responsibilities which the international organs already have for the control of production and trade. On the other hand, consumer protection measures are more applicable to industrial pharmaceuticals, while many psychoactive drugs are used in their natural form. Also, the intoxication-seeking factor in psychoactive drug use is an added argument for distinguishing between psychoactive drug control policies and consumer protection measures. Nevertheless, the feasibility of coordinating measures subsumed under these two types of control is a matter deserving further exploration.

Long-range Recommendations

Our earlier discussion of the issue of goals has already provided us with our first recommendation, which is that the goal of the international control system be reformulated as: the minimization of the harmful effects of drug use. The ensuing reorganization of the scheme of control would entail two essential changes: first, the rejection of "medical usefulness" as the authoritative standard against which drugs are to be evaluated for purposes of control (and therefore the old antithesis between medical and nonmedical use); and second, the inclusion of guarantees that controls will be flexibly adjusted to differences between societies. Before we move from generalizations about goals to more concrete proposals, we should dwell a little on the distinction between the national and international planes. Although it has been generally agreed that the ultimate responsibility for determining controls must lie with the individual state, in practice international legislation is the textual source and point of departure of many national laws. Although we have argued for international controls to buttress national ones and vice versa, we have argued also for international controls that are sensitive to national needs. But there is no inevitable dilemma in these two requirements, for we see the primary function of international control as the regulation of transnational trade. Domestic drug policy becomes a matter of international concern as soon as drugs cross national borders. Since control over export trade cannot be sustained by isolated individual effort there have to be organized systems of mutual self-discipline between and among countries, which ensure that drugs travel across national borders only under specific conditions, conditions which would vary however, from drug to drug. The elaborate system of control set up for narcotics could not, for instance, be adapted to the regulation of alcohol trade. Yet it should be within the capacity of an international body to see to the working of the principle of maintaining the volume of trade in a particular drug at an agreed level, or of a gradual diminution of trade such as was exemplified by the arrangement between the British and the Chinese for a one-tenth annual reduction of the Indian opium trade. Control of the quantity and range of drug imports is likely to bear on drug use in two ways: in the case of a consuming country with a perceived drug problem, the restriction of supplies provides a breathing space while the country tackles its problem on other fronts simultaneously; in countries where there is no already existing demand, it militates against the creation of new, and possibly artificial, needs.

We are on more uncertain ground when we come to the question of controls over production. Such controls would give added strength to those established enterprises which are already enjoying the benefits of a monopolistic market (Arndt and Lind, 1973). Yet as drug manufacturing industries and distilleries grow and gain access to overseas markets, they will try to extend the geographical reach of their distribution network (cf. the Report of the Committee to Study Problems of the Pharmaceutical Industry, 1972). Some world regulatory authority which matches these enterprises in geographical reach and which is capable of collectively considering the interests of all the countries affected is necessary. Multinational corporations characteristically establish foreign subsidiaries when their export position is threatened; to reduce costs they may situate their production units closer to their foreign markets; to penetrate and compete in these markets they usually have to increase the tempo and range of their production. International agencies have a responsibility for tempering such expansion and for ensuring that an interest in satisfying human needs, as opposed to creating them, remains, on balance, in the forefront.

More specifically, possibilities for control in the following areas should be considered: marketing techniques; advertising; differing standards of responsibility observed by manufacturers and distributors in different countries (these tending to be lower in poor countries); conditions for new product introduction and the prescribing of psychoactive drugs whose indications are highly equivocal. A standard regime under the Single Convention includes the requirement of governmental authorization for participation in all phases of the narcotics trade; such a requirement may be met either by licensing or by state ownership. The premise on which this rests is clear: public-health needs are better served by governmental ownership and control. A matter which deserves debate, say in the Commission, is whether the displacement, by governmental intervention, of the need of private drug industry in general to make profit (often at the expense of public health), might not in the long run better the chances of effective drug control. We do not assume that governments are necessarily more mindful of the health interests of the drug consumers of other countries than private industry, but we do assume that such questions are pertinent to international drug control work. Further questions worth considering are: the sale of duty-free alcohol in international airports, and whether there might be an analogy between access to exceptionally cheap liquor by diplomats and easy access to other drugs by the medical profession.

All this must be accompanied by the collection of sound data on an international scale. Because of the worldwide structure of drug and alcohol economies, reporting should be an international obligation, and the statistical office of the Division to which an earlier recommendation referred could become the clearinghouse for such data.

Forms of drug use and distribution which occur outside legitimate formal organizations—such as are typical of cannabis, coca leaf, opium, and heroin today—should be of lesser concern to the international system, not only because that concern is now exaggerated, but also because the effective capacity of international agencies to influence the situation is severely limited. It will be remembered that opium and heroin were more susceptible to control when their circulation took place in legitimate institutional structures. There is room, nonetheless, for innovations in international arrangements for the control of illegal drug activities (see Blum, Kaplan, Lind, and Tinklenberg, 1974).

We do not mean by all this to undermine the importance of cultural setting and other informal influences on drug use behavior. The informal systems of drug supply, such as through peer groups and friends, do merit attention, but international action, lacking the means of reaching such groups, probably has to limit itself to such circumscribed tasks as the promotion of local research, and advice-giving. Earlier we suggested that control measures might fare better if they were addressed to the social milieu rather than to the individual within it. Indeed, individual self-control is grounded in socialization, and formal agencies of control are relatively unimportant, compared to the power of social norms, in enforcing self-control. To influence demand by social norms requires long-term action—not specifically directed at drugs or drug use—encompassing the whole range of social planning for child-rearing and family life, for work opportunities, leisure-time activities, improved living standards, and community life. Such long-range social reforms are necessary if the aim is to influence individual demand permanently. Some agencies in the UN family have already ventured into such fields as social development and organization of work and public services, and may have experiences, expertise, and administrative resources to share with the national social planner. However, even though these matters are, in practical terms, more directly the concerns of organs other than the drug control ones, the latter's conceptualization of the problems of drug use should always include consistent awareness of them.

However, we must make a reservation here about international technical assistance. We share the skepticism expressed in many quarters about the "international expert" who is sent on a mission to a foreign country for a few weeks and returns with a report and a set of recommendations for action. When we suggest an international flow of expertise, we are thinking of people able and prepared to carry out penetrating investigations and work at the local level for long periods. As to the help they give, this might bear on treatment, pricing policy, questions of drug availability and substitution, and so on. To be in a position to assist nations, international bodies must have at their disposal a new and broader range of competence. They must be able to turn from pharmacologists to social anthropologists, from clinical medicine to social medicine, from law to sociology and economics, and from specialists to generalists.

A long-term program geared to a revised set of ends can only be roughly outlined at this elementary stage; detailed elaboration can only come after more and better disclosure of facts and after the various issues have been allowed to surface and have been thoroughly debated. There is a great deal of work to be done, and we will end by summarizing some of the tasks ahead.

1. The overall goal of international drug (including alcohol) control should be scrutinized by the Commission. We suggest that efforts be directed at the minimization of the harmful effects of drug use rather than of "drug abuse" or "drug dependence."

2. The international system should develop the habit of discussing drug problems against a background of other social problems; in prescribing controls, emphasis should be laid on the need to set these within the broader context of social policy in general.

3. Cultural differences in drug use should be respected in devising international controls.
4. Drugs should not be prohibited on the grounds of medical unserviceability.
5. The primary target of control efforts should be international trade conducted through legitimate, organizational channels.
6. Production for the purpose of overseas distribution should be closely watched by international agencies so that proper restraint can be applied in time to marketing practices tending to generate new demands by the enterprises of one country among the population of another.
7. Since, under its terms of reference, the Commission may consider all drugs whose use constitutes an international problem, it should discuss the problems posed by the use of alcohol and consider measures to alleviate them.

Appendixes

Declarations and Reservations Made to the Single Convention on Narcotic Drugs, 1961, as of 31 December 1967

Country	Relevant article and paragraph	Declaration or reservation
Algeria	48, 2	Considers that for any dispute to be referred to the International Court of Justice, the agreement of all parties to the dispute is necessary in every case.
Argentina	48, 2	Does not recognize the compulsory jurisdiction of the International Court of Justice.
	49	Reserves the right to permit temporarily coca-leaf-chewing and trade in the drug for this purpose.
Bulgaria Byelorussian Socialist Republic Czechoslovakia Hungary	12, 2 & 3	Does not consider itself bound, with regard to states not entitled to become parties to the Single Convention, by the provisions that: the Board shall request governments of nonparty countries to furnish estimates, and shall establish them if a state should fail to furnish them;
Poland	13, 2	the Board shall examine the statistical returns with a view to determining whether a party has complied with the Convention provisions;
Ukrainian Soviet Socialist Republic USSR	14, 1 & 2	the Board may ask for explanations from a government in cases of noncompliance, and may recommend an embargo on the import and/or export of drugs from/to the country concerned;
	31, 1(b)	the parties shall not knowingly permit the export of drugs to any country except within the limits of the total of the estimates for that country.
Burma	49, 1(b) and (e)	Reserves the right (1) to allow addicts in the Shan state to smoke opium for a transitory period of twenty years with effect from the date of coming into force of the Single Convention; (2) to

Country	Relevant article and paragraph	Declaration or reservation
		produce and manufacture opium for this purpose; (3) to furnish a list of opium consumers in the Shan state after the Shan state government has completed the making of such a list on 31 December 1963.
India	49, 1(a), (b), (d), and (e)	Reserves the right to permit temporarily the quasi-medical use of opium, opium smoking, the use of cannabis, cannabis resin, extracts and tinctures of cannabis for nonmedical purposes, and the production and manufacture of and trade in these drugs for the purposes mentioned.
		Does not recognize the signature of the Convention by a Nationalist Chinese representative as a valid signature on behalf of China.
Indonesia	40, 1	Does not agree to the formulation which does not permit any state which wishes to do so to become a party to the Single Convention.
	42	Does not agree to the formulation which may prevent the application of the Convention to nonmetropolitan territories.
	48, 2	Does not consider itself bound by the provision of a mandatory reference to the International Court of Justice of a dispute: agreement of all parties to the dispute shall be necessary.
Pakistan	49, 1(a), (d) and (e)	Will permit temporarily the quasi-medical use of opium; the use of cannabis, cannabis resin, extracts and tinctures of cannabis for nonmedical purposes and the production and manufacture of and trade in these drugs.
Peru	49, 2(b) and 4(b)	Reservation (subsequently withdrawn) to the provision that (1) the right to permit temporarily the quasi-medical

Country	Relevant article and paragraph	Declaration or reservation
		use of opium, opium smoking, coca-leaf-chewing, nonmedical use of cannabis, and the production and manufacture of and trade in these drugs for the purposes mentioned be subject to the restriction that no export of these drugs may be permitted to a nonparty; (2) the right referred to in (1) ceases to be effective if the party concerned fails to comply with the request of the Board or the secretary for certain specified information.
United Arab Republic		Declares that ratification of the Convention does not mean in any way the recognition of Israel, and that no treaty relations will arise between the UAR and Israel.

SOURCE: UN Document ST/LEG/SER.D/1, 1967.

APPENDIX B
Powers and Composition of the Board

The Board's "enforcement measures" and powers under the Single Convention are as follows.

1. It can ask for explanation from a government if it believes that the aims of the Convention are being seriously endangered by the country's failure to carry out the provisions of the Convention. The INCB can bring the matter to the attention of the parties, the Commission, or ECOSOC if the country proves intransigent and the situation is not remedied.

2. It can recommend embargoes, that is, it can recommend to parties that they stop the import or export of drugs (or both) from or to a country if other sanctions fail to bring about the desired result.

3. It can publish a report and submit it to ECOSOC, which can circulate it among parties.

4. It can authorize new countries to produce opium for export (in amounts not exceeding five tons annually) or recommend against such production.

5. Through the operation of the estimates and statistical returns system, it can require the limitation of manufacture or importation.

The Permanent Central Board was composed of eight experts, appointed in their personal capacity, first by the League of Nations Council, and later by ECOSOC for five-year periods. The procedure for appointment was one whereby each signatory of the 1925 Convention, each member of the Council, Germany, and the United States would submit two names each for the candidature.

The Drug Supervisory Body was composed of four members, appointed by each of the following: The Advisory Opium Committee, the PCB, the International Health Office in Paris, and the Health Committee of the League of Nations. After 1946 the appointing bodies were the Commission on Narcotic Drugs and the PCB, which appointed one member each, and WHO, which appointed two. The members were appointed in their personal capacities.

The International Narcotics Control Board consists, under the Single Convention, of eleven members elected in their personal capacity by ECOSOC for a three-year term on the following basis: three members with medical, pharmacological, or pharmaceutical experience from a list of at least five persons nominated by WHO, and eight members from a list of candidates nominated by UN members and by parties which are not UN members. Under the protocol of 1972 amending the Single Convention, the Board is to comprise thirteen members to be elected by ECOSOC as follows: three members with medical, pharmacological, or pharmaceutical experience from a list of at least five persons nominated by WHO; and ten members from a list of persons nominated by UN members and by parties which are not members of the UN. The members are to serve for a period of five years and may be reelected.

APPENDIX C

Membership and Resolutions of the Commission on Narcotic Drugs

As the original members of the Commission were designated by ECOSOC, the procedure for their election was not laid down until 1949, when the subject came up for discussion at a Council meeting and caused some difficulty. The Commission itself had emphasized the need to preserve the maximum degree of continuity in the composition both as regards the states represented as well as the representatives of those states—a requirement dictated by the "particular character of the fundamental problems of the international control of narcotic drugs which can be solved only over a period of years" (E/1109). The idea of permanent membership which was subsequently developed was based on British proposals; the U.S. did not support it, preferring instead the method used by all other UN commissions, that is, three-year terms of office. Nevertheless, when "indefinite" appointments were made in 1949, the U.S. was given a place along with nine other countries—Canada, France, India, China, Peru, Turkey, the USSR, the U.K., and Yugoslavia.

Elections and reelections to the five remaining places were held during ECOSOC sessions. Votes were taken by secret ballot, the candidates being those countries which had indicated by suitable communications to the secretariat an interest in being elected. In 1961, when the term of office was changed to one of three years, which was to be applicable to all members, the Council had to decide which of the ten members elected in 1949 for an indefinite period should have their terms of office terminated in 1964; this was done by the drawing of lots. Similarly, the decision as to which of the newly elected countries should serve for three years, two years, or one year was based on the drawing of lots. In 1968, the terms of office of members was increased from three to four years.

Accompanying the enlargement of the Commission in 1961 was a change in the criteria of membership selection; whereas previously only members of the UN were eligible, election was now extended to members of the specialized agencies and parties to the Single Convention, who were not necessarily members (for example, Switzerland, which was promptly elected). Moreover, while representation of producing and manufacturing countries, and countries with problems of illicit trafficking, was to continue to be a basis for selection, countries with drug addiction problems would now equally qualify. The pattern of election changed again when membership went up from twenty-one to twenty-four in 1967; in addition to the criteria which had hitherto been employed, the encroaching principle of "equitable geographical distribution" entered the picture finally. Thus when elections were held in 1968, candidates were specified in reference to their membership in geographical groups: "The delegate of the Phillipines named as candidates of Asian countries: Iran, Lebanon, Pakistan, and Republic of Korea. The delegate of Tanzania named as candidates of African countries: Kenya and United Arab Republic" (ECOSOC: 44th, 1968). Despite such shifts in criteria, the actual variation of the core membership has been negligible. Apart from Taiwan, which went out after 1969, the original ten "permanent" members have stayed in continuously, while Iran, Mexico, and Egypt, though not permanent in any formal sense, have also had unbroken representation in the Commission.

The members of the Commission in 1974 were: Argentina, Australia, Brazil, Canada, Chile, Egypt, France, Federal Republic of Germany, Hungary, India, Indonesia, Iran, Jamaica, Japan, Kenya, Mexico, Morocco, Nigeria, Pakistan, Peru, Rumania, Sweden, Switzerland, Thailand, Togo, Turkey, USSR, U.K., U.S., Yugoslavia.

Number of Commission Resolutions by Year and Type, 1946-71

Year	Total number of resolutions	Country or region-specific resolutions	Drug-specific resolutions
1946	4	2	2
1947	4	2	3
1948	8	2	6
1949	5	1	3
1950	5	3	4
1951	3	1	2
1952	5	1	3
1953	4	–	2
1954	14	1	10
1955	16	–	7
1956	10	3	7
1957	10	2	9
1958	13	3	6
1959	12	–	4
1960	8	3	1
1961	3	–	1
1962	7	2	2
1963	4	3	2
1964	2	1	2
1965	2	1	2
1966	2	–	1
1968	7	2	4
1969	4	1	2
1970, 1st	1	–	1
1970, 2d	1	–	–
1971	5	1	3
Total	159	35	89

APPENDIX D
Articles in the Bulletin of Narcotics 1949-61 and 1962-71

	Number of articles 1949-61	1962-71	Total
Most prevalent subject areas			
Physics, chemistry, pharmacology, physiology	94.0	55.0	149.0
Medicine, treatment	18.0	27.5	45.5
Social and behavioral sciences, epidemiology	23.0	44.5	67.5
Law enforcement, illicit traffic	27.5	13.0	40.5
International legislation and administration	30.5	11.0	41.5
National legislation and administration	22.5	9.0	31.5
Reports on the work of CND, INCB, etc.	36.0	29.0	65.0
Most prevalent drugs			
Opium / opium poppy	40.0	17.0	57.0
Morphine	21.5	5.0	26.5
Heroin	16.5	10.0	26.5
Cannabis	13.0	26.0	39.0
Cocaine / coca leaf	16.0	11.0	27.0
Barbiturates	6.0	3.0	9.0
Geographical setting			
North America*	13.0	23.5	36.5
India	11.0	7.0	18.0
United Kingdom	–	10.0	10.0
Other Western European countries	10.0	11.0	21.0
Eastern Europe	4.0	5.0	9.0
Middle East	12.0	5.0	17.0
Other African countries	4.0	5.0	9.0
Other Asian countries	12.0	14.0	26.0
Latin America	17.0	13.0	30.0
National background of author			
U.S.	26.0	36.0	62.0
Canada	18.0	7.5	25.5
United Kingdom	3.0	16.5	19.5
Other Western European countries	33.0	29.0	62.0
Eastern Europe	11.0	10.0	21.0
Middle East	13.0	5.0	18.0
Other African countries	1.0	4.0	5.0
India	9.0	8.0	17.0
Other Asian countries	10.0	10.0	20.0
Latin America	12.0	7.0	19.0
Australia	–	2.0	2.0

*Earlier period: U.S. 12.0, Canada 1.0
 later period: U.S. 20.0, Canada 3.5

Method of classification: First, the unit of classification used is the article. Despite the very great variation between articles in length and quality this was the unit chosen because this is the form in which contributions to the *Bulletin* are made. Secondly, all articles are examined and where possible classified in terms of subject area, drug, geographical focus or setting, and the author's national background. For the purposes of the analysis a category within each of the four groupings is assigned a frequency of 1 if an entire article is devoted to it, a value of 0.5 if it shares an article with one other category, a value of 0.25 if it shares an article with three other categories, and so forth. There was no attempt to cover all articles by all classifications; more articles are classifiable by subject area and author's national background than by drug or geographical setting. So as to treat the range of contents in a set of categories large enough to be meaningful, we omitted infrequent categories in the classification of articles by drug and subject area, whereas the range of geographical setting and author background categories exhaust all the articles that are classifiable along these dimensions. However, articles of unknown authorship were left out of the table.

APPENDIX E

Influential Persons in International Narcotics Control 1921–71

Name of person	Country	Advisory Committee/ Narcotics Commission — No. of sessions	Advisory Committee/ Narcotics Commission — Times in Bureau	Years in office of individuals re-elected to DSB PCOB/ INCB	Times in WHO DD expert committees	International civil servants, heads of key agencies
Schultz	Austria	9	4			
Carnoy	Belgium	12				
La Barre	Belgium				10	
Parreiras	Brazil			9*		
Curran	Canada	9	4			
Hossick	Canada	9	4			
Sharman	Canada	15	2	9		
Hoo	China	11				
Liang	China	11				
Chehab	Egypt	8	3	8*		
Russell	Egypt	13	1			
Bourgois	France	24	10			
Mabileau	France	12	5			
Reuter	France			24		
Tiffeneau	France			9*		
Vaille	France	10	4	4		
Anselmino	Germany	8	2	8		
Halbach	Germany					14
Wolff	Germany					6
Joachimoglu	Greece			9*	13	
Campbell	India	19	2			
Chatterjee	India			15		

Krishnamoorthy	India					
Ardalan	Iran	13	3			
Cavazzoni	Italy	12		8		
Gallavresi	Italy				4	11
Theodoli	Italy					
Hosoya	Japan			6		
Miyajima	Japan					
Rabasa	Mexico	10	4			
Kruysse	Netherlands	11				
van Wettum	Netherlands	18	3		4	
Zapata-Ortiz	Peru					
Chodzko†	Poland	11	3			
Ferreira	Portugal	11	1			
de Vasconcellos	Portugal	11	2			
Charoon	Siam	10				
Lorenzo-Velasquez	Spain				6	8
Ekstrand	Sweden					
Goldberg	Sweden				11	12
Atzenweiler	Switzerland	11				
Bertschinger	Switzerland	18	5	9		
Carrière†	Switzerland		6			5
Dittert	Switzerland			9*	4	
Fischer	Switzerland			9*	4	
Kielholz	Switzerland			9		
Tavat	Turkey	9	5			
Özkol	Turkey	7	4			
Beedle	U.K.					
Crowdy	U.K.					11
Delevingne	U.K.	18	4	13*		

Name of person	Country	Advisory Committee/Narcotics Commission		Years in office of individuals re-elected to DSB PCOB/INCB	Times in WHO DD expert committees	International civil servants, heads of key agencies
		No. of sessions	Times in Bureau			
Felkin	U.K.					13
Green	U.K.	10				
Greenfield	U.K.	1				
Lyall	U.K.			24		
Nicholls	U.K.			11		
Yates	U.K.				12	12
Castro	Uruguay	11				
Anslinger	U.S.	22	4			
Cameron	U.S.					5
Eddy	U.S.	2			18	
Fuller	U.S.	11				
Isbell	U.S.				4	
Lande	U.S.					5
May	U.S.			33*		
Steinig	U.S.			9		17
Vasilieva	USSR	13	2		6	
Kusevič	Yugoslavia			8		5
Nicolič	Yugoslavia	21	5			

*In both bodies
†Member of Health Committee, League of Nations 1921-36

SOURCES: All the permanent missions in Geneva of the countries of origin of the seventy key persons (except Sweden) were approached by letter for information on age, professional training, and occupation of each of their respective nationals. Twelve out of twenty-seven countries responded, namely, Austria, Belgium, France, West Germany, India, Iran, Japan, Mexico, the Netherlands, Poland, Spain, and Yugoslavia, with the Netherlands and Yugoslavia providing information on two persons each.

Other sources of data include the following: obituaries and articles in the UN *Bulletin on Narcotics*; Renborg's (1964) article in the same journal; Musto (1973); Anslinger and Oursler (1961); PCB and INCB annual reports; reports of the WHO expert committees, and the lists of participants at the various plenipotentiary conferences.

APPENDIX F

Record of UN activities in connection with crop substitution programs

1949   Commission of Inquiry on the Coca Leaf to Peru and Bolivia.

1956   Following the prohibition of opium cultivation in Iran, an FAO exploratory mission was sent to determine the kind of assistance that might be given.

1957–58 An FAO survey mission to determine crop substitution and agricultural development needs in former opium lands.

1958   Under United Nations Technical Assistance (UNTA) sponsorship, a consultant was assigned to advise on socio-economic measures to replace opium cultivation in Afghanistan.

1960   Under UNTA sponsorship, an expert was assigned to advise on the resettlement of hill tribes engaged in opium cultivation in Thailand.

1962   Sponsored again by UNTA, an expert was assigned to advise on resettlement of hill tribes engaged in opium cultivation in Thailand.

1964   UNTA sponsored a preliminary joint survey of the economic and social needs of opium-producing regions in the Union of Burma, with participants from WHO, the Burmese government, and the Division of Narcotic Drugs.

1966   A survey mission to Thailand to assess the economic and social requirements of the opium-producing regions with a view to eradicating poppy cultivation; experts and secretariat services were contributed by UN, FAO, ECAFE, and the Division of Narcotic Drugs' outposted officer.

1967   A member of the Divison of Narcotic Drugs visited Lebanon to obtain information on the sunflower operation in the Baalbek/Hermel region.

1970   UN mission to Thailand.

1971   UN mission to Thailand to draw up and sign a Plan of Operations for Drug Abuse Control in Thailand.

1972   Head of UNFDAC visited Burma, Thailand. A UN/FAO exploratory mission visited Afghanistan. A UN/FAO mission visited Lebanon and drew up recommendations for cannabis replacement.

Note on Sources

The main sources of information for this study have been the published and mimeographed documents of the League of Nations and the United Nations system. Foremost among these have been the reports submitted by the key drug organs at the end of each session to a higher body. In the text we have referred to these in an abbreviated way, as these examples show.

CND: 23d, 1969   Report of the twenty-third session of the Commission on Narcotic Drugs in 1969.

PCB, 1960   Annual report of the Permanent Central Board to the Economic and Social Council on the work of the Board in 1960.

INCB, 1970   Report of the International Narcotics Control Board for 1970.

INCB/Statistics, 1969   Statistics on narcotic drugs for 1969, published by the INCB as an addendum to its annual report.

INCB/Estimates, 1971   Estimated world requirements of narcotic drugs in 1972, published by the INCB as an addendum to its annual report in 1971.

DSB, 1965	Statement of estimated world requirements of narcotic drugs in 1966, issued by the Drug Supervisory Body in 1965.
OAC Minutes: 5th, 1923	Published minutes of the fifth session of the Advisory Committee on Traffic in Opium and Other Dangerous Drugs of the League of Nations in 1923.
OAC: 5th, 1923	Report of the Advisory Committee to the Council of the League of Nations in 1923.
WHO/EC DD, 1969	Report of the WHO Expert Committee on Drug Dependence, published in 1969. (Reports of the expert committees are usually published in the year following their meetings.)

In our reference to mimeographed documents we have reproduced the official UN documents series symbols. These identify the issuing organ and the document type. Thus, documents of the Commission on Narcotic Drugs bear the symbols E/CN.7/..., while General Assembly and ECOSOC plenary documents are prefixed by the symbols A/... and E/... respectively, followed by four digits. The symbol series E/CONF.63/C.1/SR.4 indicates that the document is the Summary Record (SR) of the 4th meeting of Committee 1 (C.1) of the plenipotentiary conference on amendments to the Single Convention (E/CONF.63/ ...).

The symbols used by the League of Nations denote the body to which the document was distributed, its date and number. The letters A, C, and M refer to the Assembly, the Council and the League Members in general, while the initials OC and CH refer to the Opium Committee and the Health Committee (Comité d'Hygiène).

Not always specifically cited, but extensively used as sources, are the documents, records, and publications named below.

General Assembly: Official Records: Budget Estimates and Information Annexes.*

Economic and Social Council: Official Records (in particular the documents of the Committee for Program and Coordination).*

The International Labor Organization: Minutes of the Governing Body.*

World Health Organization: Official Records.

* Used mainly as sources for the budgetary data in chapter 4.

UN Division of Narcotic Drugs: Information Letter.
Department of Economic and Social Affairs, Division of Narcotic
Drugs: *Bulletin on Narcotics.*
League of Nations: Official Journal.

Also consulted were the minutes and working papers of the
international drug conferences, particularly the following.

International Opium Commission, Shanghai, China 1909. Vol. 1,
Report of the Proceedings. Vol. 2, Reports of the Delegations.
(Shanghai: North China Daily News and Herald Ltd, 1909)
First Opium Conference, 3 November 1924–11 February 1925.
Minutes and Annexes. (Geneva: League of Nations Documents,
1925).
Records of the Second Opium Conference, 17 November 1924–19
February 1925. Plenary Meetings. Meetings of the Committees
and Sub-Committees. Vols. 1 and 2. (Geneva: League of Na-
tions, 1925)
Conference for the Suppression of the Illicit Traffic in Dangerous
Drugs, Geneva, 1936. Records of the conference, 8–26 June
1936. Text of the Debates. Series of the League of Nations publi-
cations. XI. Opium and other Dangerous Drugs. 1936. XI.20.
United Nations Conference for the Adoption of a Single Conven-
tion on Narcotic Drugs, New York, 1961. Official Records.
Volumes 1 and 2 (New York: UN Publications, 1964, Sales
Numbers 63.XI.4, 63.XI.5)
United Nations Conference for the Adoption of a Protocol on
Psychotropic Substances, Vienna, February 1971. Official
Records. Vols 1 and 2, New York: United Nations, 1973.
United Nations Conference to Consider Amendments to the Single
Convention on Narcotic Drugs, 1961. Records of the confer-
ence, 6–24 March 1972, Geneva. UN Documents E/CONF.
63/...

We also learned much from our interviews with the following
people, who have been concerned, in one way or another, with the
subject of this study: L. Atzenweiler, Richard H. Blum, O. J.
Braenden, Dale C. Cameron, Joseph Dittert, Harry Greenfield,
Hans Halbach, F. R. Hassler, Lawrence J. Hoover, Jr., Susanne
Imbach, Ansar Khan, E. S. Krishnamoorthy, Vladimir Kušević,
R. Migone, Joy Moser, Sten Mårtens, Robert E. Popham, P.
Raton, Bror Rexed, Michael Sacks, S. P. Sotiroff, Leon Steinig,
Walter von Wartburg.

Bibliography

Adams, Leonard P., II. China: The Historical Setting of Asia's Profitable Plague, Appendix in Alfred W. McCoy, *The Politics of Heroin in Southeast Asia*. New York: Harper and Row, 1972.

Alger, Chadwick F. The United States in the United Nations. *International Organization*, 1973, *27*, 1:1-27.

Anderson, Nels, and Nijkerk, K.J. International Seminars: An Analysis and an Evaluation. *Administrative Science Quarterly*, September 1954, *3*.

Anslinger, Harry J., and Oursler, Will. *The Murderers. The Story of the Narcotic Gangs*. New York: Farrar, Straus and Cudahy, 1961.

Arndt, Sven, and Lind, Robert. Handcuffing the Octopus: the Elusive Tentacles of Drug Supply. Paper prepared for the meeting of the International Research Group on Drug Legislation and Programs at Helsinki, June 1973.

Becker, Howard S. *Outsiders: Studies in the Sociology of Deviance*. New York: Free Press, 1963.

Becker, Howard S., and Horowitz, Irving Louis. Radical Politics and Sociological Research: Observations on Methodology and Ideology. *American Journal of Sociology*, 1972, *78*: 48–66.

Berkov, Robert. *The World Health Organization: A Study in Decentralized International Administration*. Geneva: Librairie Droz, 1957.

Bertrand, Maurice. *Report on Personnel Problems in the United Nations*. Geneva: United Nations, 1971 (JIU/REP/71/7).

Blum, Richard H., and associates. *Society and Drugs. Social and Cultural Observations*. San Francisco: Jossey-Bass, 1969.

Blum, Richard H., and associates. *The Dream Sellers: Perspectives on Drug Dealers*. San Francisco: Jossey-Bass, 1972.

Blum, Richard H.; Kaplan, John; Lind, Robert; and Tinklenberg, Jared. Elements for Drug Policy: International Implications for Crime and Justice. In *International Review of Criminal Policy*. No. 2. New York: United Nations, 1974.

Breckon, William. *The Drug Makers*. London: Eyre Methuen, 1972.

Buell, R.L. *The International Opium Conference*. Boston: World Peace Foundation, 1925.

Bureau of Narcotics, Advisory Committee. *Comments on Narcotic Drugs: Interim Report of the Joint Committee of the American Bar Association and the American Medical Association on Narcotic Drugs*. Washington, D.C.: U.S. Treasury Department, undated (1958?).

Cabinet Committee on International Narcotics Control. *World Opium Survey*, July 1972.

Cameron, Dale C. The Nature of Alcohol and Drug Abuse and Their Relationship: Policy and Implementation. In L. G. Kiloh, ed., *29th International Congress on Alcoholism and Drug Dependence*. London: Butterworth, 1971.

Christie, Nils, and Bruun, Kettil. Alcohol Problems: The Conceptual Framework. In Mark Keller and T.G. Coffey, eds., *Proceedings of the International Congress on Alcohol and Alcoholism.* Vol. 2. Highland Park, N.J.: Hillhouse Press, 1968.

Claude, Inis L. *Swords into Plowshares: Problems and Progress of International Organization.* London: Univeristy of London Press, 1965.

Cox, Robert W., and Jacobson, Harold K. *The Anatomy of Influence: Decision-Making in International Organizations.* New Haven and London: Yale University Press, 1973.

Dickson, Donald D. Bureaucracy and morality: An organizational Perspective on a Moral Crusade. *Social Problems,* 1968, *16,* 2: 143–56.

Downs, A. *Inside Bureaucracy.* Boston: Little, Brown, 1967.

Eisenlohr, Les. *International Narcotics Control.* London: George Allen and Unwin, 1934.

Ekstrand, Eric Einar. *Jorden runt på trettio år: En fortsättning.* Stockholm: Norstedt, 1944.

Fleming, Denna Frank. *The United States and World Organization 1920–1933.* New York: Columbia University Press, 1938.

Foote, Wilder, ed. *Dag Hammarskjöld, Servant of Peace: A Selection of His Speeches and Statements.* New York: Harper and Row, 1963.

Fort, J. Paper delivered at the Twenty-ninth International Congress on Alcoholism and Drug Dependence, Sydney, 1970.

Gabrielsson, Johannes. *Consommation des boissons alcooliques dans les différents pays.* Stockholm and Paris, 1915.

Gaffney, George H. Narcotic Drugs—Their Origin and Routes of Traffic. In Wittenborn, J.R.; Brill, Henry; Smith, Jean Paul; and Wittenborn, Sarah A., *Drugs and Youth: Proceedings of the Rutgers Symposium on Drug Abuse.* Springfield, Illinois: Charles C. Thomas, 1969: 55–56.

Galtung, Ingrid Eide. The Status of the Technical Expert: A Study of UN Experts in Latin America. *Journal of Peace Research,* 1966, *3*: 359–79.

Galtung, Johan. *EG—den nya supermakten.* Stockholm: Prisma, 1973.

Gerth, H. H., and Mills, C. Wright, eds. *From Max Weber: Essays in Sociology.* London: Kegan Paul, Trench, Trubner and Co., 1948.

Ghosh, Bimail. "Report on the Activities of the 'Misión Andina.'" Off-print from *Zur Integration der Indianischen Bevölkerung in die moderne Gesellschaft Lateinamerikas.* [On the integration of the Indian population into modern Latin American Societies]. Colloquium organized by the Working Unit on German Latin American Research at Freiburg, May 1967. Freiburg: Arnold-Bergstraesser-Institut, 1968.

Gibberd, Kathleen. *The League in Our Time.* Oxford: Basil Blackwell, 1933: 143.

Goldberg, Peter B., and DeLong, James V. Federal Expenditures on Drug Abuse Control. In Drug Abuse Survey Project, *Dealing with Drug Abuse.* New York: Praeger, 1972.

Gross, Nelson G. Interview in *U.S. News and World Report,* 25 September 1972: 49–60.

Grove, J.W. *Government and Industry in Britain.* London: Longmans, 1962.

Hadwen, John G., and Kaufmann, Johan. *How UN Decisions Are Made.* Leyden: A. W. Sythoff; New York: Oceana Publications, 1962.

Hercod, R., ed. *Proceedings of the International Conference against Alcoholism at Geneva.* Lausanne, 1925.

Holahan, J.F. The Economics of Heroin. In Drug Abuse Survey Project, *Dealing with Drug Abuse.* New York: Praeger, 1972.

Hordern, Anthony. Psychopharmacology: Some Historical Considerations. In Joyce, C.R.B., ed., *Psychopharmacology:*

Dimensions and Perspectives. London: Tavistock Publications, 1968.

Horowitz, I.L., and Liebowitz, M. Social Deviance and Political Marginality: Toward a Redefinition of the Relation between Sociology and Politics. *Social Problems*, 1968, *15*, 3: 282.

Hubbard, Ursula P. *The Co-operation of the United States with the League of Nations, 1931-1936.* International Conciliation. No. 329. New York: Carnegie Endowment for International Peace, 1937.

Immonen, E. J. Toiminta väkijuomien salakuljetusta vastaan kieltolain aikana [Fight against smuggling during the Finnish prohibition]. *Alkoholikysymys,* 1965, 33: 73–81.

Jackson, Sir Robert G. A. *A Study of the Capacity of the UN Development System.* Vols. 1 and 2. Geneva: United Nations Publication DP/5, 1969.

Jansson, Jan-Magnus. Valta [Power]. In *Yhteiskuntatieteiden käsikirja II.* Porvoo: Werner Söderström, 1964.

Kalant, O. J. Report of the Indian Hemp Drugs Commission, 1893-94: A Critical Review. *The International Journal of the Addictions,* 1972, *7*, 1:77–96.

King, Rufus. *The Drug Hang-Up: America's Fifty-Year Folly.* New York, W. W. Norton, 1972.

Kinney, Jack A.; Christensen, Ronald; Welch, Wilfor H.; Bush, Gerald W.; and Lowenthal, Arthus A. *A Study of International Control of Narcotics and Dangerous Drugs.* Submitted by Arthur D. Little, Inc. to the Bureau of Narcotics and Dangerous Drugs. U.S. Department of Justice, May 1972.

Mayor's Committee on Marihuana. *The Marihuana Problem in the City of New York.* (The La Guardia Report.) Lancaster, Pa.: Cattell, 1944.

Lande, A. Principles of Effective Drug Abuse Control. Paper presented at the International Institute on the Prevention and Treatment of Drug Dependence. Lausanne, 1970.

Landy, Ernest Alfred. *The Effectiveness of International Supervision. Thirty Years of ILO Experience.* London: Stevens and Sons, 1966.

Lanouette, William. Legislative Control of Cannabis. Ph.D. dissertation, University of London, 1972.

Lindesmith, Alfred R. *The Addict and the Law.* Bloomington Ind.: Indiana University Press, 1965.

de Lint, J., and Schmidt, W. Consumption Averages and Alcoholism Prevalence: A Brief Review of Epidemiological Investigations. *British Journal of Addiction*, 66: 97–107, 1971.

Lowes, Peter D. *The Genesis of International Narcotics Control.* Geneva: Librairie Droz, 1966.

Lowry, Ritchie P. Towards a Sociology of Secrecy and Security Systems. *Social Problems*, 1972, *19*: 437–50.

Martini, G. A., and Bode, Ch. The Epidemiology of Cirrhosis of the Liver. In *Alcoholic Cirrhosis and Other Toxic Hepatopathias.* Stockholm: Skandia International Symposia, 1970.

McCoy, Alfred W. *The Politics of Heroin in Southeast Asia.* New York: Harper and Row, 1972.

Monopolies Commission. *A Report on the Supply of Chlordiazepoxide and Diazepam.* London: HMSO, 1973.

Murphy, Morgan F., and Steele, Robert H. *World Heroin Problem: Report of a Special Study Mission.* U.S. Congress, House Report. 92d Congress, 1st session, no. 92–298, 1971.

Musto, David F. *The American Disease: Origins of Narcotic Control.* New Haven and London: Yale University Press, 1973.

Myrdal, Gunnar. *An American Dilemma: The Negro Problem and Modern Democracy.* New York: Harper and Row, 1944.

Mäkelä, Klaus. Consumption Level and Cultural Drinking Patterns as Determinants of Alcohol Problems. Paper delivered at the International Congress on Alcoholism and Drug Dependence. Amsterdam, 4–9 September 1972.

Neligan, A. R. *The Opium Question with Special Reference to Persia.* London: John Bale, Sons and Danielsson Ltd., 1927.

Owen, P.E. *British Opium Policy in China and India.* New Haven: Yale University Press, 1934.

Pastuhov, Vladimir D. Experience in International Administration. Memorandum on the Composition, Procedure and Functions of the Committees of the League of Nations. Washington, D. C.: Carnegie Endowment for International Peace, 1943 (mimeographed).

—— *A Guide to the Practice of International Conferences.* Washington: Carnegie Endowment for International Peace, 1945.

Pickard, Bertram. *The Greater United Nations.* New York: Carnegie Endowment for International Peace, 1956.

Ranshofen-Wertheimer, Egon. *The International Secretariat: A Great Experiment in International Administration.* Washington, D. C.: Carnegie Endowment for International Peace, 1945.

Renborg, Bertil A. *International Drug Control: A Study of International Administration by and through the League of Nations.* Washington, D.C.: Carnegie Endowment for International Peace, 1947.

—— The Grand Old Men of the League of Nations. *Bulletin on Narcotics,* 1964, *16,* 4: 1–11.

Report of the Committee to Study Problems of the Pharmaceutical Industry. Ministry of Industrial and Scientific Development/Ministry of Public Health (France), July 1972 (mimeographed).

Russell, Bertrand. *Power: A New Social Analysis*. London: George Allen and Unwin Ltd., 1937.

Sainsbury Committee. *Report of the Committee of Enquiry into the Relationship of the Pharmaceutical Industry with the National Health Service, 1965–1967*. London: HMSO, 1967.

Sharp, Walter R. *Field Administration in the United Nations System*. New York: Praeger, 1961.

Skjelsbaek, Kjell. Non-governmental Influence on IGO Decisionmaking. Paper given at the meeting of the International Research Group on Drug Legislation and Programs at Helsinki, June 1973.

Sjöström, Henning, and Nilsson, Robert. *Thalidomide and the Power of the Drug Companies*. Harmondsworth: Penguin Books, 1972.

Skolnick, Jerome H. Coercion to Virtue: A Sociological Discussion of the Enforcement of Morals. Mimeographed submission to the President's Commission on Law Enforcement and Administration of Justice, 1967.

SOU: *Statens Offentliga Utredningar 1969:36, Läkemedelsindustrin* [Official reports of the Swedish state: the drug industry], Stockholm, 1969.

Spong, Senator William B. *Report to the Committee on Foreign Relations*. U.S. Senate, 92d Congress, 2d Session, September 1972.

Steinig, L. The International Aspects of Drug Control. Paper delivered at the Round Table Conference: Non-medical Use of Dependence Producing Drugs—Current Problems and Approaches. Council for International Organizations of Medical Sciences, CIOMS/RTC/6/17, 1971.

Sulkunen, Pekka. Alkoholijuomien tuotannosta ja kulutuksesta [On the production and consumption of alcoholic beverages]. *Alkoholipolitiikka*, 1973, *38*: 111–17.

Symonds, Richard, and Carder, Michael. *The United Nations and the Population Question, 1945–1970*. London: Chatto and Windus, 1973.

Taylor, Arnold H. *American Diplomacy and the Narcotics Traffic, 1900–1939*. Durham, N.C.: Duke University Press, 1969.

Terry, Charles E., and Pellens, Mildred. *The Opium Problem*. New York: Haddon Craftsmen, 1928.

Thörnander, Gunnel. *Algeriets fredliga revolution*. Stockholm: Prisma, 1971.

UN Commentary on the Single Convention on Narcotic Drugs, 1961. New York: United Nations, 1973.

United Nations Office of Public Information. *Everyman's United Nations*. 8th ed. New York: United Nations, 1968.

UNESCO and International Institute of Administrative Sciences. *National Administration and International Organization*. Brussels, 1951.

United States National Commission on Marihuana and Drug Abuse. *Marihuana: A Signal of Misunderstanding*. Washington, D.C.: Government Printing Office, 1972.

United States Senate, Committee on Foreign Relations. Hearing of 27 June 1972. *Protocol Amending the Single Convention on Narcotic Drugs*. Washington, D.C.: Government Printing Office, 1972.

Vaitsos, C.V. Bargaining and the Distribution of Returns in the

Purchase of Technology by Developing Countries. *Bulletin of the Institute of Development Studies*, 1970, 3:16–23.

Voionmaa, Tapio. An International Survey of the Production and Consumption of Alcoholic Beverages. In *Proceedings of the Twenty-Second International Congress against Alcoholism*. Helsinki, 1939.

Voionmaa, Väinö. The Problem of the Smuggling of Alcohol in Finland. In *Proceedings of the International Conference against Alcoholism*. Geneva, 1–3 September 1925.

Walters, F. P. *A History of the League of Nations*. London: Oxford University Press, 1952.

Wartburg, W. P. von. Problems of International Drug Abuse Control with Regard to Psychotropics. *The Australian Journal of Forensic Sciences*, 1970, *2*, 4: 1–11.

White, Lyman Cromwell. *International Non-Governmental Organizations*. New Brunswick: Rutgers University Press, 1951.

World Health Organization. *Pharmaceutical Advertising. A Survey of Existing Legislation*. Geneva, 1968.

World Health Organization/Finnish Foundation for Alcohol Studies. *Alcohol Control Policy and Public Health*. Report on a Working Group, Helsinki, 1973. Copenhagen, 1974.

Willoughby, W. W. *Opium as an International Problem: The Geneva Conferences*. Baltimore: The Johns Hopkins Press, 1925.

Wilson, C.W.M.; Banks, J.A.; Mapes, R.E.A.; Korte, Sylvia M.T. Influence of Different Sources of Therapeutic Information on Prescribing by General Practitioners. *British Medical Journal*, 1963, September 7:599–604.

Winnington, Alan. *The Slaves of the Cool Mountains*. London: Lawrence and Wishart, 1959.

Wolff, Pablo Osvaldo. *Marihuana in Latin America, the Threat it Constitutes.* Washington, D.C.: The Linacre Press, Inc., 1949.

———— The Activities of WHO in Drug Addiction. *British Journal of Addiction,* 1952, *50,* 1: 1–17.

Woodcock, Jasper. Administrative Considerations. In Blum, Richard H.; Bovet, D.; and Moore, James, eds., *Controlling Drugs: An International Handbook for Drug Classification.* San Francisco: Jossey-Bass, 1974.

Woodward, Eliot G. The Development and Future Structure of the Pharmaceutical Industry. *Svensk Farmaceutisk Tidskrift,* 1973, *77:* 356–66.

Worthen, Dennis B. Prescribing Influences: An Overview. *British Journal of Medical Education,* 1973, 7: 109–17.

Wortzel, Lawrence H. *Technology Transfer in the Pharmaceutical Industry.* New York: United Nations Institute for Training and Research, Report No. 14, 1971.

Zacune, Jim, and Hensman, Celia. *Drugs, Alcohol and Tobacco in Britain.* London: William Heinemann Medical Books, 1971.

Index of Names

324

Index of Subjects

Addiction. *See* Dependence

Administrative Management Service (AMS), 34

Advisory Committee on the Traffic in Opium and Other Dangerous Drugs, 54, 58; antiopium pressure on, 151–52; appointment of DSB members by, 299; and cannabis question 184–88, 203; creation of, 13; crop substitution discussed by, 205–6; and drug manufacturers, 155, 224, 272; ineffectiveness of, 9, 13, 15; influential countries in, 116; key persons in, 119, 120, 125, 304–6; London meeting of, 152; membership of, 13n, 14; nicknamed "Old Opium Bloc," 13; perception of illicit traffic by, 223, 236; relation to Board of, 76, 104–5; reporting of seizure information to, 226; and Scheme of Stipulated Supply, 151–52; secretariat (Opium

Traffic Section) of, 61–62, 65, 93, 190; and U.S., 14, 135

Afghanistan: criminal code of, 238–39; and crop substitution in, 213, 215, 308; as source of cannabis, 233; as source of illicit opium, 208, 232; and U.S., 144, 146

Africa: alcohol control in, 9, 13, 28, 165–68, 180; and *Bulletin*, 101, 302; cannabis in, 181, 190, 193, 199, 233; UN missions to, 109, 240; and U.S., 144, 145; and Vienna Convention, 260, 267

Alcohol, 165–80; access of diplomats to, 291; in agricultural development, 219, 288; and Anslinger, 125, 137; and cannabis, 98, 190, 195; combined approach to, 16; control in Africa, 9, 13, 28; deaths from, 3; excluded from international negotiations, 253;

326